Making a Mass Institution

New Directions in the History of Education

Series editor, Benjamin Justice

The New Directions in the History of Education series seeks to publish innovative books that push the traditional boundaries of the history of education. Topics may include social movements in education; the history of cultural representations of schools and schooling; the role of public schools in the social production of space; and the perspectives and experiences of African Americans, Latinx Americans, women, queer folk, and others. The series will take a broad, inclusive look at American education in formal settings, from prekindergarten to higher education, as well as in out-of-school and informal settings. We also invite historical scholarship that informs and challenges popular conceptions of educational policy and policy making and that addresses questions of social justice, equality, democracy, and the formation of popular knowledge.

Diana D'Amico Pawlewicz, *Blaming Teachers: Professionalization Policies and the Failure of Reform in American History*

Kyle P. Steele, *Making a Mass Institution: Indianapolis and the American High School*

Making a Mass Institution

• •

Indianapolis and the
American High School

KYLE P. STEELE

Rutgers University Press

New Brunswick, Camden, and Newark, New Jersey, and London

Library of Congress Cataloging-in-Publication Data

Names: Steele, Kyle P., author.
Title: Making a mass institution: Indianapolis and the American high school / Kyle P. Steele.
Description: New Brunswick: Rutgers University Press, 2020. | Series: New directions in the history of education | Includes bibliographical references and index.
Identifiers: LCCN 2019042540 | ISBN 9781978814394 (paperback) | ISBN 9781978814400 (hardcover) | ISBN 9781978814417 (epub) | ISBN 9781978814424 (mobi) | ISBN 9781978814431 (pdf)
Subjects: LCSH: Education, Secondary—Indiana—Indianapolis—History—20th century. | High schools—Indiana—Indianapolis—History—20th century. | Segregation in education—Indiana—Indianapolis—History—20th century. | Indianapolis (Ind.)—Social conditions—20th century.
Classification: LCC LA285.I5 S74 2020 | DDC 373.772/52—dc23
LC record available at https://lccn.loc.gov/2019042540

A British Cataloging-in-Publication record for this book is available from the British Library.

♾ The paper used in this publication meets the requirements of the American National Standard for Information Sciences—Permanence of Paper for Printed Library Materials, ANSI Z39.48-1992.

www.rutgersuniversitypress.org

Manufactured in the United States of America

For Emily

Contents

Making a Mass Institution

Introduction

• •

> Where'd you go to high school?
> —The quintessential St. Louis question

For people who grew up in St. Louis, Missouri, my hometown, there is one question, and one question alone, that dominates the experience of meeting someone new. If one St. Louisan meets another, one of them will invariably ask, "Where'd you go to high school?" in the first few exchanges of their conversation—probably immediately after "Hello" and "What's your name?" The question has become so ubiquitous that it has developed into something of an inside joke in the Gateway to the West. You can buy T-shirts, coffee mugs, and onesies for babies emblazoned with the question. The question has its own Facebook page (seeking to connect high school classmates) with hundreds of followers. The *Riverfront Times*, a local alternative newsweekly, developed an online quiz with the title "Where You *Should've* Gone to High School," for those St. Louisans who grew up elsewhere but, nonetheless, want in on the fun.[1]

Like any good joke, the question, "Where'd you go to high school?" has two basic, universalizing assumptions, both of which are at the heart of this book and are of great consequence to the history of American education. The first assumption is that everyone in St. Louis—and by extension the United States—attends high school, which simply was not always the case. In 1890, as historians have described well, a mere 6 percent of the nation's fourteen-to-seventeen-year-olds (359,949 pupils) received any form of secondary education. By 1930, that figure had mushroomed to 51 percent (4,804,255 pupils), as school leaders and state and local governments scrambled to construct an average of one new building per day just to house the throngs of incoming students.[2] Three decades later, by 1960, almost everyone between fourteen and seventeen years old in America (roughly 90 percent) was enrolled, and graduation rates, indicative of the amount of time students spent in school, rose above 60 percent for the first time. Plainly put, the growth of the high school that occurred between 1900 and 1960, the period at the heart of this book, is one of the most remarkable—perhaps *the* most remarkable—educational and cultural phenomena of the first half of the twentieth century.[3]

The second assumption is that in St. Louis—or any metropolitan area—no other seemingly straightforward question can tell you as much about a person. Indeed, the *Atlantic* ran a story in 2014 pointing out that St. Louis, while perhaps the first city to silkscreen "Where'd you go to high school?" on clothing, was far from unique. Residents of cities as diverse as Louisville, New Orleans, Cincinnati, Baltimore, and Charlotte, among others, reported that the question was commonplace in their hometowns, too. And for good reason. As the article's author, Deborah Fallows, wrote, asking the question is, on the face of it, "actually another way of asking 'Where do you live?'" "*But*," she continued, "you aren't seeking a simple answer of name or geography. You are using those questions to seek valuable information about the socio-economic-cultural-historical background of a person. It helps you orient that person in the context of the world as you live it and interpret it."[4]

On the one hand, Fallows implied, most people agree that "Do you go to church?" and "What's your racial background?" and "How much money do your parents make?" and "Who did you vote for?" are deeply personal questions that have no place in polite conversation, certainly when meeting someone new. On the other hand, "Where'd you go to high school?" though far from perfect in its ability to capture any one person's complex identity, is seen as innocuous and wholly acceptable. The extent to which "Where'd you go to high school?" is demographically and culturally revealing, therefore, reflects the precision with which our society sorts children within systems of secondary schools. High schools are powerful social institutions, and they tend to reflect the neighborhoods and communities in which they operate.

To explore and bring the assumptions of "Where'd you go to high school?" to life in one American city—Indianapolis, Indiana—this book employs a three-tier analytical approach, one that presents the high school from multiple angles. It explores national educational trends, to understand the high school as a distinctly American invention, guided from above by policy elites; the character of Indianapolis and its people, to recognize high schools as place-based institutions, the creation of local government, politics, and contending interests; and student life, to remember that young people, and their youth culture, have shaped secondary schools in different ways historically.

Through this analysis, this book makes two unique contributions to the historical literature. First, it describes how an American city created a divided and unjust system of high schools over the course of the twentieth century, one that sought socially reproductive ends by effectively sorting students geographically, economically, and racially through various means, including the curriculum. The Indianapolis high school system mirrored the multiple forces of mass society that surrounded it, as it became more bureaucratic, more focused on identifying and organizing students based on perceived abilities, and more anxious about teaching conformity to middle-class values. As the high school became a mass institution, therefore, it maintained the status quo far more often than it challenged it.

Indianapolis presents an ideal case study in this regard because its secondary program evolved in a similar fashion to those in other urban centers of the North, notably its neighbors in Cleveland, Detroit, St. Louis, Chicago, and Milwaukee. Indianapolis started with a small "academic" high school in the 1860s, expanded by adding an industrial training school in the 1890s, implemented "comprehensive" schools in the 1910s, instituted racially segregated schools in the 1920s, developed "custodial" institutions in the 1930s, experimented with "life adjustment" education after World War II, and was altered dramatically and permanently by suburbanization in the 1960s. These represent *the* key changes to public high schools nationally, and Indianapolis created and maintained institutions at each turn that were near archetypes.[5] The local character of the city is integral to this story, but to experience the schools in the pages that follow is to experience the development of the American high school in the twentieth century.

Of course, there could never be a perfectly representative case study in the history of American education. As with defining America, defining an American school system or the American high school comes with challenges. Nonetheless, Indianapolis is unusually well suited—in its implementation of nationally popular educational policy, to be sure, but even geographically and culturally. It is certainly not an eastern or western city, but most consider it part of the Midwest. It is certainly neither fully northern nor southern, but most consider it somewhere in the middle. It is the capital of a technically free state developed by white southerners, or a city north of the Mason-Dixon line, but it is divided in two by the old National Road (US Route 40), long considered the true North-South divide.[6] It is not without significance, too, that many people in Indianapolis, throughout the twentieth century, spoke of their city as occupying a place near the "heart"—literally and figuratively—of the American experience. Even in the present, the official motto of Indiana is "The Crossroads of America."[7]

Second, this book highlights the experiences of the students themselves, and the formation of a distinct, school-centered youth culture, which hitherto has remained peripheral to historical inquiry.[8] While many scholars recognize the existence of the institution's youth culture, surprisingly few historians have studied its genesis or meaning. Historicizing the student perspective, in concert with the more conventional, curriculum-focused narrative, helps re-create how young people experienced high school. Ultimately, this book argues, the high school, as it evolved into a mass institution, was never fully the domain of policy elites, school boards and administrators, or students but rather a complicated and ever-changing, contested meeting place of all three.[9]

Unearthing the student perspective requires access to a wide variety of student-generated documents, and Indianapolis has preserved an unusually vast and rich supply of archival materials on its secondary schools. In addition to an impressive number of yearbooks, student senate reports, commencement addresses, and personal correspondence, several of the schools maintained vibrant weekly or monthly newspapers, and one (the prestigious Shortridge High School) produced a *daily* newspaper, the first of its kind nationally, throughout much of the twentieth century. The size and scope of these accounts of student life are unprecedented, are severely underutilized in academic writing, and, in combination with other sources on Indianapolis's high schools—namely, school board reports, city council records, and newspapers—illuminate worlds rarely explored in the history of American education.[10]

With the aid of this exceptional source material, tracing the development of Indianapolis's high school system allows for a nuanced study of the city's (and the nation's) most perplexing and enduring problems, as the people of Indianapolis (like Americans generally) rarely saw their schools in one-dimensional terms, as sites of learning and nothing else. Rather, high schools were and continue to be prisms through which we view society writ large.

As described in chapter 1, for example, when population growth and factory automation sent more working-class children to the North Side's academic Shortridge (the first high school, founded in 1864) at the turn of the century, administrators promptly opened a second, separate high school on the city's more blue-collar South Side. This new institution offered some academic classes, but it specialized, first and foremost, in industrial training and was unabashedly named the Manual Training High School.

Given the location and curriculum of Manual High, school leaders suggested that it was best for the so-called hand-minded and those "from homes of a *different* sort."[11] While the curricular disparities between Shortridge and Manual merit serious investigation, the ways in which the students perceived the class-based differences are made plain in school newspapers and yearbooks, a point of view that administrative reports failed to capture. In the annual football game between Shortridge and Manual, for instance, the rivalry provoked Thanksgiving Day fistfights, caused scores of injuries and arrests, and forced school leaders to ban interscholastic sports altogether in 1907.[12]

When escalating enrollments necessitated a third high school, the city opened Arsenal Technical High in 1912, which eventually featured more than a dozen buildings spread out over a scenic seventy-six acres. Tech would soon be Indianapolis's largest high school by a wide margin, and it was the city's first fully "comprehensive" high school, meaning it ostensibly offered Shortridge's curriculum, and Manual's curriculum, and other, new vocational "tracks" for students to pursue on their paths to graduation. Put another way, if Shortridge and Manual sorted students on the North and South Sides of Indianapolis, then Tech sought to do the same within one massive, multibuilding campus.[13]

City school leaders again divided the student population in the 1920s, as revealed in chapter 2. Under pressure from white supremacy groups linked to the national resurgence of the Ku Klux Klan, local officials ended the policy of racially integrated high schools and quickly constructed Crispus Attucks High, which welcomed its first all-black class in 1927. While Attucks immediately asserted itself as an important and beloved hub of African American life and was resolutely led by black administrators and a highly educated, nearly all-black faculty, a close reading of its student yearbooks, as well as the city's black newspapers, reveals the challenges that civil rights leaders would face for decades, both in education and in all walks of life.[14] That is, black parents and students debated whether it was best to pursue integration as the only path to true equality or, given widespread white intransigence and racism, their own, separate institutions. Would separate schools, like Attucks, best promote black students' welfare?[15]

Chapter 3 explores the effects of skyrocketing enrollment on the character of the high school during the Great Depression. School leaders and administrators drastically expanded the institution's rules and regulations, as well as its after-school clubs and activities, both of which broadened the social and cultural importance of the high school. In the process, a robust student culture arose in the 1930s, one that stressed conformity and was rooted in the nation's middle-class, white, Christian, patriarchal, and heteronormative values. While this middle chapter departs from the book's focus on the ongoing processes of sorting students in Indianapolis, therefore, it demonstrates that maintaining social order became ever more important as increasing numbers of pupils entered the system.

The story of race in the postwar era—the focus of chapter 4—illustrates the importance of high school sports in shaping the city, more so, in many ways, than the legal system or the larger civil rights movement. When a 1949 state law finally banned school segregation (after years of lobbying by civil rights leaders), gerrymandering and segregated housing patterns meant that it had little effect on the city's classrooms. Nevertheless, in 1942, the state athletic association began allowing the Attucks High boys' team (and teams from other all-black schools) to participate in the state basketball tournament, from which it had been barred for decades. When Attucks made a number of deep runs in the early 1950s, eventually winning the tournament in 1955 and 1956, it was for a time the toast of the town among both white and black people. Representing the limits of the racial understanding that athletics can engender, however, little changed beyond the boundaries of the basketball court once the tournament had ended. Racism and discrimination remained the norm for Attucks's students, faculty, and community. By the time the historic *Brown* decision was handed down in 1954, the city's black students recognized fully the limited effects that the public high school, whether legally segregated or not, could have on their futures in a prejudiced society.

As chapter 5 demonstrates, between 1955 and 1971 Indianapolis discovered new ways to divide its students along racial, class-based, and gender-based lines. In the mid-1950s, school leaders vigorously implemented the nationally popular "life adjustment" movement, which claimed that most high school pupils needed to be prepared for "life" (for managing a home, or for working in low-skill service industry jobs, among other concerns), as opposed to being prepared for college or high-skill industrial or technical jobs. It was a form of "watering down" the academic curriculum that had taken place in previous decades at Manual, and, as before, school leaders experimented with it most explicitly on the more working-class South Side. Reasoning, once again, that working-class children needed less challenging subject matter, they built a new Manual High and opened a specialized, job-preparation school named Harry E. Wood High on the old Manual site. Both schools were located south of downtown; both schools were heralded as bastions of the "life adjustment" movement.

Back at Shortridge, on the North Side, middle-class and wealthy students prepared primarily for college, and in 1957 the school was named among the nation's best by *Time*, *Newsweek*, the *Wall Street Journal*, and several other publications. In less than a decade, however, rapid suburbanization, primarily of the northern suburbs, had dramatically changed the city's first and most celebrated high school. By the middle of the decade, Shortridge's student population was nearly three-fourths African American, and its remaining white families and powerful alumni base demanded that school leaders somehow "save Shortridge." As an answer, the board—led by Shortridge alumnus and future Indianapolis mayor and US senator Richard Lugar—implemented the Shortridge Plan, which proclaimed Shortridge the system's official "academic" high school and announced that its admissions would be guarded by a rigorous examination. Although the board ended the Shortridge Plan before 1970, and it did little to stop the exodus of affluent white families from the North Side, it verified that local elites would go to remarkable lengths to keep the school as it had been for generations: academically prestigious, mostly white, and mostly well-to-do.

In the late 1960s, the Justice Department successfully sued the Indianapolis public schools for taking illegal steps (gerrymandering its boundary lines, in particular) to keep its schools racially segregated. Just as United States District Judge Samuel Hugh Dillin reached his decision, however, Mayor Lugar lobbied successfully for the passage of the so-called Unified Government—or Unigov, for short—which united the city and county governments and legislative bodies for the sake of tax and public-service efficiencies. To make Unigov politically viable to white citizens, Lugar and his Republican colleagues removed the city and surrounding suburban school districts from the plan. Including them would have killed Unigov before it began, for many white suburbanites had moved out of the city explicitly so their children could attend racially homogenous schools. While school leaders had sorted high school students within the city for decades, this new urban-suburban divide, bolstered by Unigov, would continue that trend indefinitely. It was basically the same system with a new name.

Taken as a whole, therefore, a study of Indianapolis's high school system from 1890 to 1971 demonstrates that "Where'd you go to high school?" has been a powerful question for generations. Whether at the academic Shortridge High, the "hand-minded" Manual High, the "comprehensive" Tech High, the racially segregated Attucks High, or the "life adjustment" Wood High, school leaders and administrators made a high school system, one that sought primarily to sort students in a socially reproductive and unjust way. For their part, the students who attended these schools, often with little say in the matter, brought their distinct cultures to life. They wore their school colors, they published newspapers and yearbooks, they formed cross-town rivalries, they attended dances, and they hoped to make better futures for themselves. Administrators, teachers, and students all created a complicated "mass institution," one that endures, in slightly modified forms all over the nation, to the present.

In 1940, seventeen-year-old Kurt Vonnegut Jr. graduated from Shortridge. After commencement, Vonnegut enrolled at Cornell, joined the army (where he witnessed the Battle of the Bulge and the raid of Dresden), tried his hand at "public relations" for General Electric, and eventually penned some of the nation's most important postwar fiction, including *Cat's Cradle* (1963) and *Slaughterhouse-Five* (1969). And yet, despite an adulthood filled with haunting and undeniably memorable experiences, Vonnegut never fully shook the consequences of his time as a high school student in the midwestern city's capital. His mind, it seemed, returned time and again to the halls, playing fields, and classrooms of Shortridge. "High school," he told *Esquire* in 1970, "is closer to the core of the American experience than anything else I can think of. We have all been there . . . [and while] there, we saw nearly every sign of justice and injustice, kindness and meanness, [and] intelligence and stupidity, which we are all likely to encounter later in life."[16]

The high schools in Indianapolis demand significant scholarly attention, then, because they facilitated the creation of a tax-supported institution, a mass institution, that, as Vonnegut put it, "is closer to the core of the American experience than anything else." That is, in many ways, to begin to understand the American high school is to begin to understand America.

1

Shortridge, Then Manual, Then Arsenal

• •

Indianapolis Defines and
Develops a High School
System, 1890–1919

> But it is the province of the public
> high school—heaven help us!—to reach
> for good every boy and girl in its
> community.
> —Indianapolis's Arsenal Technical High
> School principal Milo Stuart in 1917

Published in 1917, Principal Milo Stuart's assessment of the public high school's "province," as he put it, would have seemed bizarre to most Americans only thirty years earlier.[1] At the time of his writing, nonetheless, the notion that every adolescent in the country would, or at least should, attend high school was becoming pervasive, and Stuart was riding the wave of the institution's growth to national acclaim. "Universal education . . . through the secondary school period is an obligation now generally accepted by the American people," he wrote. "Popular devotion to it as the open sesame to human happiness has crystalized into a vital faith."[2] If the American high school was indeed the key to human happiness, as Stuart believed, then he was among its most devoted

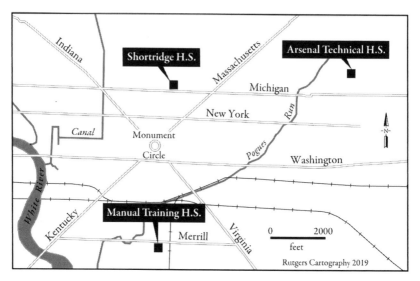

FIG. 1.1 Map of Indianapolis high schools, 1919

disciples, committed to spreading it as far and wide as possible over the course of his long career.

By 1917, Stuart oversaw Indianapolis's Arsenal Technical High School, or Tech, the city system's third, newest, and soon-to-be largest secondary school. At the start of that school year, Tech's fifth year of existence, he was responsible for more than two thousand students, scores of teachers and staff members, and more than a dozen standalone buildings on a seventy-six-acre campus. Drawing from his professional experience, he wrote about the high school prodigiously; trumpeting his cause, he toured the country to speak about school administration; and, as a result, he was chosen to serve as one of only twenty-six members on the commission formed by the National Education Association (NEA) to write the *Cardinal Principles of Secondary Education*, a group whose findings "reflected . . . the winds of change that had swept the education world in the previous quarter-century."[3] By any measure, he was among the quintessential school leaders of the Progressive Era, a bona fide "administrative progressive," as historian David Tyack once called them.[4]

When Stuart and his fellow members on the commission published their findings in 1918, they forcefully rebuked the high school curriculum of yesteryear for being too bookish, academic, and disengaged from "real life." Furthermore, they assailed the mission of the high school writ large for failing to meet the needs of "the entrance of large numbers of [high school] pupils," who were, they believed, "of widely varying capacities, aptitudes, social heredity, and destinies in life." As anxieties about the nation's rapid urbanization, industrialization, and immigration surged, the *Cardinal Principles* report became, according to celebrated historian of the curriculum Herbert Kliebard, "the era's most-cited statement on the nature of the high school."[5] Undeniably, in Indianapolis, only one of dozens of cities on the rise, school leaders were compelled to transition from one high school with 539 students in 1883 to three high schools with more than 7,000 students in 1919. The cause for alarm was real. The desire for a clear path forward, which the *Cardinal Principles* unapologetically provided, was palpable.

Compared with that of other cities, the expansion of Indianapolis's high school system in the Progressive Era was far from unique. Owing to a variety of national phenomena intertwined with the swelling of urban areas—including factory automation, an escalating standard of living for segments of the working class, and a succession of child labor laws—the involvement of young people in industry declined steadily from 1880 to 1920, propelling more children, especially adolescents, into school. In the three decades preceding 1920, for example, the number of fourteen-to-seventeen-year-olds enrolled in high schools across the country grew from 7 percent to 38 percent, an increase of nearly five million pupils.[6] To keep up with the remarkable pace, one historian noted, "Americans built an average of one new high school per day between 1890 and 1920, not all of them palaces, but an indication of impressive demand."[7]

Even though the secondary school system's growth in Indianapolis was not unique, its effect on the lives of the city's young people was unmistakable, a reality historians more often imply than describe. In her memoir, *My Rear View*, for example, Dorothy Dugdale chronicled her time as a student at Tech from 1918 to 1922, and the details of her experience are apropos here. Though she presented merely one white high schooler's perspective, her words not only offer a window into the early days of the modern American high school but also accentuate how her experiences differed from those of students a generation earlier. When Dugdale walked through Tech's wrought-iron gates as a freshman in 1918, she encountered a secondary school system more similar to that of the 1960s than to that of the 1890s. While the student population would mushroom beginning in the Great Depression, the system's essential features, which later enabled it to accommodate nearly every adolescent in the city, were in place by 1920.

To begin with, if Dugdale had been born in 1864 instead of 1904, she likely would not have attended high school at all. In the late 1870s, only a few hundred children, most of them white and middle class, attended school beyond eighth grade in Indianapolis. The city's original high school, modest from its inception, was just a decade old, employed a handful of teachers, and strained to graduate fifty or so students per year. While Superintendent Abram Shortridge, who founded the school in 1864 and became its namesake, claimed it unified, elevated, and democratized public education, its earliest years were plagued with insufficient funding and a succession of inadequate, often temporary buildings. Eventually, it settled on the city's North Side, at Michigan and Pennsylvania Streets, but it required near-constant additions and renovations to adequately house its pupils.

By the late 1880s, as railroads, factories, and high-rise office buildings transformed the local landscape, the public high school had emerged as a permanent fixture in Indianapolis, leaving the school board scrambling to match the speed of the city's broader growth. Between 1883 and 1893, for example, Indianapolis's total population leapt from less than 70,000 to nearly 150,000, and secondary school enrollments, in turn, also more than doubled, finally eclipsing one thousand pupils. As demand for secondary education surged, especially among working-class children, Shortridge High looked like a mid-nineteenth-century institution struggling to keep pace in an industrial age.

When the city was forced to expand to two high schools, creating Manual High in 1895 and embarking on the creation of a high school system, its school leaders followed a geographical and socioeconomic path worn by decades of industrial capitalism and the inequality it produced. Thus, Shortridge High, the original and decidedly academic high school, would continue to serve the North Side of the city, where most middle-class and wealthy neighborhoods were located. And Manual High, which, as its name implied, offered manual training courses alongside a small number of academic courses, would serve the more working-class and multiethnic South Side of the city. Even though Dugdale went to Tech, she grew up in the affluent North Side neighborhood of Woodruff Place, which was "an area restricted to residential homes . . . [with] three drives with esplanades, featuring fountains and statuary." Had she enrolled in high school in 1905, therefore, she would have gone to Shortridge, as she wrote, "like our older sisters did, because at the time there were only two high schools," each distinct in character.[8]

In utilizing Shortridge and Manual to sort students geographically and socioeconomically, Indianapolis's school leaders exacerbated class antagonism and educational inequality. In the short term, this division produced wide disparities in their secondary school curriculum offerings and, beyond the classroom, led to numerous class-based, interscholastic football riots, several so violent that the school board banned all competitions between the schools in 1907. In the long term, this division engendered disparities in college attendance rates and, one can safely presume, the career trajectories of its graduates. By 1910, about two out of three Shortridge students went to college, while roughly one out of ten Manual students did so. Naturally, Dugdale's two older sisters attended college after Shortridge, and she, a typical child of the North Side, did so too. She and her twin brother "graduated from college on the same day, [she] from Indiana University in Bloomington, and he from Northwestern University in Evanston, Illinois."[9]

In 1912, overcrowding at Shortridge and Manual prompted the opening of Tech and the move to prominence of its bold and tireless principal, Milo Stuart. Given the combination of Stuart's clear-cut educational philosophy and Tech's massive campus, with its multiple buildings, Dugdale and her classmates had several curricular options. Some, like Dugdale, paved their way to college by taking academic courses, including history, mathematics, English, and modern languages; others were directed to working-class jobs by taking vocational courses, including electrical work, printing, building trades, and automobile repair; and all of the students, by attending school together and receiving the same diploma, made Tech the epitome of the "comprehensive high school," which Stuart and the *Cardinal Principles* report both revered and propagated. If Shortridge and Manual sorted students on the North and South Sides, Tech did the same within its many beautiful acres. To the Bloomington-bound Dugdale, "it was a marvelous school to go to, just a marvelous school."[10]

Finally, though the fact is omitted from her memoir, Dugdale, her twin brother, and their older sisters attended racially integrated high schools, a distinctive feature of the secondary school system in Indianapolis since the 1870s. As droves of new students, a considerable number of them African American, enrolled during the Progressive Era, however, school leaders faced a mounting tide of segregationist and white supremacist sentiment, which would only intensify with the national reemergence of the Ku Klux Klan in the 1920s. While differences in social class helped to define the spread of the high school before World War I, therefore, race and racism would quickly move to the fore afterward. The high school system Abram Shortridge established in 1864 was radically different—significantly more diverse and patently more complicated—by the end of the 1910s. It was a situation that school leaders, alongside students themselves, would grapple with for the next half century.

There was no returning to the past, when high schools were small and exclusively academic. Indianapolis, like the rest of urban America, had made an ever-expanding high school system.

Indianapolis's First Public High School: A Mid-Nineteenth-Century Institution Struggling to Keep Pace in an Industrial Age

Abram Shortridge was a native Indianan, a career educator, and superintendent of the Indianapolis public schools from 1863 to 1874. And he, more than any other person, led the charge to establish the first permanent high school in his beloved state's capital.[11] Only slightly later than cities similar to Indianapolis, such as Cleveland (which founded a public high school in 1846), Cincinnati (1847), and Chicago (1856), the energetic, slender, and mustachioed Shortridge proved successful in his quest by 1864, only his second year in office.[12] After deftly winning over the school board and several members of the city government who were indifferent to "advanced education," Indianapolis High, as it was originally called, consisted of two spare rooms in an existing ward grammar school. Soon after it opened with little fanfare, Shortridge inexplicably went blind, eventually regaining some sight but forever "living in perpetual moonlight," as he once told a reporter. Despite the tragedy that befell him, the modest two-room high school, which eventually bore his name, set in motion a local system of secondary education that surpassed the pioneering superintendent's wildest expectations.[13]

As in towns and cities throughout the Northeast and then the Midwest in the second half of the nineteenth century, Indianapolis's first high school required cumbersome admissions examinations, employed only one teacher (and his assistant), enrolled a very small number of male and female students (twenty-eight in its first year), and graduated even fewer of them well into the 1870s (five in the first graduating class, that of 1869). Nonetheless, by expanding on the basic subjects taught in the lower branches, and ostensibly welcoming all pupils deemed morally and academically fit, Abram Shortridge and the high school's earliest reform-minded champions insisted that it met three crucial needs. First, it would help unify the public system, for its rigorous examinations, the results of which were made public, would effectively dictate the curricular direction taken by the city's lower branches. Second, it would elevate the status of the public system, for, by providing an alternative to private secondary schools (namely, academies), it would attract the support of the "respectable classes." And third, it would serve to democratize the public system, for by offering "advanced learning" at the taxpayer's expense, it would reward merit regardless of one's ability to pay.[14]

"No encouragement should be given to the false anti-republican idea," proclaimed the High School Committee in the 1870s, "that the better class of schools should be for the wealthy." Indeed, "work can be done so . . . that [the public high school] will be, in fact, the best that can be had."[15] Arguing similarly in 1879, board president William Bell stated proudly, "The crowning glory of the public-school system is the *free* High School." For in the public high school alone, Bell believed, "the child of the humblest citizen can acquire an education that will enable him to compete even-handed in the battle of life with the child of the millionaire."[16] While President Bell echoed a widespread belief among public school leaders nationally that tax-supported education could reward personal merit and prevent the hardening of social class divisions, the children of Indianapolis who labored on the streets and in factories, who left school so frequently by the age of twelve, likely saw the issue differently. The "people's college," as it was often called, then came with an opportunity cost too great for most families.

For those who could afford to attend, a number that was growing appreciably by the close of the century, the curriculum and instruction were heavily textbook based and reliant on rote memorization, and they included courses in English, mathematics, science, history, geography, and foreign language (either Latin or "modern languages," such as German or French). In addition to fostering "mental discipline" (the strengthening of the mind's "faculties"), the content of each subject purposefully contributed to the pupil's "cultural development," or his or her understanding of nineteenth-century political economy from a middle-class perspective. For example, courses in chemistry not only "trained the mind" but also included lessons in "scientific temperance" and encouraged students to apply various scientific principles to "the processes of human industry."[17]

In algebra, a staple of the nineteenth-century curriculum, textbooks instructed students on the class-related problems students might face after high school, often posing questions about "dispensing charity to the poor" and the difficulties of managing potentially "maladjusted" factory laborers.[18] In courses on history and geography, books by S. Augustus Mitchell (1860s) and Arnold Guyot (1870s), which sold at impressive rates, informed students about the lesser Catholic and pagan African nations, and the challenges and opportunities of the "white man's burden." And even in English class, which on the surface appeared less ripe for moral posturing, students were bombarded with spelling and syntax textbooks with references to "a dutiful child" and "an importunate beggar," as well as axioms such as, "Idleness and ignorance is the parent of many vices." Wherever young scholars looked, therefore, the destitute were demeaned, individual merit was exalted, and moral purity, based in the teachings of pan-Protestant Christianity, reigned supreme.[19]

While critics routinely charged the high school with teaching an elite, college-preparatory curriculum to the children of aristocrats, in truth, Shortridge High, like most of the nation's public high schools, offered what was referred to (and best described) as "advanced, practical learning."[20] Aside from its moralistic overtones, educators designed the curriculum to prepare some students for college (roughly 15 percent nationally in 1890), but just as many for white-collar, often gender-specific, occupations, including teaching.[21] In fact, the only substantive change the Indianapolis school board made to the curriculum between 1864 and the early 1880s was the addition of classes in "commercial papers," "penmanship," and "bookkeeping." These courses sought to produce a new generation of managers, secretaries, and accountants for the increasingly complicated and stratified economy.[22] Early high school students in Indianapolis encountered a daily instructional environment rooted in what historian David Labaree characterizes as "citizenship training," "moral education," "a practical curriculum," and a "meritocratic pedagogy."[23]

As enrollment jumped from twenty-eight in 1864 to more than five hundred by the early 1880s (see table 1.1), school leaders in Indianapolis, faced with intermittent financial crises, regularly scrambled to pay their teachers and house

Table 1.1
Enrollment and Graduates at Indianapolis (Shortridge) High, 1870–1893

	Enrollment	Graduates
1870	103	10
1873	206	13
1876	339	21
1879	385	49
1883	539	41
1893	1,263	130

SOURCE: Indianapolis Board of School Commissioners, *Report of the Principal of the High School* (Indianapolis: Indianapolis Board of School Commissioners, 1880), 103.

their students. After quickly outgrowing its two rooms in the grammar school on Vermont and New Jersey Streets, the high school relocated to the Second Presbyterian Church on the Circle (the heart of downtown), where it operated for six years, in nearly all of which the school was beyond capacity. By 1872, as demand for secondary education grew, the old church was bursting at the seams, forcing another move, this time four blocks north to the corner of Michigan and Pennsylvania Streets. The new site's property and building had once belonged to Robert Underhill, an iron and flour magnate, but came under the control of the Baptist Young Ladies Institute when the former owner went bankrupt in the Panic of 1857.[24]

After buying the Ladies Institute, which itself (along with many private academies) had folded under the weight of the public high school's ongoing success, the school board secured funds to remodel the original building and added another, a project that totaled an astounding $94,000, or more than $3 million today. Thousands of curious and proud citizens attended the evening ceremony that dedicated the new facility in April 1872. They heard speeches from Superintendent Shortridge and Indiana governor Thomas A. Hendricks, and toured the impressive new campus, which also contained the school board's offices and the first home of the Indianapolis Public Library. While the beautiful library—featuring double parlors, a dining room, a reading room, and nearly fifteen thousand volumes—was an unqualified asset to the high school's teachers and students, the board reluctantly moved it (along with its offices) to the Sentinel Building on the Circle two years later, in 1875. Predictably, as it had since its inception, the high school again needed space for more classrooms.[25]

As in most other cities, the seemingly endless demand for the public high school was driven by Indianapolis's broader growth, in both industry and inhabitants. The population more than tripled between 1870 and 1900, and industrial production moved symbiotically with it. Indianapolis enjoyed an economy built on slaughtering animals and meatpacking, foundries and machine shops, printing and publishing houses, and liquors and malts; however, its central location nationally, steady railroad development, and easy access to raw materials (on surrounding farms and in forests) led to staggering growth, a growth that matched that of Milwaukee, Detroit, Cincinnati, and Minneapolis in the late nineteenth century.[26]

In the late 1870s, Indianapolis mayor John Caven boasted, "Our city will be girt about with a cordon of industries, like the pillar of cloud by day and the pillar of fire by night," since "the angel of prosperity is going before us and leading us on." Caven's passionate rhetoric was common in an age of boosterism and competition between developing cities, but the outspoken mayor was quickly proved correct. By 1880, more than ten thousand industrial employees created more than $27 million worth of goods in Indianapolis. That figure would double by 1900—and double *again* by World War I.[27]

While more and more of Indianapolis's men and women labored with their backs and hands in the expanding industries, others went to their white-collar jobs in new and modern office buildings. With time, a twentieth-century skyline appeared in the Mile Square district that surrounded the Circle, the very center of which, in 1889, was adorned with the 248-foot limestone obelisk named the Indiana State Soldiers and Sailors Monument, which honored Civil War veterans. Several high-rise buildings, equipped with elevators, central heating, telephones, and electric lights, soon surrounded the famed Monument Circle, including the Majestic Building (1896, ten stories), the Indianapolis News Building (1897, ten stories), the Merchants Bank Building (1913, seventeen stories), and the Fletcher Trust Building (1915, fifteen stories).[28] Streetcars and interurban lines carried people in and out of the city with new efficiency. Residential apartment complexes appeared almost overnight. And the markers of urban commercialism, such as English's Opera House and Hotel, the Spencer House, and the Bates House, among many others, entertained and delighted unprecedented numbers of fun-seekers, both day and night. Moving in line with the swiftly rising economy, city expenditures and the tax coffers that buttressed them rose from just $80,000 in 1860 to nearly $6 million in 1908. As a result, a colossal and ornate city hall was finally completed in 1909, giving the municipal government its first permanent home.[29]

The depth and pace of urban change were unparalleled, and they excited, frightened, and mystified Americans, not just in Indianapolis, but in cities from coast to coast. While a generation of writers, social scientists, poets, historians, politicians, and others ventured to see the forest for the trees, Indianapolis's own Booth Tarkington—the Pulitzer Prize–winning novelist, onetime Shortridge High student, and critic of the industrial age—was among the most articulate and widely read. "That small city, the Indianapolis where I was born [in 1869]," he wrote, "exists no more today than Carthage existed after the Romans had driven ploughs over the ground where it had stood." "Progress," he added wryly, "swept all the old life away."[30]

As Tarkington knew, the prosperity attending industrialization was everywhere applied unevenly. And the railroads, which had turned his city's central location into a competitive advantage, only assisted in exacerbating class-based residential segregation and racial inequality. Established in the late 1840s and expanding briskly, railroads such as the Madison and Indianapolis (1847) and Belt Line (1877) were concentrated on the near South and East Sides of the city. Eventually, the South Side in particular, just four blocks south of the Circle, became home to more than fifteen different rail lines and a palatial new Romanesque revival–style Union Station, which was completed in the late 1880s and is still standing today. Besides spurring the economy, the railroads attracted waves of new immigrants to Indianapolis, not only to keep the lines in service but also to work in their adjacent industries and in the residential neighborhoods that sprang to life around them.[31]

By the turn of the century, Indianapolis's southern half was decidedly blue collar. Furthermore, the neighborhoods that populated the city to the south and east of the Belt Line railroad ("on the other side of the tracks," as the expression goes) were infused with the German, Irish, Jewish, and Italian cultures of their working-class inhabitants (see table 1.2). Germans, always the largest white ethnic group, had arrived in large numbers following the failed revolution of 1848. They settled first on the near East Side, near Lockerbie Square, and later established "thriving commercial districts along Virginia Avenue as far south as . . . Fountain Square." The Irish, who had lived alongside the city's African American residents in the 1830s and 1840s, settled Irish Hill by the 1860s, an area bound by railroad tracks to the north and south and Dillon and Nobel Streets to the east and west, respectively.[32] And Jews, arriving in larger numbers from Russia and Poland after 1900, often settled around Meridian and Morris Streets, where they established synagogues, mutual aid societies, and other cultural institutions, such as the still-celebrated kosher-style Shapiro's Delicatessen. "All of these groups," historian James Divita explains, "established distinct ethnic neighborhoods . . . [and] only the North Side remained the city's affluent, white, native-dominated district, a location that was attractive to the upwardly mobile immigrant descendants."[33]

While southern Indianapolis became synonymous with multiethnic, working-class life, "the combination of smoke, noise, and traffic from railroads . . . and industries," as scholar Lamont Hulse suggests, drove "middle and upper class residents to new neighborhoods away from the South and East Sides." Because floodplains and the Central Canal (built in the 1830s by Irish laborers) blocked the well-to-do from moving west, they found themselves hemmed in on three sides, leaving, to their minds, no option but to establish

Table 1.2
Foreign-Born Population of Indianapolis, 1870–1930

	Total population	% foreign-born	Total foreign-born	Born in Germany	Born in Ireland	Born in Italy	Born in Poland	Born in Russia
1870	48,244	22.1	10,657	5,286	4,318	18	34	3
1880	75,056	16.8	12,610	6,070	3,660	50	81	110
1890	105,436	13.7	14,487	7,893	3,547	112	62	140
1900	169,164	10.1	17,122	8,632	3,765	282	322	338
1910	233,650	8.5	19,842	7,518	3,255	658	—	1,255
1920	314,194	5.4	17,096	5,097	2,414	754	378	1,309
1930	364,161	3.8	13,740	3,888	1,383	794	498	905

SOURCES: Population statistics for 1870: Department of the Interior, Census Office, *Volume I: The Statistics of the Population of the United States* (Washington, DC: Government Printing Office, 1872), 380, 386–391; for 1880: Department of the Interior, Census Office, *Volume I: The Statistics of the Population of the United States* (Washington, DC: Government Printing Office, 1882), 536–537, 538–541; for 1890: Department of the Interior, Census Office, *Part I: Report on Population of the United States at the Eleventh Census* (Washington, DC: Government Printing Office, 1895), xcii, cxxvi, cli; for 1900: Department of the Interior, Census Office, *Census Reports, Part I* (Washington, DC: United States Census Office, 1901), clxxv; for 1910: Department of Commerce, Bureau of the Census, *Volume II, Population 1910: Reports by States, with Statistics for Counties, Cities, and Other Civil Divisions, Alabama–Montana* (Washington, DC: Government Printing Office, 1913), 576; for 1920: Department of Commerce, Bureau of the Census, *Abstract of the Fourteenth Census of the United States* (Washington, DC: Government Printing Office, 1923), 378–383; for 1930: Department of Commerce, Bureau of the Census, *Population, Volume III, Part 1, Alabama–Missouri* (Washington, DC: Government Printing Office, 1932), 721.

exclusive new neighborhoods of their own farther and farther north of the Circle. Before long, wealthy enclaves such as Meridian-Kessler and Woodruff Place were designed and developed, featuring their signature "shaded esplanades, green lawns, and parkways." Similarly, the Mapleton–Fall Creek neighborhood, platted in the 1870s, gained a reputation for its spacious Victorian homes and "landscaped meadows and hills in the adjacent Crown Hill Cemetery." Although these communities gave their residents easy access to downtown, where many of their patriarchs worked, they were intended, as Hulse notes, "to contrast the rurality of suburban life with the industrializing city."[34]

By the close of the century, two interrelated facts became clear to Indianapolis's school leaders and power brokers. First, the railroads and industry had altered the city's landscape permanently. While the population and economy were booming, the South Side, with its train whistles and plumes of smoke, became more and more working class and multiethnic; and the North Side, with its tree-lined streets and country clubs, became wealthier and predominantly populated by native-born whites. Second, the public high school, which educated more than 1,200 children in 1893, was in dire need of reform. Its campus on the North Side, celebrated as it was in the 1870s, was plainly inadequate for the middle-class and wealthy children who lived nearby. To complicate matters, significantly more working-class children, as well as small numbers of African American children, also wanted to attend the public high school, and they found Shortridge too far from their homes, not to mention overcrowded. The city had changed, and the high school, with one foot still in the 1860s, had failed to keep up.

What the city's school leaders resolved to do, though neither unusual nor irrational, affected the character of Indianapolis's neighborhoods and the high schools that served them for generations: they mapped the growth of the secondary school system onto the city's emerging social-class divisions. They would remodel and expand Shortridge in 1884 and again in 1905. Given its location at Michigan and Pennsylvania Streets, it would primarily serve the increasingly college-bound children of the North Side. In addition, the board would open a second high school on the South Side in 1895, unabashedly named Manual High, and it would offer, alongside the traditional academic curriculum, "manual" or "industrial" courses. In contrast to Shortridge, it would primarily serve working-class children, whom school leaders euphemistically referred to in official reports as "the great masses," the "hand-minded," or those "from homes of a *different* sort."[35]

In short order, and as the direct result of school policy, the children of Shortridge High, dressed in their school colors of blue and white, were nicknamed the "Northsiders." And their foes from Manual, dressed in red and white, were the "Southsiders." Accordingly, "blue and white" and "Shortridge" stood for "North Side" and "wealthy"; "red and white" and "Manual" stood for "South Side" and "working class"; and when the two schools met on those terms, on the football field and elsewhere, the results were predictable. The realities of twentieth-century class antagonism, however implied in their actions, were woven into their fight songs, their mascots, their pom-poms, and their letterman jackets from the start.

Shortridge, Manual, and the Hardening of a Class-Based High School System

The class-based divisions that ultimately defined the tension between Shortridge and Manual were evident even before the latter school was built. According to board minutes, the city briefly opened "High School Number 2" in 1891, hoping to make secondary education more accessible for children on the South Side. The product of several petitions and protests from parents who felt Shortridge was too distant for their sons and daughters, the temporary school opened in space it shared with the "old Calvin Fletcher Primary School" on Virginia Avenue, six blocks southeast of Union Station. Aside from its makeshift, second-rate facility, the board further undercut the school's authority to offer a complete program of "advanced education" by insisting that it was merely a feeder school "to provide instruction for only the first three years of the regular course . . . [so that] pupils would come to . . . [Shortridge] for their last year" and graduation. Only "serious" and "proven" South Side students, it said, could travel north of the Circle to earn a diploma.[36]

Just as High School Number 2 opened its doors, resources for a second, separate high school came to fruition, courtesy of a groundswell of interest in and support for "manual" or "industrial" education (the two terms were often used interchangeably). Since the mid-1880s, a growing number of citizens in Indianapolis, many of German heritage, had agitated for "a free trade school" to educate adolescents, as in several European nations, for their likely blue-collar careers. In many respects, the local movement was led by Otto Stechhan, a German-born mechanic. Stechhan had traveled throughout Europe to study the schools there, briefly opened the Mechanics' Institute in Indianapolis (which failed because of excessive costs), and eventually won over the powerful Central Labor Union, which joined him in his pursuit of public funds. "Free trade schools," Stechhan believed, "would bring recognition to the mechanic, the artisan, [and] the laborer," giving the student, unlike the on-the-job "factory system" of training, "a comprehensive view of his whole work."[37]

In March 1891, under persistent pressure from Stechhan, various labor groups, and the habitually cash-poor school board, the Indiana state assembly approved House Bill 611. On the last day of its legislative session, it voted to permit "the collection of five cents on every hundred dollars taxable property in Indianapolis," the proceeds reserved for "the establishment of an industrial training school."[38] While it took four years for the institution, Manual Training High School, to open officially, planning began immediately, which allowed school leaders to set the tone for the institution's future, curricular and otherwise.

First, they decided to place Manual on the South Side—a triangle of "frontage of 420 feet on Meridian Street, 183 feet on Merrill Street, and 331 feet on Madison Street"—to meet demand for secondary education south of the Circle and allow them to close the unpopular and ill-conceived High School Number 2. Second, they chose to supplement the school's manual training offerings with "a good general education" program. While Manual would ensure its graduates were "thoroughly fitted for . . . those important industries . . . [of] the modern industrial, commercial, and social world," the board believed that also requiring some academic subjects would guard against the school's training "descend[ing] to the mere practical details of some handicraft, making its possessor . . . without intelligent comprehension of the principles on which such a practice is founded." And third, they chose as the school's principal Charles E. Emmerich, who embodied Manual's respectably working-class, hybridized approach. Born, raised, and educated in Coblenz, Germany, Emmerich moved to the United States at twenty-one, was recruited by Abram Shortridge to teach high school Latin and German, and, after service in the army, had led High School Number 2 as principal since its inception.[39]

Until his retirement in 1910, Emmerich oversaw the singular "General Course of Study" for students at Manual, which was meant, the school's motto indicated, to achieve an "education of mind, hand, and heart." The curriculum, therefore, was "a combination of the subjects usually taught in High Schools *and* in Manual Training Schools, with a feeling, which has not been disappointed, that the union was good of both." That is, while Manual students had to take a few courses in English, algebra, physics, and chemistry (and could take all academic courses by choice), they were bombarded by "multiple subjects per term in Manual Training." By graduation, the great majority of young women had completed multiyear, intensive programs in the "cooking" or "sewing" department; and most young men, by comparison, were educated broadly in the "manual training" department, which offered numerous courses in woodworking (in year one), forging (year two), patternmaking and foundry (year three), and machine fitting (year four). The hope was that they would leave Manual, Emmerich wrote, with the ability to "think clearly, to reason logically and thus . . . enter any vocation they choose, with a reasonable chance of success."[40]

The impetus for Manual High was local, but it was intimately tied to the national movement for manual and industrial education, which, in many ways, was led and embodied by the work of Calvin M. Woodward, the founder of the Manual Training School of Washington University in St. Louis (1880). Woodward's three-year program in St. Louis—combining shop work with math, penmanship, science, and drawing—moved quickly to national prominence, and he was soon delivering regular addresses to the NEA, which brought together school leaders nationwide to debate pedagogy and education policy.[41] Though Woodward's ideas met some resistance, the movement ultimately gained traction, especially in urban centers: Baltimore opened the first tax-supported manual training school in 1884, and it was soon followed by Philadelphia (1885), Toledo (1885), and St. Paul (1888). By the turn of the century, roughly one hundred districts had adopted Woodward's ideas in some capacity, either in standalone schools or in departments within existing schools.[42]

Many leading proponents of manual education came to Indianapolis to tour Emmerich's school, and their praise, demonstrative of Indianapolis's wholesale embrace of the movement, was routinely published in Manual's annual yearbook. In 1897 alone, they printed remarks from ten different visitors. E. R. Booth, for example, the principal of Cincinnati's industrial school, noted, "[The] building is the most complete I have ever seen; in fact, I believe it is the best in the country. Neither the hand nor the mind is neglected." The superintendent of the Brooklyn public schools, William Maxwell, suggested that "it is indeed a model for other cities to initiate." And A. J. Lane, superintendent of the Chicago public schools, congratulated "the young people of Indianapolis on the magnificent provision that has been made ... for their mental and manual education," finding that they were offered "advantages equal to those presented in the very best institutions in the country."[43] These commentators were preaching to the choir, but their approval of Emmerich and the board's execution of manual training was indisputable.

Manual's students, too, wrote often about their pride in their school and its impressive facilities, but they found occasions to address its implied second-class status vis-à-vis Shortridge. "But who should feel proud of this school, and is it situated so as to best accommodate its pupils?" asked a student in 1896. The writer continued, Manual "is not one of a community [neighborhood], nor even one half of the city [the South Side]. It belongs to and is for the benefit of the people." In other editorials, the student-authors addressed Manual's location on the more industrial side of town, as well as its relative distance from the Circle, with a defensive tone. "Some, probably, object [to the location] on account of its being beyond the railroad tracks. But such an objection!" One writer questioned whether the freight trains "running at a rate at which they travel in this city [were] any more dangerous than our street cars," which Shortridge students rode to and from school regularly. Furthermore, another student noted, "You surely do not criticize its location on account of distance. You must admit that the center of a circle is equidistant from all points in circumference. Were you ever informed that our school is situated very near the center of the city?"[44] These turn-of-the-century entries were the exception, not the rule, but they proved that some Manual students contemplated the differences—educational, spatial, and otherwise—the city's two high schools presented.

While commentators in Indianapolis and beyond applauded Manual for its "practical" and "efficient" approach to secondary education, Shortridge continued to grow in academic prestige, presumably in pursuit of its remarkably different motto, which said nothing of learning with one's hands: "A disciplined mind and a cultivated heart are elements of power." In terms of the curriculum, students on the North Side had few options outside of the traditional academic subjects. Indeed, the Department of Commerce, which offered classes in "commercial law," "penmanship-spelling," and "business organization," expanded modestly in the early twentieth century, but it had existed, in one form or another, since the 1870s. Most students opted instead for classes in the well-regarded departments of English, mathematics, foreign language, history, art, physics, chemistry, and biology. A study of each school's assigned textbooks, for example, shows that Shortridge alone enabled college-bound children the chance to study multiple works of Chaucer, Spenser, Shakespeare, Bacon, Palgrave, and Paulding, as well as William Vaughn Moody and Robert Morss Lovett's *History of English Literature*—all within a single semester of English.[45]

Beyond the classroom, Shortridge became nationally prominent for its literary societies, magazines, and other student publications. William T. Harris,

FIG. 1.2 Shortridge High School exterior, 1906. (Courtesy of Bass Photo Co. Collection, Indiana Historical Society.)

for example, the US commissioner of education and pedagogical pioneer, once praised the staff of its monthly magazine of poems and short stories, the *Comet*, writing, "A stream of influence comes from . . . [your school] which must surely exert a wide and wider influence for the benefit of the whole country."[46] Perhaps more impressively, however, was the introduction of a daily student newspaper, the *Echo*, which began at the urging of students in 1898. While student newspapers had existed in public high schools since their beginnings in the mid-1800s, a *daily* newspaper was without rival. To sustain it, the *Echo* required multiple teacher sponsors (called censors), a complete staff of students for each day of the week, and—as a sign of Shortridge's political standing—generous school board funding for its very own on-campus printing press.[47]

"To publish a daily paper in a High School is a very dangerous undertaking . . . [and] has never been done before," the editorial team wrote on its first day in print. "However," they continued with the confidence instilled in them by their teachers, parents, and school board, "if any High School is capable, it is . . . [ours], and with that faith in its ability, we have commenced publication."[48] The *Echo* was published continuously for more than five decades, and it served as a fitting symbol of Shortridge's hyperliterate, copiously resourced, and self-possessed culture.

Table 1.3
Occupations of Shortridge and Manual Pupils' Fathers, 1906

	Occupations of Shortridge pupils' fathers (%)	Occupations of Manual pupils' fathers (%)
Managers, corporate officers, merchants, manufacturers	23.2	11.8
Bankers, lawyers, doctors, dentists	8.9	2.6
Engineers, architects	3.0	4.2
Shopkeepers, store owners	4.5	2.4
Real estate agents, salesmen	12.7	7.4
Teachers, nurses, policemen, firemen	2.9	1.5
Skilled tradesmen, artists	13.8	22.0
White-collar clerical workers	16.2	13.5
Clergymen, missionaries	2.4	1.8
Unskilled laborers	4.6	13.9
Railroad employees	3.2	6.9
Farmers	2.9	3.1
Retired	1.3	0.0
Unemployed	0.4	8.9

SOURCE: Indianapolis Public Schools, *Annual Report, 1905–1906* (Indianapolis: Indianapolis Public Schools, 1906), 56–57.

School leaders, possibly hoping to offset Shortridge's rising reputation for academic excellence and exclusivity, wrote often in the early 1900s about the high school system's broad appeal and inclusive spirit. Eager to make its case, the school board in 1906 went as far as collecting and publishing the occupations of every secondary school student's father (see table 1.3). "These tables indicate," it wrote in an introduction to the results, "that the high school is not an institution for the rich alone, but for the poor as well; they both recite in the same classes." The high school, it alleged, "breaks down social barriers; it is a powerful means of promoting the right kinds of understanding between different classes of people."[49] It was a compelling and egalitarian argument for the board to assemble, one rooted in mid-nineteenth-century notions of merit, republicanism, and the noblest purposes of public education. But the numbers, even at first glance, told a different and more nuanced story.

The results of the survey may have substantiated the claim that the high schools in Indianapolis were more middle class than either poor or wealthy, but they also—inadvertently, perhaps—confirmed the existence of a class-based gulf between Shortridge and Manual. By publishing the results by school, the board revealed that Shortridge's families were twice as likely to be headed by "Managers, Corporate Officers, Merchants, Manufacturers," more than three times as likely to be headed by "Bankers, Lawyers, Doctors, Dentists," and roughly twice as likely to be headed by "Shopkeepers, Storeowners." In contrast, the fathers of students at Manual were almost twice as likely to be "Skilled Tradesmen, Artists," or "Railroad Employees" and three times as likely to be "Unskilled Laborers."[50] Moreover, children attending high school at Manual in 1906 were over twenty times as likely to have fathers struggling with unemployment, a painful and unstable position far less common on the North Side.

While students at Shortridge and Manual probably ignored such reports about their fathers' occupations, or the class implications of such studies, they could hardly ignore one another at their annual football game on Thanksgiving Day. Football being the quintessence of masculinity then as today, the two sides had met since 1895 on the fourth Thursday in November at a neutral location (most years in Washington Park). There, the players, coaches, students, parents, alumni, and large swaths of the city repeatedly gathered to "settle the score." As a sign of the game's growing importance by the early 1900s, local newspapers, including the *Indianapolis Sun*, covered the contest with great enthusiasm in the weeks leading up to kickoff. Even though the game carried its own sufficient drama, reporters wrote excitedly, often in the language of war, printing headlines such as, "Teams Anxious for the Whistle," and "Coaches Give Charges Last Bit of Advice," and "Teams Ready to Fight like Tigers."[51]

Although surprisingly little has been written about turn-of-the-century high school football, scholars have well documented the rise of college football in the period, and similarities between the two were marked.[52] As historian Brian Ingrassia has argued, college administrators, along with the politicians who supported them, welcomed the rapid expansion and popularity of football for self-interested reasons. Not only did the sport allow previously elite and almost exclusively academic institutions (including Harvard, Yale, Michigan, and Notre Dame) to build regional and even national fan bases, but it also allowed them to deepen and imbibe in the era's fascination with male vigor. "Besides training young men in the strenuous ways of modern life," Ingrassia argues, football helped "publicize universities and disseminate prevailing ideas about the body and social order." By the early 1900s, the annual Harvard-Yale game, a contest between two of the most storied schools in America, was perhaps the most anticipated athletic contest of the year. Known simply as "the Game," it too was played at Thanksgiving.[53]

None other than President and Harvard alumnus Teddy Roosevelt, who publicly promoted the nation's embrace of masculinity, helped popularize and shape the future of football. Roosevelt viewed football, along with big-game hunting, "big stick" diplomacy, and advocacy of the "strenuous life," as an antidote to the softening of the American man, or the "life of slothful ease, a life of peace . . . [of that] lack either of desire or of power to strive after great things," as he once stated famously.[54] By 1905, however, college football had become so violent, and at times deadly, that Roosevelt was forced to bring the game's leading figures to the White House to save it, "especially by reducing the element of brutality in play," as the *Washington Post* reported.[55] While they succeeded in part by changing the rules of the game—adding the forward pass and halting play when the ball carrier fell to the ground—it was an inescapable fact that more than forty-five young men had died playing football between 1900 and 1905, most of them from traumatic brain injuries sustained at the bottom of a pile of bodies. Roosevelt conceded that football-related deaths should be avoided, but he noted, "I have no sympathy whatever with the overwrought sentimentality that would keep a young man in cotton wool" and "a hearty contempt for him if he counts a broken arm or collar bone as of serious consequence when balanced against the chance of showing that he possesses hardihood, physical address, and courage."[56]

In Indianapolis, the newspapers and many of the city's residents inscribed their own ideas about male strength and bravery onto the annual Shortridge-Manual football game. In the *Sun* as well as in the respective school newspapers, Shortridge's team was known as the "Northsiders" and Manual's team as the "Southsiders," implying that the final scores mattered well beyond the painted lines of the field. Nonetheless, as the games' programs disclosed, the combatants, physically speaking, were merely children. In the 1906 game, for instance, the average Shortridge player was only sixteen years old, five feet eleven inches tall, and a paltry 143 pounds; the average Manual player, in turn, was seventeen, five feet eleven, and 148 pounds.[57]

Though they carried the weight of the city's class-based, cross-town rivalry, risking life and limb in the process, they were far from men. They were high schoolers, but by the early 1900s, in Indianapolis and elsewhere, that meant engaging in far more than academics. Even the schools' young women, who could avoid the punishment of the football field, were unable to fully escape the scope of the class-based contempt. As the Shortridge students chanted derisively of the many female "cooking" or "sewing" students of Manual: "Girls in white, girls in red; They're the gals that make the bread."[58] It appeared that all was fair in love, war, and Indianapolis high school football.

By 1907, the viciousness surrounding the game had reached a boiling point, and student commentators in the school newspapers looked to capture the boyish, but very real, violence for which the event had become known. "For several years," one student explained, "our conflicts . . . have been followed by brawls of the bloodiest nature." As if the game itself, with its actual risk of injury or death, was not enough, the student continued, "Occasionally, the two factions [have] even journey[ed] downtown after the final whistle . . . [to have] their pitched battle on Monument Circle, with the weaker contestants being dumped into the fountains."[59] On other occasions, rioters on the losing end of a fight were thrown into the dangerous White River. Scrapes, cuts, and bruises were common. More critical injuries were always a possibility.

In the *Echo*, Shortridge students nevertheless wrote jokingly, albeit gruesomely, about "football: a system of manslaughter very fashionable with boys."[60] In some years, they included witticisms disguised as linguistics studies, such as, "From the Latin words 'Footibus,' meaning 'put the boots to him,' and 'balloona,' meaning 'up in the air, or who hit me with a public building?' A body of students surrounded by ambulances."[61] Before the 1905 contest, one student captured the bloodthirst in poetry, of all forms.

> Sing a song of football,
> Pockets full of salve,
> Two and twenty legs in all,
> Punctured at the calf.
> Captain in the hospital,
> Full-back in the soup,
> Twenty-seven faces,
> Broken in the group.

Next to the poem was a detailed and conventionally written news report, blandly noting that the game "between the Blue and White and the Red and White" had generated "record-breaking" ticket sales. The spectacle always drew a crowd.[62]

In 1907, after yet another postgame, Monument Circle melee, the school board banned all interscholastic sports, fearing the hostility would only escalate. The year prior, in fact, it had "cautioned both student bodies against such a demonstration . . . with the suspension of athletic activities . . . as the penalty for an outburst."[63] While an observer later described the board's warning as "waving a red flag at a bull," it had no choice but to make good on its threat. Students on both sides circulated petitions against the ban but eventually accepted their fate, reduced to organizing intramural football leagues. As Manual students wrote in their yearbook, the *Mirror*, for 1907, "When the board did finally take action, in spite of the bitter disappointment felt by many, our school settled down again in the spirit of loyalty and obedience to law, for which it has always been noted."[64] Perhaps because they had won seven of the thirteen contests since 1895 (a point they made clear in the *Mirror*), the "Southsiders" felt comfortable taking the high road. Either way, not until 1920 did the city's high schools again clash in football.[65]

While many viewed the Shortridge-Manual game and its accompanying riots as simply the product of a "boys-will-be-boys" culture in the era of Roosevelt, the class-based significance of their bloody Thanksgiving Day meetings was unambiguous. Two years after the ban on interscholastic sports, Superintendent Calvin Kendall, the city's most powerful school leader, articulated the sorting the two high schools had accomplished, however unintentional it had been. "Critics of the . . . public schools," Kendall wrote in 1909, "overlook that in the old-time schools, the children were more largely from educated families than now." The sons and daughters of "the uneducated," he continued, "did not attend school, or, if they did, they attended irregularly . . . [and the] high school or academy pupils were almost exclusively from cultivated homes." Today, however, "large numbers of . . . our high school [students] come from homes of a *different* sort."[66] Since Kendall and his colleagues had developed a secondary school system in which children from "cultivated homes" mostly attended Shortridge, and children from "homes of a *different* sort" mostly went to Manual, they should have anticipated fights after football games. Their actions carried much further than the gridiron.

Sorting students geographically, socioeconomically, and through the curriculum had both short- and long-term implications. And while the average Manual student was probably better off than the average adolescent a generation earlier (since the former's family could forgo their wages), the higher status of Shortridge was obvious. By 1910, less than 30 percent of graduates citywide planned to attend college, but more than 60 percent of Shortridge's seniors had such plans.[67] Further, some of the school's recent graduates, who had gone on to institutions of higher learning, even wrote to the *Echo* about why others should follow in their footsteps. College-going became so common that they crafted testimonials that amounted to advertisements for Yale, Wellesley, the University of Chicago, and several other prestigious schools. "Go to Cornell!!" one former student wrote. "It will make you a man, self-reliant, vigorous and conquering."[68]

Although the bulk of Shortridge graduates attended the respectable and in-state Butler, Indiana, and Purdue Universities, the Ivy League and its peers were regular destinations. Bergen Herod, a senior in 1910, "scored first place in the Yale entrance exam out of all the applicants nationwide." The Harvard Society of Indianapolis had numerous members and offered Shortridge students admitted to America's oldest college "a scholarship of $200 per annum." The *Echo* noted that college graduates were offered similar aid to attend Columbia and Wesleyan.[69] In 1909, the school board proudly printed a letter from William Sabine, dean of the Harvard School of Applied Science, who wrote, "I think I am safe in saying that the pupils of few schools average as high in their college record as those from Shortridge."[70] Since Sabine had been explicitly asked to comment on the city's *entire* high school system, the omission of Manual was glaring. Perhaps he did not even know that the South Side school existed.

Despite the official documents that claimed the secondary school system mixed "different classes of people" and "br[oke] down social barriers," Shortridge's and Manual's principals held sharply diverging ideas, steeped in class-based assumptions, about their respective schools. And the board, sometimes

SHORTRIDGE DAILY ECHO

Vol. 12. No. 77.　　SHORTRIDGE HIGH SCHOOL, INDIANAPOLIS, TUESDAY, JAN. 11, 1910.　　Two Cents

JUNIORS HOLD IMPORTANT MEETING

Class Selects Class Motto—Mrs. Carey presented with a Beautiful Ring

AT THE HELM

MR. WEYANT TO ADDRESS SCHOOL

Subject of Talk in the Auditorium Tomorrow Morning Will Be, "The Air."

GRAYS ARE STILL IN THE LEAD

Teams Will Again Battle This Afternoon for Supremacy in the League

OFFICIAL NOTICES

Indianapolis Public Schools

MORRIS SOCIETY TO MEET

FIG. 1.3 Shortridge High School *Echo* front page, January 11, 1910. (Courtesy of Indianapolis Public Schools and Indianapolis Public Library Digital Collections.)

brazenly, printed statements from both men, almost side by side, in its annual reports. Shortridge principal George Benton, for example, bragged in 1909 that his school's "present requirements have placed us upon the list of accredited schools, recognized by the North Central Association of Colleges and Secondary Schools, of which this school was a charter member." As such, "a large number of our graduates find their way into the various colleges and universities which accept our certificate for work done." Benton admitted that "it is no longer possible to enter college on presentation of [our] diploma [alone]," but he assured the board and the parents of his students that "any boy or girl . . . may prepare in full in this school for any institution of higher education in the land."[71] To Benton, college attendance after Shortridge was relatively common-place, and his school assisted many students on their paths to dorm rooms, lecture halls, and beyond.

By contrast, Manual's principal Emmerich applauded his students who went on to college, but he was unequivocal on the institution's central purpose. "I wish to give expression to my earnest opinion," he wrote in 1909, "that the high school should arrange its courses to meet the demands of the great majority of its pupils who cannot go to a college or university." In other words, "it should not be a preparatory school for higher institutions of learning—only incidentally so—and the only real object . . . should be to lay a deep and broad foundation." For at least 90 percent of his pupils, he asserted, the high school was "the 'people's college,' and it should, therefore, not adapt . . . to the entrance requirements of the colleges and universities."[72] To Emmerich, college attendance after Manual was relatively rare, and his school assisted many students on their paths to factories, secretarial pools, construction sites, and beyond.

By 1910, the ban on interscholastic sports had allowed the Shortridge-Manual rivalry to cool, but the school board, yet again, was preoccupied with overcrowding in its secondary schools. At Manual, school leaders built two additional classrooms in 1903 and, in 1904, two entirely separate building annexes, one of which was three stories tall and included a full-size gymnasium. On the North Side, at Shortridge, they constructed an eight-classroom annex in 1901 and, in 1905, an entirely new three-story building. It contained forty new classrooms, a full-scale cafeteria, a 1,606-seat auditorium, and a gymnasium with an indoor track. Yet both schools still needed more space, despite the fact that the system's operating budget—supervised by the city auditor and treasurer and distributed by the board—reached $1 million.[73] "If the present rate of increase . . . continues," Emmerich pleaded in his signature plainspoken style in 1909, "the time will soon come when some measure will have to be taken to relieve this state of affairs."[74]

In May 1911, the school board concluded that it had exhausted "the property adjacent to either school sufficient to build an adequate addition," and that a third high school was necessary. The school that opened in 1912, Arsenal Technical High School, came to bear three essential characteristics, all of which portended the future of secondary education in Indianapolis. First, it was situated on a massive seventy-six-acre, multibuilding campus. It had once been home to a US arsenal (1864–1902) and, later, the privately funded Winona Agricultural and Technical Institute (1904–1919). Because of Winona's run, however short-lived, the site was ready for immediate use, already outfitted for "technical" and "vocational" education and primed for almost limitless expansions, all of which the school board would need in the coming decades.

Second, the board chose Milo Stuart as Tech's principal, a position he would hold until 1932. Stuart, who had served as Manual's principal since Emmerich's death in 1910, was a rising star in the field of secondary education administration, and Tech would function as a laboratory and proving ground for his ideas, most of which he shared and developed with many prominent administrators throughout the country. In the 1910s, he helped shape Tech into a fully "comprehensive" high school. As the influential *Cardinal Principles* report (1918) prescribed, it would offer both Shortridge's and Manual's curriculum and a whole host of other vocational courses all within its one, extraordinary location. While Indianapolis had once sorted students between its North Side and South Side high schools (and would continue to do so), Tech, under Stuart's guidance, would do the same from building to building and classroom to classroom.

Third, Tech would be racially integrated, for the time being at least. As the next chapter explains, all of the city's high schools, unlike its elementary schools, had been racially integrated since the 1870s. When larger numbers of black children began enrolling in the high school, however, school leaders, pressured by a growing number of whites and white supremacists in Indianapolis, soon questioned the practice. If class distinctions among whites had shaped the high school system's growth before 1900, race, too, would join it as a major issue for the remainder of the century. Including more children—especially of different races, classes, and perceived ability levels—would forever challenge the meritocratic and egalitarian rhetoric that gave birth to the public high school.

Arsenal Technical: The First Signs of a "Mass Institution," an Embrace of the *Cardinal Principles* Report, and the Strains of Inclusivity

Bound by Tenth Street to the north, East Michigan Street to the south, and Oriental Avenue to the west, Tech's sprawling, college-like campus drove much of its reputation. As Principal Stuart wrote in his school's founding year, the board had, in his opinion, demonstrated "a rare far-sightedness" in capitalizing on the existing Arsenal grounds, for their many acres represented "an expansive plan for improvements that will adequately care for the high school problem . . . for years to come."[75] Thanks to its previous use as the Winona Agricultural and Technical School, moreover, it had multiple buildings already outfitted for schooling. In shrewdly making use of the old and erecting the new, Stuart and the board, by 1919, would earn a ten-page, feature-length article in the respected magazine *Architectural Forum*. Tech's campus, then featuring a football stadium, multiple new classroom buildings, a picturesque quadrangle, and access to the bucolic stream Pogue's Run, the *Forum*'s editors wrote, was "of unusual advantages, qualities, and beauty."[76] Their interest and praise were a sign of the times.

Aside from accommodating the secondary school system's future growth, Tech's location, a little over a mile northeast of Monument Circle, was in the heart of the city's quadrant most in need of a new high school. To make this point clear to the board, Stuart, a master communicator, prepared detailed maps of the city divided into quarters, writing in conjunction with them that "the [eighth-grade] graduates of [our grade] schools . . . all live nearer the Arsenal grounds than to either of the other [high] schools, giving [Tech] a position of central vantage." Furthermore, the ever-bold Stuart proved unafraid of speaking directly to the city's patterns of class-based residential segregation, unlike the board. He added, in no uncertain terms, "that the northeastern section of the city, being composed of the substantial middle class, furnishes a very large per capita quota of high school pupils."[77]

Given that Tech would likely draw students from the North and East Sides of the city, catching overflow from both Shortridge and Manual along the way, Stuart favored a curriculum with an exceptionally broad appeal. In describing his career, his daughter recalled that Shortridge "had gained an excellent academic reputation . . . [by] preparing students for college with rigorous courses in Latin, Greek, history, mathematics, English, and modern languages." Meanwhile, Manual "primarily offered practical vocational training courses along with basic courses for students not likely to go to college." Consequently, as more and more children attended the high school, Stuart concluded that both curricula were valuable and necessary. And offering them within one high school—a "comprehensive high school," as leading school administrators called it—was paramount. "Milo H. Stuart had a dream," his daughter wrote. "His ideas were innovative, and his energy boundless."[78]

With Stuart's leadership, Tech marched in step with the recommendations of the NEA's paradigm-shifting *Cardinal Principles* report, which he had helped author. Though principally written by former high school teacher Clarence Kingsley, the report clearly reflected Stuart's larger (and highly influential) educational ideology, arguing that the nation's current model of secondary education failed to meet the needs of both individual students and society.[79] In stark contrast with a "purely academic" curriculum, which Shortridge High had more or less offered since the 1860s, the *Cardinal Principles* enumerated seven broad objectives for America's high schools: "health," "command of fundamental processes" (basic literacy), "worthy home membership," "vocation," "citizenship," "worthy use of leisure time," and "ethical character." While laden with vague language, the report clearly advocated for an expansion of the vocational and nonacademic curricula, which would presumably cultivate the nation's "industrial growth," "efficiency," and "democracy."[80]

On the subject of pupil organization, the report stated, "In short, the 'comprehensive school' is the prototype of a democracy in which various groups must have a degree of self-consciousness as groups and yet be federated into a larger whole."[81] Although it stopped short of explicitly connecting social class, race, or gender to its explanation of "various groups," as Stuart was sometimes wont to do, it insisted that diverse training was required for students.[82] The striking variations in the career trajectories of graduates who studied Latin and mathematics and those who studied manual arts and stenography, therefore, were "natural" and were accepted as welcome features of comprehensive high schools pursuant to the *Cardinal Principles*.

While the comprehensive high school, which would dominate American secondary education after World War I, remained associated with the *Cardinal Principles* report, Stuart was the man who "wrote the book" on the subject. Published in 1926, his treatise, *The Organization of a Comprehensive High School: A Presentation of Plans and Devices of the Arsenal Technical Schools, Indianapolis, Whereby the Interest of the Individual Is Kept Paramount*, took nearly 150 pages to describe what the *Cardinal Principles* report had said in five. Getting at the heart of his philosophy as an educator and administrator, he wrote, "A public secondary school . . . has no choice but to meet the interests, abilities, and the economic necessities of its every individual student," no matter if the student was "dull, normal, or brilliant, and irrespective of his position, wealth, creed or race."[83] It was a burden Stuart was willing to shoulder, but a burden no less, and the stakes were momentous: "'Keep him in' [keep the student in school] must be the verdict . . . if future society is to be spared an unduly institutionalized population."[84] In facing industrialization head on, Stuart opined, Americans could either build comprehensive high schools or be prepared to build prisons, mental hospitals, and other providers of social services instead.

To historian Jeffrey Mirel, the arrival of the comprehensive high school—in which graduates received "the same ultimate credential, a high-school diploma, despite . . . very different education programs and . . . very different standards"—marks a clear, and inequitable, turning point. While Kingsley, Stuart, and similarly aligned administrators and school leaders claimed to act in the name of "democracy" and "efficiency," their actions cemented systems of tracking into secondary education's future. Fittingly, Mirel calls it "the faux equality of diversity"; of great consequence, the public high school would never look back.[85]

Apart from its comprehensive organization, Tech was designed to be explicitly vocational for students on nonacademic tracks. Spurred by mandates and funding from both the state of Indiana's Vocational Education Law (1914) and the federal Smith-Hughes Act (1917), it was able to offer, by 1919, seven different courses of study in vocational subjects: "machine shop practice, automobile construction and repair, electrical work, printing, agriculture, building trades, and salesmanship."[86] Manual High, of course, had offered training for children interested in working-class jobs since the 1890s, but school leaders did not view Manual as purely vocational, for it was broadly concerned with and blended job preparation with academic courses. At Tech, however, "vocational education . . . means just what the term implies—an education which aims to an individual or group of individuals for a particular occupation or trade." Thus, the board stipulated, future electricians would enroll in "electrical work," future mechanics in "automobile construction and repair," and future carpenters in "building trades."[87] Each program had only one purpose.

To further the nascent tradesman's development, the school board determined that every subject in the vocational track would promote vocationalism, even those that were previously considered academic. For example, "the course in English in [the] printing" track, the board wrote, "would include spelling, punctuation, proofreading; [and] compositions would be written on the history of printing and printing materials." Moreover, "the [young printer's] course in mathematics would include problems in the cutting of stock and in estimating the cost of materials."[88] Not a minute was to be wasted in the fast-paced high school of tomorrow, especially on frivolous pursuits such as Plato's *Republic*, the sonnets of Shakespeare, and the principles of physics. "The vocational instruction does not conflict with the regular and fundamental work done by the public schools," Stuart reassured those who might question the changes. "Vocational and general education are merely different phases of the same educational process."[89]

Meanwhile, students at Tech who hoped to attend college were supported fully in Stuart's system, as they had been at Shortridge for decades. Like their vocational-track classmates, they too wore the "green and white" (the school's colors) and considered themselves "loyal Techites," as they were called, but they *did* have the chance to study Plato, and Shakespeare, and physics, and several other academic subjects. The comprehensive high school's built-in system of tracking put college-bound young women and men in different classrooms and in different buildings, and the results were pronounced. By 1925, Tech's twelfth full year, 405 of its 750 graduates went on to institutions of higher learning. Though handfuls of them matriculated at pharmacy schools, normal schools, and fine arts academies, most went to respected four-year universities, including Butler (a remarkable 150 graduates), Purdue (68), Indiana (43), and DePauw (13). Even matching Shortridge's elite reputation to a degree, other members of Tech's class of 1925 enrolled at the University of Chicago (2), Princeton (2), Columbia (2), Wisconsin (1), Michigan (1), Swarthmore (1), and Notre Dame (1). Demonstrative of the comprehensive high school's reach and popularity, Stuart was elected president of the NEA's National Vocational Guidance Association in the same year.[90]

While Tech and its trailblazing principal set about redefining secondary education, little changed at Shortridge and Manual in the 1910s aside from escalating enrollments. If anything, Shortridge became more unapologetically elite in its reports to the school board, particularly in describing its cultivation of students interested in higher education. As longtime principal George Buck noted in 1916, "an important line of work we have been doing for several years . . . concerns the Course of Study . . . [pupils] may desire to pursue . . . especially for those students who are preparing for some particular college." A team of teachers, for example, devoted "ten periods a week to conferences with students and their parents" to discuss entrance requirements, and the school kept "catalogues of different colleges and universities . . . on file," both of which worked "toward making the high school course a means to an end." To Buck, the concerted effort led to "better balance, less scattered courses, and a higher grade of work by candidates for college entrance."[91] At Shortridge, it seemed, the task of having more secondary school students was challenging but straightforward: it simply meant preparing more students for postsecondary education than ever before.

As the next chapter explains, the broad expansion of secondary education after 1900, besides precipitating the comprehensive high school, had unexpected consequences for race relations in Indianapolis. Building over time, the number of young black women and men enrolled across the Shortridge, Manual, and Tech campuses reached almost eight hundred by the early 1920s. Black students constituted only 9 percent of the city's secondary school enrollment, but their growing numbers had an effect on school leaders similar to that seen when more working-class white children enrolled in the 1880s and 1890s. If public secondary education was conceived with white, middle-class children in mind, the arrival of new and different groups of children, especially in combination with limited resources, forced the board, among others in the city, to examine the depths of the commitment to equity through tax-supported education.

If Shortridge, Manual, and Tech enabled school leaders to effectively sort students based on their ideas about social class, what, within their class-based framework, would be their approach to race? Furthermore, when it became clear in the 1920s that race would trump class in the sorting of secondary school pupils, why did the board build an all-black high school where integrated secondary schools had existed since the days of Abram Shortridge? How would black citizens react to the idea of a segregated high school? And once the all-black school—named Crispus Attucks High School—opened in 1927, how would it function in service of its community? The answers reveal much about the creation of a high school *system* in Indianapolis, one perpetually in discord with its nearly century-old pledge of inclusivity and equality.

2

Forced Segregation and the Creation of Crispus Attucks High School, 1919–1929

●●●●●●●●●●●●●●●●●●●●

> Labor Omnia Vincit.
> —Motto of the 1928 senior class of
> Crispus Attucks High School

The inaugural yearbook of the all-black Crispus Attucks High School, published in the spring of 1928 and simply named *The Attucks*, was modest yet elegant, distinguished yet restrained. Heavy to lift with just one hand, the hardcover volume was wrapped in dark green cloth and featured impressive gold inlays (to match the school colors), and within its ninety-eight pages, it included a dedication, a motto, a class poem, and senior class profiles. To showcase the breadth of Attucks's extracurricular activities and the vibrancy of its student life, it also had reviews of its drama club's performances of Shakespeare's *As You Like It* and Oscar Wilde's *The Importance of Being Earnest*; the outcomes of its interscholastic competitions in football, baseball, and, of course, basketball; and page after page of the names and pictures of the bright-faced young women and men who made up the student council, the Big Sisters society, the orchestra, and a variety of other clubs. By almost any definition, then, *The Attucks* had the look and feel of any other high school yearbook of the era. It followed the

FIG. 2.1 Images from the inaugural yearbook of Crispus Attucks High School, 1928.
(Courtesy of Crispus Attucks High School Museum Archives.)

conventions that could be found on the pages of annuals not just throughout Indianapolis, or even the Midwest, but throughout the country—North and South, urban and rural, rich and poor, and black and white.[1]

Just below the surface of the images and text, however, were the realities of a high school fraught with adversity. Crispus Attucks, by 1928, was a high school that was forced to operate within a city teeming with racism and white supremacy. It was part of a public school system grappling with the recent segregation of its secondary schools. And it was charged with serving an African American community that was united in purpose but often divided over the best path forward for its children. *The Attucks's* art and copy, so carefully chosen by the yearbook staff and the school's administrators, seemed to serve as a mirror for it all, and it brimmed with the tension and conflict that had dominated the preceding decade.

Further, to those with a knowing eye, *The Attucks's* first fifteen pages, all of them in black and white, told much of the story. Though in yearbook form, each of them addressed—implicitly and at times explicitly—the most critical, perplexing, often exasperating questions facing black people in Indianapolis at the close of the 1920s. How did segregated education come to be in a city where integrated secondary schools had existed for fifty years? How could the city's African American people admire or revere a school whose creation many had opposed? And once it opened, what kind of school would Attucks become, and how would it serve its community?

In the first five pages, after a list of the yearbook staff members and a brief foreword, the graduating class of 1928, the school's first, had chosen to dedicate *The Attucks* in two parts. It began by thanking the school's principal, Matthias Nolcox, an intense, Harvard-educated, and experienced African American school leader from nearby Princeton, Indiana, "whose love and devotion to our common cause has inspired us." Next, it thanked the school's dynamic and highly educated, all-black faculty, whom Nolcox himself worked tirelessly the previous year to recruit, and "whose guiding hands have directed us to the completion of our High School career."[2]

Dedications were common in high school yearbooks, but they had special importance here. They spoke to the deep pride the students had in Attucks, confirming that the city's black community leaders, despite having opposed the creation of a segregated high school throughout the 1920s, had embraced the task of choosing capable administrators and passionate teachers. Indeed, in a very short period of time, Attucks was becoming a beloved hub of black life in Indianapolis. If a segregated high school was to exist, the city's black citizens seemed to reason, it had better be great.

Following the dedications, nonetheless, were portrait-style pictures of the Indianapolis public schools' all-white board of school commissioners, a group that consisted of, moving counterclockwise, President Theodore F. Vonnegut (whose family had long been influential), Vice President Lillian G. Sedwick, Charles W. Kern, Fred Kepner, and Lewis E. Whiteman. Rounding out the page was Charles Miller, the district's recently appointed superintendent.[3] Though presented without comment, the inclusion of these five men and one woman, in a place of such prominence, undoubtedly reminded the readers of *The Attucks* that their much-loved school—indeed, its entire existence—was the result of the unprecedented political power and electoral viability of white supremacist groups in their city and state, a phenomenon linked directly to the national resurgence of the Ku Klux Klan in the 1920s. And while multiple white citizen groups in Indianapolis had led the charge for the segregation of the city's high schools for nearly a decade, it was this particular group of people, all of whom ran successfully on the Klan-backed "United Protestant School Ticket" in 1925, who embodied its ascendancy.[4]

In stark contrast, page 8 of the yearbook presented a detailed pencil drawing of an ornate, block-long flatiron building, under which it read, "New Home of Madam C. J. Walker Manufacturing Co."[5] Walker, perhaps the most powerful black businessperson in the city, had incorporated her burgeoning beauty company, which sold products designed specifically for black women, in 1911 and promptly transformed the business into a smashing success and an economic and cultural anchor in black Indianapolis. Between 1910 and her death in 1919, it grossed more than $100,000 a year, reportedly making Walker the first female self-made millionaire, of any race, in America.[6]

By proudly including an artistic rendering of her company's new headquarters (which also housed a drugstore, a restaurant, medical offices, and the soon-to-be famous Walker Theatre) in their yearbook, Attucks's students paid homage to the importance of Walker's life as an activist and philanthropist.[7] More pressing for this moment in 1928, however, they demonstrated the impressive reach of her legacy, which was evidenced by the many organizations—businesses, churches, voluntary associations, and schools, among others—she supported that dotted the chain of black neighborhoods on the city's northwest side, the heart of which was the northwest-to-southeast Indiana Avenue, known locally as "the Avenue."

One of the voluntary associations that Walker had long supported, the Colored Men's Branch of the YMCA, was featured on page 9, and its sister organization, the new Phyllis Wheatley Branch of the YWCA, occupied all of page 10.[8] By the first printing of *The Attucks*, the Senate Avenue Y (as the men's branch was known), claimed hundreds of members, ran an array of athletic leagues, offered night classes for adults, and hosted weekly Bible study groups. Moreover, under the leadership of its longtime executive director, the charismatic Faburn DeFrantz (who served from 1915 to 1951), it became the most active and visible forum for the community's debates over the effects of, and the appropriate response to, racism and Jim Crow.[9]

Black people from all walks of life were drawn to the Y under the magnetic DeFrantz's leadership because it provided a place where they could hear speeches from renowned black orators, listen to their neighbors, and, at times, engage in vigorous debate. Was it best, they asked, to pursue integration as the only path to true equality; or, given widespread white intransigence and racism, should they pursue their own, separate institutions—places like Crispus Attucks High School—which they could govern for themselves and with their children's interests in mind? Images of the YMCA and YWCA in *The Attucks*, therefore, owing to their stature socially and politically, demonstrated their significance in the community's past and the school's future. At the same time, they gestured to their connection to national debates over racial equality.

On the one hand, for example, none other than Booker T. Washington, the era's foremost accommodationist and longtime president of the Tuskegee Institute in Alabama, was instrumental in securing funds for the completion of the expansive building that housed the Senate Avenue Y. When it was dedicated in 1913, he stood proudly on the building's steps with the city's black leaders as they posed for photographs that were circulated widely. On the other hand, when DeFrantz attempted to bring the integrationist, and at times directly anti-Washington, perspective to Indianapolis, he sought out men such as Walter F. White and the incomparable black intellectual W. E. B. DuBois of the National Association for the Advancement of Colored People (NAACP). White and DuBois visited and spoke multiple times in Indianapolis, and DeFrantz corresponded with them and confided in them regularly. White and local NAACP lawyer Robert L. Baily organized the legal battle against the creation of Crispus Attucks High School in the mid-1920s.[10]

Pages 12, 13, and 15, which completed *The Attucks*'s introduction, included an image of the new building's handsome exterior (two blocks off Indiana Avenue), a close-up of its intricate entrance (replete with Greek columns), and its senior class's motto, *Labor Omnia Vincit* (Work conquers all).[11] In the space of fifteen pages, ending with an image of the brand-new school building itself, the 1928 yearbook not only helped to contextualize the events of the previous decade that had hastened its existence, but it also signaled what blacks in Indianapolis would hope for, and more often demand of, Crispus Attucks in the coming years.

It tacitly acknowledged the prejudice that had led to a segregated city, an all-black high school, and an entirely Klan-backed school board. At the same time, it celebrated the many recent accomplishments of the school's principal, teachers, and students. And while those associated with Attucks never reached a consensus on how they should rebut the hate and violence of the local white supremacy movement—whether it was Washington's self-sufficiency and accommodationist approach, or White's civil rights and integrationist approach—the opening pages of the yearbook solidified the school's most vital mission: to stand alongside black Indianapolis's numerous other institutions, places like the Madam C. J. Walker Company, the Senate Avenue YMCA, and the Phyllis Wheatley YWCA, as a symbol of community pride. Moreover, Attucks should stand, as the senior class's motto indicated, as a bastion of undeterred hard work, whether in the classroom, in the struggle for equality, or, in the coming decades, on the basketball court.

Black Indianapolis and Life on "the Avenue"

As multiple scholars have noted, migration patterns to Indianapolis were somewhat unique. Its black population was not the direct result of the Great Migration, the decades-long process by which African Americans, beginning in the 1910s and 1920s, relocated from the predominantly rural South to the industrializing North.[12] Unlike Detroit (1.2 percent), Chicago (2.0 percent), and Milwaukee (0.3 percent), for example, Indianapolis already maintained a considerable black population (9.3 percent) in 1910, and the population only grew in size and cultural significance. Bolstered to a degree by the Great Migration, it boasted one of the nation's most vibrant black communities in the decades before World War II. At 13 percent of the city's population in 1940, only Philadelphia claimed a concentration of African Americans as large.[13]

For all its vibrancy by the early 1900s, the city's black residents had faced racism at every turn since Indiana's founding. Before the Civil War, free African Americans, as in most states, were prohibited from voting, serving in the state militia, testifying against a white person in court, and marrying outside their race. In the face of labor market discrimination, they persisted in finding work and paying their taxes, but their children were excluded from the city's burgeoning public, tax-supported school system until well after the Civil War.[14] Article XIII of the 1851 state constitution—while frequently ignored and eventually voided by the Supreme Court—barred African Americans from crossing the state's border to take up residence. Though slavery was eliminated in Indiana by the 1820s, any semblance of racial equality was missing.[15] As renowned African American historian Emma Lou Thornbrough writes, blacks, before and even after 1900, "almost never ventured into a 'white' hotel or restaurant [in Indianapolis], and signs announcing that the proprietor 'catered to white trade only' were not uncommon."[16]

Excluded from white neighborhoods and white Indianapolis writ large, African Americans mostly settled just north and west of the heart of downtown, where, with time, Indiana Avenue and its adjoining streets formed the nexus of the community's economic, social, intellectual, and spiritual life.[17] Forged in the fires of racism, which were fueled by discriminatory housing laws and real estate practices, churches such as Bethel African Methodist Episcopal (founded before the Civil War), Allen Chapel African Methodist Episcopal

(1866), and New Bethel Baptist Church (1875) united their congregations in faith. Newspapers such as the *Indianapolis World* (1882), the *Indianapolis Freeman* (1888), and the *Indianapolis Recorder* (1897) engaged their readership in the politics of race. And businesses such as the Willis Funeral Home (1890), the law offices of J.T.V. Hill (1882), and the Walker Manufacturing Company (1911) met the needs of their nearly all-black clientele.[18]

By the start of World War I, in remarkable fashion, the commercial and residential districts along the Avenue were home to more than two-thirds of the city's black residents, as well as thirty-three restaurants, twenty-six grocery stores, seventeen barber shops, and thirteen dry goods stores. If in need of shoe repair, patrons could choose from among fourteen different cobblers, most within walking distance of one another. Capturing the self-sufficiency of the neighborhood's all-encompassing nature, and perhaps the simultaneous pride and anger its race-based isolation caused, one longtime resident noted that it "was a world within itself. We had everything that we wanted right there on Indiana Avenue. We didn't have to go downtown," whether welcome or not, he stated.[19]

The impressive development of the Avenue and its environs was in many ways the product of the black community's widespread commitment to the racial worldview espoused by Booker T. Washington. As historian Eric R. Jackson has found, Washington's accommodationist approach, which he famously outlined in his Atlanta Exposition speech in 1895, had gained broad acceptance in the city by the early 1900s. Rather than agitating for integration in public spaces, including public schools, Washington urged African Americans to pursue economic self-sufficiency first (often beginning in segregated industrial and normal schools), and he implored them to "own most, if not all, of the social institutions that operated in their [segregated] neighborhood[s]."[20] Echoing Washington's message nearly verbatim, the more conservative-leaning *Freeman* editorialized in 1916, "We have learned to forgo some rights that are common, and because we know the price." As the community was already surrounded by welcoming public spaces along the Avenue, it continued, "we would gain but little in a way if certain [white] places were thrown open to us. We have not insisted that hotels should entertain our race, or the theatres, rights that are clearly ours."[21]

Further demonstrative of Washington's influence in Indianapolis, the newspaper *Colored World*, as early as 1900, referred to him as "a great educator [and] a great reformer." In the same year, a group of influential black business-people formed the Afro-American Local Council, an organization committed to the "Tuskegee principles" and, its leaders stated, "look[ing] after those matters affecting the interests of colored men."[22] Likewise, the Flanner House, which opened in 1900 under the direction of a biracial board and had a wide-ranging social mission, developed an educational program "intended to train blacks for domestic service and other jobs that were customarily open to them."[23]

Perhaps the pinnacle of Washingtonian accommodationism at the time, the expansive Senate Avenue Y was completed in 1913. Given its early commitment to providing a racially segregated space for physical and spiritual health and for imparting "practical" vocational skills, the Y was a testimony to the principles advocated by Washington, who fittingly spoke at its dedication. There, before the city's black press, Washington stood shoulder to shoulder with Madam C. J. Walker, George Knox (the editor of the *Freeman*), Freeman B. Ransom (Walker's attorney and business manager), Joseph Ward (a prominent physician), and other black elites. Historian Thornbrough calls it the epitome of "the Age of Accommodation" for African Americans in Indiana.[24]

Although Washington's political philosophy held sway and shaped the Avenue's character before World War I, the Y (somewhat ironically) would soon become an integral part of the city's civil rights movement, including the legal challenges to housing and school segregation in the 1920s.[25] As the black population continued to expand in the 1910s (see table 2.1), it naturally required more space, both in hitherto white neighborhoods and in the public school system, which was then facing an unprecedented level of overcrowding. In search of new neighborhoods, homes, and schools, the city's African Americans faced an increasingly active segregationist Indianapolis and, by the early 1920s, the powerful racist forces attending the reemergence of white supremacy and the

Table 2.1
African American Population of Indianapolis, 1870–1940

	Population of Indianapolis	African American population	% African American	% African Am. growth over prev. decade
1870	48,244	2,931	6.1	—
1880	75,056	6,504	8.7	121.9
1890	105,436	9,133	8.7	40.2
1900	169,164	15,931	9.4	74.4
1910	233,650	21,816	9.3	36.9
1920	314,194	34,678	11.0	58.9
1930	364,161	43,967	12.1	26.8
1940	386,927	51,142	13.2	16.3

SOURCES: Population statistics for 1870 and 1880: Department of the Interior, Census Office, *Statistics of the United States at the Tenth Census: Population* (Washington, DC: Government Printing Office, 1880), 417; for 1890: Department of the Interior, Census Office, *Statistics of the United States at the Eleventh Census: Population, Part I* (Washington, DC: Government Printing Office, 1890), 704; for 1900: Department of the Interior, Census Office, *Fifteenth Census of the United States: Population, Volume I* (Washington, DC: Government Printing Office, 1901), cxix; for 1910: Department of Commerce, Bureau of the Census, *Negro Population, 1790–1915* (Washington, DC: Government Printing Office, 1918), 768; for 1920 and 1930: Department of Commerce, Bureau of the Census, *Fifteenth Census of the United States: Population, Volume II* (Washington, DC: Government Printing Office, 1933), 69; for 1940: Department of Commerce, Bureau of the Census, *Volume II, Characteristics of the Population, Part 2: Florida–Iowa* (Washington, DC: Government Printing Office, 1943), 813.

Ku Klux Klan. Elements of Washington's accommodationist approach, especially the notion of economic self-sufficiency, would never fully recede, but a new wave of black leaders and their institutions—DeFrantz, the Y, White, and the local branch of the NAACP (founded in 1913)—came to the fore to influence the struggle for civil rights locally for decades.

Housing First, Elementary Schools Second, a High School Third: Segregation, White Supremacy, and the Ku Klux Klan

As soon as African Americans sought to take up residence outside the city's historically black neighborhoods, often looking farther to the north and west, they were met with fierce opposition. Almost immediately, a number of white citizens' groups (often in the form of "homeowners' associations") coalesced, demanding that their members sign so-called restrictive covenants, or documents pledging to never sell or lease their properties to nonwhite families.[26] In 1921, for example, a group of segregationist whites formed the Capital Avenue Protective Association. Similarly, the Mapleton Civic Association, which counted many influential businessmen as members, organized in 1923, declaring that its chief aim was "to prevent members of the colored race from moving into our midst, thereby depreciating property values fifty percent, or more."[27] Perhaps owing to its elite membership, the people of Mapleton tended to wrap their racism in the subtler language of accounting, finance, and business.

With time, however, these organizations became more numerous and took actions that were more overtly racist. By the mid-1920s, the unabashed White Supremacy League and White People's Protective League had surfaced as two of the most vocal opponents of integrated housing in Indianapolis. While the city managed to avoid the race-based riots that erupted in places like East St. Louis (1917), Chicago (1917 and 1919), and Washington, DC (1919), violence and intimidation generated by these groups and their sympathizers were commonplace.[28] When African American families moved into neighborhoods claimed by the Capital Avenue Protective Association, for example, their neighbors on all three sides regularly built abnormally tall "spite fences" to wall off the "intruders"; on at least one occasion, in 1924, a grenade was thrown through the front window of a home of a black family who had ignored the informal housing decrees; and throughout the decade, fearful white citizens distributed race-baiting flyers in neighborhood after neighborhood, many emblazoned with hateful messages such as, "DO YOU WANT A NIGGER FOR A NEIGHBOR?"[29] None of these tactics was unique to Indianapolis, but each represented the rising tide of animosity.[30]

Less than a year after the formation of the Capital Avenue Protective Association, various city organizations turned their attention from housing to public education, though the two were nearly inseparable. Their goal: to pressure the board to formally segregate the entire school system. In early 1922, the Federation of Civic Clubs, a group that had previously sidestepped explicitly racial policies, demanded at a board meeting that the schools segregate, citing health concerns. Quoting statistics from the Marion County Tuberculosis Society, they argued that tuberculosis disproportionately infected the city's black residents. They maintained that the illness was especially common among African American children, many of whom lived in "congested housing" and were "in the incipient stage" of the disease. For the sake of all the city's children, the Federation of Civic Clubs insisted without irony, it was time not for an aggressive campaign to combat childhood tuberculosis but for the creation of completely "separate colored schools."[31] The potential exposure of white children, it implied, posed the greatest threat to the city's program of education.

At the same board meeting, in a move that indicated intergroup collusion regarding school segregation, the Mapleton Civic Association and the White Supremacy League presented their respective cases. In addition to health concerns, they claimed that segregated schools were actually in the African American community's best interest. As one historian summarizes their case, they concluded that "the African American student population would benefit [from separate schools] . . . because [they] would take more pride in their work and in their behavior in such facilit[ies]."[32] By this logic, if their arguments were accepted as sincere, taking the city's recent groundswell of racist activism to its logical conclusion—a comprehensively apartheid society—was the most prudent step the government could take in care of the futures of its people, both white and black.

In the face of mounting pressure, the board acquiesced in March 1922 by creating a "district within a district" for the city's black elementary school children. As a matter of policy, too, it began removing black children from previously mixed-race elementary schools and placing them in segregated ones closest to their homes. Although residential segregation and the maintenance of several "colored" elementary schools had already created a segregated elementary system before the turn of the century, this shift in policy provoked exasperation and anger among many African Americans, particularly those whose children were directly affected. As a result of the school board's actions, scores of black parents were forced to tell their five-to-twelve-year-olds why schools they themselves had often attended would no longer welcome them.

Using a legal strategy that resembled that of the plaintiffs in the landmark *Brown v. Board of Education* (1954) decision more than thirty years later, two different groups of parents in Indianapolis sued the Indianapolis school district. They alleged that the new race-based boundaries made it too complicated, expensive, and emotionally burdensome for their children to attend school. While it was a brave and important step on the road to challenging de jure school segregation, the parents lost both cases. Signaling deference to local school governance, the court claimed ambiguously that "the Indianapolis School Board had the right to implement its own policy."[33]

Surprisingly, given the city's racist elementary school policies, racial integration in Indianapolis's high schools was nearly as old as the institution itself. In 1869, Abram Shortridge and a handful of other prominent, white citizens who had formerly been abolitionists, all with, in Shortridge's language, "an enlightened attitude in regard to colored children," petitioned the state legislature to amend its public school law, which had banned blacks from schools outright for decades. While they were successful in May 1869, Shortridge noted, "two or three years after the law . . . was enacted, few [black children] had mastered the course of study in the district schools and were prepared to enter the high schools." By 1872, however, Mary Alice Rann, "a bright, well-dressed girl," as Shortridge described her, came to the superintendent with "a wish to enter the high school."[34]

Shortridge, perhaps determining that forgiveness would be easier to obtain from the board than permission, took the matter into his own hands. As he later told a reporter, "Without asking any questions, I walked her to the room of the principal [George Brown]," and, "without any explanation or request, I said, 'Mr. Brown, here is a girl that wishes to enter the high school,' and then I went back to my work."[35] Five years later, in 1877, the state legislature made Shortridge's bold course of action part of Indiana law. In line with the doctrine of "separate but equal" included in the *Plessy v. Ferguson* (1896) Supreme Court decision, the law stipulated "that in case there may not be provided separate schools for the colored children, then such colored children shall be allowed to attend the public schools with white children."[36] Inauspiciously, therefore, the Indianapolis high schools were integrated, as there was no separate, all-black high school.

While few records exist on the high school experience for black children before World War I, student publications at Shortridge and Manual indicated a substantial insensitivity to race, and an undercurrent of racism, common in turn-of-the-century America. At Shortridge, the students produced regular minstrel shows and made frequent use of blackface, both in an effort to demean black culture for the sake of comedy.[37] In 1899, for example, the Shortridge yearbook recounted the school's much-anticipated and raucous final performance of the year, noting, "The minstrel show came first. We can distinctly hear, even now the long-drawn 'Oh—!' which came involuntarily from the big audience when the red curtains were mystically separated and revealed two tiers of black faces, mighty collars, flaring red ties, and white gloves. At each of the two extremities, sat two comical figures who were soon destined to provoke tremendous applause by their fun-making."[38] At Manual, in the same vein, the school newspaper, the *Booster*, featured a recurring character in blackface,

Sylvester Simkins, who did and said foolish things week after week. One can imagine how black students, unable to escape these features of high school life, felt about their standing in the halls and classrooms of Shortridge and Manual. The schools' walls offered no protection.

In 1904, a Shortridge student was expelled for refusing to sit next to a black female classmate in, as fate would have it, a civil government class. When the principal, George Benton, reviewed the matter, he sided with the classroom teacher, who had dismissed the student; when the incident escalated, and then required the attention of Superintendent Calvin Kendall, he, too, backed the principal and his teacher. The boy and his family, incensed by the ruling, hired a local attorney to handle the matter, and in an appeal to the school board, the lawyer demanded that the student be reinstated. "The seat adjacent was occupied by a young woman who was personally objectionable to him," the attorney wrote without irony. By the time the board met again, the young woman had already asked to be transferred to another class, "in order to relieve her from the embarrassment which the acts of the suspended pupil" caused her.[39] *She* was embarrassed, but her racist classmate apparently was not.

By 1908, Superintendent Kendall, in a "secret memorandum" to civic leaders, found it necessary to weigh in on integration at the secondary level of education. At the time, there were more than twenty thousand African Americans, almost 10 percent of the total population, living and working in Indianapolis, most of them northwest of the Circle in the proud and vibrant neighborhoods along Indiana Avenue. And though residential segregation, in concert with segregated elementary schools, answered the "race question" through the eighth grade, the public high school was open to interpretation, and Kendall's assessment was emphatic: "Sooner or later, it will be necessary to remove the colored children from the present high schools."[40]

Predictably, the creation of a separate, all-black high school became the next obvious target for white supremacy and segregationist groups in the 1920s. As black children were removed, one by one, from their integrated elementary schools, a dozen or so local groups, united in racism, took aim at the approximately eight hundred young black men and women who then attended the city's three high schools: Shortridge, Manual Training, and Arsenal Tech (see table 2.2).

Table 2.2
High School Enrollment in Indianapolis by Race, 1923

	Male	Female	Total (% of total HS pop.)
White	4,021	4,048	8,069 (91%)
African American	328	464	792 (9%)

SOURCE: Indianapolis School Board, school board minutes, September 1923.

Though the effort was tinged with Indianapolis specifics, a similar pattern was emerging nationally, in both the North and the South. As historian Davison M. Douglas has pointed out, the combination of the Great Migration, racial fears among white people, and racist stereotypes of black people led to new forms of school segregation in districts from coast to coast. Alton, Illinois, introduced segregation in 1897; East Orange, New Jersey, in 1905; and Oxford, Pennsylvania, in 1909. The state of Kansas passed a law permitting segregation at the high school level in 1900, essentially leaving the issue to local boards. In 1912, Arizona mandated segregation in the elementary schools and permitted it in the high schools. Dozens of states and locales passed similar measures. In the age of Jim Crow, Indianapolis's segregationists and white supremacists were far from alone.[41]

The Indianapolis Chamber of Commerce's Committee on Education, perhaps the most powerful and outspoken champion of segregated secondary schools, was the first to present its case, bringing its three-page, typed resolution to a school board meeting in June 1922. Like the Mapleton Civic Association earlier, the committee preferred to describe its motivations in forward-looking, seemingly race-neutral language. It believed that Indianapolis needed several new and "modern" high schools, not just a segregated one. Moreover, "in the development of a comprehensive high school system for the City," it posited, "proper attention should be given to the necessity for a separate . . . completely equipped and adequate high school building for colored students," one that would comply fully with the doctrine of "separate but equal."[42] As a marker of the now-pervasive and unambiguously racist climate, no one on the all-white board asked the committee why updating the high school system required segregating it. The two goals seemed to go hand in hand in service of the city's growth and progress.

Apart from "modernizing" the high school system, creating an all-black institution was routinely framed as a sensible solution to the district's persistent problems with overcrowding, an issue that plagued the elementary and secondary school levels. Arsenal Tech principal Milo Stuart, for instance, visited the board throughout the 1920s to lobby for more space at his school, which then educated more than 4,000 students. Armed with extensive and detailed reports, the sort for which he was famous nationally, he noted that Tech was "1,500 pupils beyond capacity," that "22 rooms [were] in use [that were] never intended for school purposes," that there were "no quarters for a program . . . of physical education," and that there was "no place for assembling any reasonable proportion of the student body."[43] Meanwhile, at the esteemed Shortridge—where the largest number of black students enrolled because of its central location—students, both black and white, "were crowded into classrooms in old buildings that were in a state of deterioration." One report indicated that Shortridge's once-vaunted campus, which was meant to accommodate

1,600 students, was forced by 1920 to make room for 2,600. It was a tough pill to swallow for the white supporters of a high school that was then considered "one of the most academically prestigious public[s] . . . in the United States."[44]

For some white segregationist parents speaking before the board, the combination of racially mixed *and* overcrowded high schools was intolerable. Albert S. Pierson, for example, an employee at the powerful Lilly Company and father of a high school freshman at Shortridge, lambasted the board's inaction in an open letter. He noted up front that his "daughter set her heart upon going to Shortridge almost from the time she started to Grade School because . . . our family attended Shortridge for three generations, and to think that our children have to submit to [the crowded] conditions you are tolerating is beyond belief." What made matters worse, Pierson made plain, was that the overenrolled classrooms at Shortridge included African American children. The mere presence of these students, in search of an education like that received by his family for generations, seemed to cause his daughter added harm. "She came home [from her first day] very much disappointed, naturally, and up in arms for more reason than one," he wrote. "She was surrounded by negroes," he continued incredulously, "and [she] advises that there were more negroes in her classes than white children." Dismayed, Pierson concluded his letter with a demand, one that appeared to capture the mood of the city's segregationist movement: "I want to know just how long the citizens of Indianapolis are going to be compelled to submit to such humiliation."[45]

Pierson and his like-minded allies in the chamber of commerce, the Mapleton Civic Association, the White Supremacy League, and many other organizations received their answer quickly, for the board voted on the matter on December 12, 1922. In a unanimous decision, anticipated by the pro-segregation *Indianapolis News* a few days earlier, the board justified an all-black high school as necessary and wise. At its next meeting, three days before Christmas, it issued a public report that outlined its race-based rationale.[46]

In the language of paternalism and condescension disguised as praise, the board began by acknowledging that "the large number of colored pupils in our high schools . . . shows a laudable desire on their part and on the part of their parents for a high school education." Given that reality, it concluded (in a nod to the chamber of commerce) "that the fullest opportunity should be given for the realization of this desire." A proposed segregated high school would be "modern in construction and appointments," ensuring that its graduates would develop "initiative and self-reliance and the other qualities needed for good citizenship." In an appeal to adherents of Washington's accommodationist approach, the board added, "It is possible to secure fully qualified colored teachers who are graduates of our best colleges and universities . . . [such that] teaching can be put on the highest plane."[47] More than offering a quality education, the all-black high school would also provide well-paying jobs for the African American community's best and brightest.

The board's report read as more dispassionate than hateful, more levelheaded than emotional. While it was fully in agreement with people like Pierson, or the members of the White Supremacy League, it had little use for their fiery rhetoric. It was the decision's implications, therefore, not the tenor of the board's words alone, that were the most insidiously racist. It was the implied superiority of the decision that, in the short and long term, would cause the most harm to racial equality and understanding in Indianapolis. While the struggle for civil rights for African Americans, in Indiana's capital and elsewhere, was inextricably bound to centuries of slavery, and would again dominate the tumultuous 1960s, it was the more localized and less often physically violent decisions of this sort—in this case affecting the daily lives of black high school students and their families—that sculpted the contours of race and freedom for generations of people. Spearheaded by seemingly respectable men in suits (representing the chamber of commerce) as opposed to seemingly loathsome men in white robes and hoods (representing the Ku Klux Klan), it pointed to a form of racism that would be lasting.

According to the school board's minutes, members representing the Ku Klux Klan never spoke before the body in the 1920s. The Klan's leaders undoubtedly applauded the school commissioners' decisions in 1922, nonetheless, for their organization's growth and influence loomed over the drive to segregate the school system and build an all-black school. Indeed, it is impossible to know the extent of overlap and cooperation among the Klan and the numerous other white supremacist and segregationist groups in Indianapolis in the era. But the extent of the Klan's electoral success at the municipal level alone suggests that there was wide agreement and plenty of mutual appreciation.

From the time of the Klan's reemergence as a national force after World War I—distinct from the Klan of the Reconstruction era (1865–1877) and civil rights era (1954–1968)—Indiana, and Indianapolis especially, figured prominently in its development. After establishing its first office in the city in March 1921, its leaders set out to recruit as many members as possible and to trumpet its prohibitionist, racist, anti-Catholic, anti-Semitic, anti-immigrant, and ultimately white supremacist message. By 1922, it had begun publishing a weekly newspaper, the *Fiery Cross*, out of the downtown district's Century Building, and, buoyed by local advertising revenue, it surpassed 125,000 subscribers in less than a year. Between 1921 and 1927, at least 27 percent (and as much as 40 percent) of the city's native white men were official dues-paying members. To one historian of the Klan, Leonard J. Moore, the organization in Indiana was, "by all accounts[,] . . . the largest and most politically powerful in the nation."[48]

As several scholars have argued, the Indianapolis Klan of the 1920s was successful because it fashioned itself first and foremost as a populist bastion of nativism, and as the protector of a myopic view of the values (Protestantism, republicanism, and capitalism, it believed) on which the nation was founded.[49] While it engaged in cross-burning and other offensive displays of intimidation from time to time, it preferred to advance itself through intense nationalism, the ballot box, and a manipulation of the criminal justice system. Part and parcel of its so-called five-point plan, the Klan in Indiana, as historian Wyn Craig Wade notes, developed a platform that attracted leaders of fundamentalist Christian churches, united itself with neighborhood clubs and associations (including homeowners' associations), drove membership with popular outdoor rallies, touted an implicitly biased form of "law and order," and endeavored to make membership for females respectable.[50] Its leaders and politicians, as Moore posits, "were far more interested in patronage and power than they were in ideology."[51] Its commitment to realpolitik, therefore, was its real danger.

In fact, the Klan, as an organization, involved itself in the affairs of the public schools only after the board, citing budget shortages, dragged its feet on executing the highly anticipated "High School Building Program." A response to the 400 percent increase in the secondary school student population between 1910 and 1925, the building program of the mid-1920s was massive. It included not only the creation of an all-black high school but also a new auditorium and cafeteria at Arsenal Tech, an eighteen-room addition at Manual Training, a "modern [and] cosmopolitan" new campus and building for Shortridge, and an entirely new high school for the city's West Side (eventually named George Washington High). Including the annexation of Broad Ripple High in 1924, it hoped to double the infrastructure of the city's secondary schools at the taxpayer's expense.[52]

Although the Klan certainly favored an all-black high school, its approach to the building program was driven by more than racism. Throughout 1923 and 1924, for example, the *Fiery Cross* repeatedly attacked board president Charles W. Barry over the school system's outdated facilities. Beyond reporting that the schools were then using "outside toilets, [and] old stoves," and were subjecting their pupils to "stench and filth and revolting conditions," it also claimed that Barry's efforts to delay construction projects were, of all things, but a piece of a vast Roman Catholic conspiracy.[53] The Catholic Barry, according to the *Fiery Cross*, was being directed by local bishops in an effort to "undermine Indianapolis' public schools" and the city as a whole. To that end, when the city's Catholics raised more than $1 million for a new Cathedral High School (the city's largest private secondary school) in the mid-1920s, the Klan's editors opined, "Protestant children from congested city high schools will find a welcome there," and would thus come under the influence of the pope and his American bishops.[54]

As the 1925 school board election drew near, the opportunistic Klan and its grassroots political machine sprang to action, organizing and backing a group of five candidates sympathetic to their cause. Collectively named the "United Protestant School Ticket," in an effort to accentuate the group's commitment to God and country over its antipathy for blacks and non-Protestant whites, all five candidates were elected by wide margins. So, too, were several other Klan-supported politicians, including Republican mayor John L. Duvall, along with a city council majority to support him. By the end of the decade, owing to revelations of rampant corruption, the resignation of Duvall, and the very public downfall of its most charismatic leader (D. C. Stephenson), the Indianapolis Klan had faded into electoral obscurity. In the meantime, however, its representatives on the school board—Theodore F. Vonnegut, Lillian G. Sedwick, Charles W. Kern, Fred Kepner, and Lewis E. Whiteman—methodically carried out the "High School Building Program" year by year. In doing so, propelled by the Klan, they oversaw the completion of a segregated high school in a city where one had never existed.[55]

A Failed Legal Challenge and the Creation of Crispus Attucks High School: Black Indianapolis Embracing an Unwanted Institution

The argument against the creation of an all-black high school began before the board passed its resolution in December 1922. In November of that year, the Better Indianapolis Civic League—a group of black businesspeople, church leaders, and their allies—submitted a petition in protest. Attached to the list of names and signatures was a letter, penned by prominent lawyer Robert Lee Brokenburr, that enumerated their four primary objections. First, they noted that the public schools were made possible by the taxation of *all* people, so to divert funds in the name of discrimination was "unjust, un-American, and against the spirit of democratic ideals." Second, forced segregation, they reasoned, was likely to lead to friction and unrest among the city's people and was therefore "un-christian, anti-social, divisive in spirit, and pernicious."[56]

Third, in solely practical terms, they argued that placing black students in a completely new high school, rather than expanding the existing ones, "would create considerable added expense . . . [in the form of] teacher's salaries, administrative oversight, heat, light, overhead . . . and the like." And fourth, they asserted that a segregated high school, besides being racist, was an act of class antagonism, and "the attempt to . . . [provoke] such class feeling in the public schools, the cradle of American idealism, is to be condemned."[57] Although it was rejected, the civic league's petition was followed by another one by a delegation of black ministers in early December. Joining the ministers, in turn, were the editors at the *Freeman* and the *Recorder*, both of whom ardently criticized the idea of "the jim crow school."[58]

In fighting to keep the high schools integrated, the Better Indianapolis Civic League and the black press, as well as a majority of African Americans in the city, for that matter, demonstrated their gradual pivot away from the politics of racial accommodation. Their efforts matched a similar evolution on the national level, for the drive for equality and the development of legal challenges to segregation were hallmarks of the ever-expanding NAACP (founded in New York in 1909), as well as its widely read monthly magazine the *Crisis* (edited by DuBois until 1934). When the local NAACP branch was founded in Indianapolis in 1913, it naturally charted the same course, and when the issue of school segregation came to the fore in the early 1920s, its leaders quickly allied themselves with both the national NAACP office and the well-connected Senate Avenue Y.[59]

The local NAACP branch regularly exchanged letters with the New York office to keep the latter informed of the school board's actions and to raise money for the anticipated legal battle. So, too, did DuBois and the Y's Faburn DeFrantz. Even before the board passed its December 1922 resolution, the two men discussed how to attack segregation, and how to explain its inherent threat to democracy. In one particularly lengthy and representative exchange in June 1921, DuBois wrote to DeFrantz, "The theory of the public school is that it should be the foundation of democracy in the land." To separate children systematically, he elaborated, "usually means their virtual separation through life," and this separation solidifies "misunderstanding, friction, group, class, and racial hatred."[60] Though DuBois's prescient remarks fell on deaf ears among Indianapolis's school leaders, it helped to nurture a cohesive integrationist message in cities across the country.

In early 1923, before construction on the high school had even begun, a team of local NAACP lawyers—Robert L. Bailey, W. S. Henry, and W. E. Henderson—filed suit in the Marion County court to block the board's plans. In consultation with Walter White, of the national NAACP office and a close associate of DeFrantz's, the lawyers argued that a segregated high school in Indianapolis, even if conceived and built in good faith, could not possibly meet the demands of the doctrine of "separate but equal." Because it would ostensibly have to match the course offerings, instructional expertise, and educational equipment of the city's three existing high schools, which educated thousands of students in three separate locations, it would either fall short or drown of financial infeasibility.[61]

When the Marion County court refused to issue an injunction, White advised Bailey and his team to appeal to the Indiana Supreme Court, and he assured them that the national NAACP office would attempt to offset the fees. After hearing the arguments, the court handed down its decision in 1926. In *Greathouse v. Board of School Commissioners*, the justices upheld the lower court's ruling, determining that the suit, although potentially valid, was premature.

Because the all-black school had yet to open, there was no empirical way to measure whether black children were denied "an educational advantage accorded white children of equal advancement." Therefore, it would be unjust to infringe on the all-white board's autonomy until such a determination could be made, Justice Benjamin W. Willoughby noted dismissively, "merely to allay the fears and apprehension of individuals."[62] In a city where the Klan ran the municipal government and its schools, and in a nation where dozens of vigilante-led lynchings of African Americans were occurring every year, "fears" was likely a more accurate term than "apprehension."

Before the state's supreme court had dashed their hopes of preventing the segregation of the high schools, black leaders and average citizens alike, perhaps in anticipation of defeat, sought to effect change where they could. For the time being, that meant wresting control of the all-black school's future character by choosing its name. While the board referred to it simply as the "colored high school" in the early 1920s, it resolved, in 1925, to name it Thomas Jefferson High, apparently unaware of or unmoved by the fact that the nation's third president, however influential, owned more than six hundred slaves over the course of his life. After receiving multiple letters of protest, the board determined to change the name to Theodore Roosevelt High, in honor of the twenty-sixth president. Summarizing the black community's displeasure with the new name (though most agreed it was better than Jefferson), one parent appealed calmly to the board: "But as the school is for Colored people, why not allow it to be named after some of their own heroes . . . of noble characteristics?"[63] Eventually, a group of black leaders, including DeFrantz and Brokenburr, submitted yet another petition to the board, and this time the commissioners complied. In early 1927, they adopted the name Crispus Attucks High School, in recognition of the African American who was killed in the Boston Massacre of 1770.

Though purely symbolic, the new name served as a litmus test of sorts for the city's black residents as they came to terms with the arrival of an all-black high school. On the one hand, some people despised both the name and what it stood for, and they would never fully accept what, in their minds, would always be "the jim crow school." One particularly witty commentator, for example, noted that Crispus Attucks the man, far from a hero, was "only an inquisitive barber who ran into the street at the . . . appearance of British soldiers and was shot down with the other" white protesters.[64] On the other hand, many people viewed the school's name as an important victory, a sign that the institution was finally under African American control, and that they alone were responsible for its success. As the *Recorder* wrote in August 1927, a month before the school opened, African Americans had "protested the proposed Negro school from the start," but now they "hope[d] . . . that the faculty of the new Attucks High" would flourish.[65]

Perhaps the most crucial step in setting the tone at Attucks, as the *Recorder* indicated, was choosing its principal and the members of its faculty. Though appointed by the board, the man selected in April 1927, Matthias Nolcox, was African American, educated at Harvard, and an experienced educator from Indiana. He was, by all accounts, humble yet ambitious, soft-spoken yet demanding, and the right person to lead the school.[66]

Nolcox went to work immediately to recruit the most qualified, talented, and enthusiastic teachers he could. According to those close to him, he "interviewed and investigated hundreds of applicants," finally settling on a faculty of forty-eight experienced teachers, some of whom moved to Attucks from college teaching posts in the South, "all of whom had a bachelor's degree," and many of whom "possessed advanced academic . . . or professional degrees."[67] While fifteen teachers left after the first year, subsequent turnover was rare, and many spent their entire careers at Attucks. On the eve of the *Brown v. Board* (1954) decision, for instance, twenty-seven years after Attucks had opened, twelve of the original forty-eight hired by Nolcox remained.[68]

Because of the academic rigor at Attucks in its opening decade, as well as the students' exposure to a highly educated faculty, an impressive number of the school's earliest graduates attended colleges and universities, even though the expense of enrolling proved prohibitive for most young adults. By the early 1930s, the school's yearbooks regularly celebrated the achievements of its pupils and listed the names of its college attendees in the annual alumni directory. Those records, while far from complete, indicated that dozens of Attucks's graduates went on to Indiana University, Butler University, and Purdue University. A smaller group of students, moreover, left the state for some of the nation's most prestigious schools, including Virginia Commonwealth, the University of Chicago, Fisk University, Wilberforce University, Howard University, the University of California–Los Angeles, Dartmouth College, and Oberlin College.[69]

Apart from highlighting the academic demands of the new Crispus Attucks, its earliest yearbooks are imbued with the student body's deep and growing pride in their high school. As enrollments climbed from 1,354 in 1927 to over

Table 2.3
Enrollment in Crispus Attucks High School, 1927–1934

	Male	Female	Total
1927–1928	548	806	1,354
1930–1931	702	871	1,573
1933–1934	697	838	1,535

Source: Frederick K. Gale, "The First Twenty-Five Years of Crispus Attucks High School, Indianapolis, Indiana, 1927–1952" (master's thesis, Ball State Teachers College, 1955), 80.

1,500 in 1933 (see table 2.3), Attucks's administrators added a variety of clubs and organizations, more and more of them in service of the school's social function. In the Christmas 1929 edition of *The Attucks*, for example, the students wrote beautifully and earnestly not only in articles with titles such as "The Negroes Contribution to World's Civilization" but also (and much more frequently) in articles with titles including "School Spirit in Attucks," "The Student Council," "Up and Down the Halls at Attucks," and "A Lesson at Yelling," the last of which was a guide, for oblivious freshman of course, on cheering appropriately at sporting events.[70]

"What is school spirit?" asked Alberta Clemons, a student contributor to *The Attucks* in 1929. "Every upper grade student should know. It is something catching, like an infectious disease." As if she were speaking for all of black Indianapolis, Clemons admitted, "When I entered Attucks in September, I did not feel that I would enjoy being here." After a few months, however, she "found out that school spirit is the key and is essential to every student in Attucks." Like the city's other black institutions that came before it—the Madam C. J. Walker Company, the Senate Avenue YMCA, and the Phyllis Wheatley YWCA—Attucks would be successful, in the face of blatant discrimination, so long as it brought its community pride; so long as it evoked community spirit. Although she was no more than eighteen years old at the time, Clemons knew that much was "essential."[71]

In short order, the men's basketball team, named the Tigers, distinguished itself among the many clubs and organizations. Because the city's and state's segregation laws extended to interscholastic sports, the team's young men were forced to travel great distances to play other all-black schools. They endured painfully long bus rides (often midweek) and the indignity of finding rest stops that would welcome them. Along the way, they earned a reputation that extended well beyond the city, defeating the likes of Central High in Louisville; East High in Xenia, Ohio; Douglass High in Evansville, Indiana; and Wendell Phillips High School in Chicago. Ironically, as chapter 4 addresses, it was the ongoing success of the basketball team—including its multiple state championships in the 1950s—that allowed Attucks, as a cultural institution, to enter the white mainstream in basketball-obsessed Indianapolis. Indicating the limits of the racial understanding that athletics can engender, however, little would change beyond the boundaries of the basketball court once the games had ended. Where it mattered most, racism and systematic discrimination remained the norm for Attucks's students, faculty, and the community the school served. Enshrined in the 1920s, it was a practice that lasted well into the postwar years, even after legally mandated school segregation was eliminated in 1949.

As the next chapter explains, the emergence of intense school pride, as well as a distinctive youth culture at the secondary school level, was not unique to

Crispus Attacks High School. Though Attucks's students would always be united over the pain caused by segregation, and celebrate their accomplishments at school, their growing affinity for "the green and the gold" was part of a much larger national phenomenon, one that developed in American high schools in the 1930s irrespective of race, class, or geographic location. During the years of the Depression—as secondary school enrollments skyrocketed, as "custodialism" was on the rise, and as jobs for adolescents disappeared—the students of Indianapolis and elsewhere described the extending reach of the high school not in curricular terms but in social ones. School dances and other school-sponsored peer gatherings, which had existed alongside interscholastic sports and student clubs for decades, increasingly defined the boundaries of American youth culture.

Meanwhile, as the high school experience became the norm for Indianapolis's young people, black and white, the city's administrators responded by pursuing obedience and respect for authority above all. By implementing more rules, regulations, and procedures—in addition to expanding and controlling extracurricular activities—they attempted to create a complete social world for their pupils. The resulting peer culture, which students were required to embrace to receive the high school's benefits and resources, was rooted in the norms of the nation's broader culture, and it stressed middle-class, white, Christian, patriarchal, and heteronormative values. Conformity to the existing social order meant abiding by a host of dominant values, wherever one attended high school.

3

The High School Moves to the Center of the American Adolescent Experience, 1929–1941

● ●

> Freshman!
> Do you want to know everything that is going on in school?
> Do you want to find out who the famous upperclassmen are?
> Do you want to see what freshman are stepping out in front right away?
> Do you want to do something to make yourself indispensable to the school first thing?
> O.K.—Subscribe to The Echo!!!
> —Advertisement for the Shortridge High School daily newspaper, the *Echo*, September 6, 1932

By the close of the 1920s, Indianapolis, like much of urban America, had created a high school system. It was a system that sorted its secondary school students by race, as a matter of law, and by class, as a matter of local custom and geography. And although school leaders maintained a policy of open enrollment for all white children throughout the first half of the twentieth century (they could conceivably attend *any* high school), students and their families understood fully the race- and class-based divisions that defined the prestigious Shortridge High, the "hand-minded" Manual Training High, the comprehensive Arsenal Tech High, and the all-black Crispus Attucks High. Indeed, school leaders noted in official documents in 1934 that the city was "not rigidly districted for high schools and white pupils may make their own choice as to schools." But they admitted, quite plainly, that in reality, "pupils usually make their choice dependent upon accessibility . . . and type of work desired."[1] Some, they reasoned, desired to find blue-collar work, while others desired to find white-collar work; some had easy access to Manual, while others had easy access to Shortridge. Put another way, when students wore their school colors into the community, they carried the carefully crafted reputation of an institution with them, one that had only hardened over the last three decades.

Alfred Kuerst, for example, who graduated from Tech in 1933, grew up in Indianapolis's Irvington neighborhood, just a few miles east of Tech's massive campus. When asked as an adult about his high school experience for an alumni magazine, he immediately recalled the city's well-established way of sorting students. "Most of my [white] childhood friends [in the modestly integrated Irvington neighborhood] went to Tech," he wrote, but "black students were required to go to Crispus Attucks. One of my best friends [from childhood], Frank Shobe," he continued with regret, "had no choice but to go to Attucks."[2] To Kuerst, school-based inequality was what was most memorable.

Rosalind Petrovich, who lived on the West Side of Indianapolis in the firmly working-class Haughville neighborhood, chose to enroll at Shortridge in 1931 for its sterling "academic reputation" but quickly transferred to Tech for financial and social reasons. "I transferred from Shortridge . . . during the depression . . . [when] money was scarce," she told the alumni magazine. Because the school system did not provide transportation for its students, the long trip from Haughville to the North Side Shortridge was expensive, and "car fare was a problem" for her and her family. Furthermore, Petrovich recalled, "At Shortridge I felt like I was from the 'wrong side of the tracks.' I grew up in an ethnic neighborhood . . . [and lived among] Serbs, Greeks, Hungarians, Romanians, all mixed together, [and] we had a certain kind of fellowship and celebrated family and religious events together."[3] At Shortridge, Petrovich felt her home culture was out of place. Shortridge's "blue and white" had long stood for "North Side" and "wealthy," and that message rang loud and clear to a young woman from the East Side.

With a high school system firmly in place, school leaders and administrators faced a new and unexpected challenge beginning in the 1930s: the Great Depression. Owing to its relatively diversified economy, Indianapolis fared better than most midwestern cities, but it suffered markedly all the same. As early as 1931, for example, the *Indiana Business Review* reported that employment and business activity had declined in the city for twenty-two months in a row. By that summer, nearly every laborer in the manufacturing sector only worked part time. As historian Deborah Markisohn has written, "Finding a job was particularly difficult for middle-aged men, since men over forty-five were considered past their prime."[4] As a visible marker of the collapse, home construction slowed and then stalled in Indianapolis. In 1933, only twenty-seven dwellings were completed in the *entire* city. Though Indiana's capital never faced unemployment rates as abysmal as Cleveland's (50 percent) or Gary's (a devastating 90 percent), the decade's nadir saw numbers as high as 37 percent. The population grew by more than 20,000 in the 1930s (reaching nearly 390,000), and municipal tax coffers for routine services and maintenance, let alone relief, dwindled quickly. Breadlines, homelessness, near starvation, and desperation became ever present.[5] The city, like the nation, had fallen on hard times.

Aside from wrecking the economy, the Depression sent more teenagers into the secondary schools than ever before, for there simply were fewer and fewer jobs for them. And it was during this unprecedented spike in enrollments, scholars have pointed out, that the nation's high schools adopted a "custodial mission." Their primary function became keeping adolescents, as one historian puts it, "out of the adult world (that is, out of the labor market), instead of preparing them for it."[6] For the first time in their history, therefore, American high schools, and the administrators who led them, appeared to care as much about occupying a young person's time as they did about ushering him or her toward graduation.

The shift was a watershed in the institution's history.[7] As Thomas Hine notes in his history of the American teenager, industrialization from the turn of the century through the 1920s, especially the rise in disposable income for young people, "had glamorized and eroticized youth." But, Hine continues, "the Depression and the war that followed did something even more decisive to youth: They bureaucratized it."[8]

To take on the custodial mission, as well as to "bureaucratize youth," school leaders in Indianapolis, like their urban peers, added dozens of courses to the city's schools, nearly all of which eschewed the traditional academic subjects in favor of watered-down, "practical" courses including Community Civics, Home Living, Social Practice, and Hygiene.[9] In many ways, this was a continuance of the process of curricular diversification that began with the opening of Manual Training High in 1895 and the comprehensive Arsenal Technical High in 1912. Nonetheless, what made this administrative push for "usefulness" and "practicality" unique was that, as several historians have suggested, it also endeavored to shape the high school pupil's individual character, or what one Indianapolis principal called the student's "physical, spiritual, mental, and cultural" personality.[10]

With a goal that expansive in mind, administrators, in addition to broadening the curriculum, widened the high school's social and cultural significance. Over the course of the 1930s, they created more rules, policies, and procedures, which they enshrined in increasingly complex and ubiquitous "student hand-books," known today as "codes of conduct." Furthermore, they dramatically expanded extracurricular activities, which soon filled more hours of a teenager's day than ever before. Of course, after-school activities were as old as the high school itself, but they more than doubled in the age of custodialism, from an average of roughly twenty per school to more than forty. By decade's end, if a student had an interest, the high school probably had a formal club to address it.[11]

Combined, these two changes—for more rigidity and for more social relevance—made the Depression-era high school an "all-inclusive" experience. As Robert Lynd and Helen Lynd observe in their groundbreaking study of Middletown (Muncie, Indiana), "The high school, with its athletics, clubs[,] . . . dances and parties and other 'extracurricular activities,' is a social cosmos unto itself, and about this city within a city, the social life of the intermediate generation [that is, the adolescent generation] centers."[12] The Lynds could have just as easily been writing about Indianapolis, only sixty miles away.

Within that manufactured and heavily regulated "social cosmos," school leaders pushed for cultural homogeneity among their students, one that reflected the nation's middle-class, white, Christian, patriarchal, and hetero-normative values.[13] And while school dances, sexist policies regarding athletics, overtly Christian clubs, and near-constant adult supervision did much to accomplish this goal, what fortified its potency was how well administrators enlisted many students in the effort. In the form of student newspapers and yearbooks, in particular (which have been preserved to a remarkable degree in Indianapolis), the student culture that emerged in the 1930s sought above all to maintain order and hierarchy.

Time and again, the student voices captured in these documents called for intense school spirit, more orderly hallways and classrooms, appropriate and traditional courtships, clearly demarcated gender roles, and a strict pecking order of power and respect among students (wherein freshman were placed firmly at the bottom). There would always be resistance and youth "subcultures," but they were systematically silenced in the ever-expanding high school. To have access to the high school's abundant resources and powerful platforms—to write for the paper, to win an award, to get a scholarship, or to be featured in the yearbook—meant adopting what sociolinguist Penelope Eckert would later name a "pro-school" attitude.[14]

While the school system had effectively divided students geographically, through the curriculum, and with racist policies over the course of the previous three decades, the 1930s witnessed an added goal: for the first time, the high school aimed to move the center of the adolescent experience. And it succeeded. Through more course offerings, more rules, more clubs, and a more carefully managed youth culture, the high schools in Indianapolis produced a reliably conformist student population. It was a product that would be lasting.[15]

Becoming Custodial Institutions: An Expansion of Course Offerings (and Their Aims) in the Depression

As historians have documented well, public high schools adopted what is best described as a "custodial mission" during the Depression, or what David Angus and Jeffrey Mirel characterize as a shift from preparing students for "adult roles and responsibilities" to directing attention to the "immediate and clearly relevant problems of youth."[16] Part and parcel of that mission was the continued expansion of the number of courses for students on their path to graduation, a process that began with the arrival of manual and industrial training at the turn of the century and continued during the drive for vocationalism and "practical learning" in the 1910s and 1920s. Recall from chapter 1 that the National Education Association's *Cardinal Principles* report, published in 1918, came to symbolize this trend in the secondary school curriculum.

The report's authors, whose words eventually circulated widely, wrote with near certainty that an abundance of options for adolescents, some academic and some more "practical," was not only efficient (and therefore good for society) but also democratic and equitable (and therefore fair to the individual). "This ideal [of organizing a democratic society]," they wrote, "demands that human activities be placed upon a high level of efficiency."[17] From this perspective—one embodied by Milo Stuart, Tech principal and member of the commission that wrote the *Cardinal Principles*—efficiency and democracy went hand in hand in the twentieth century.

In line with national trends, administrators in Indianapolis added courses, year after year, to the city's high schools, often at a staggering pace (see table 3.1). At the institution's inception in the 1860s, for example, students could choose

Table 3.1
Number of Courses Taught in the Indianapolis
High Schools, 1868–1933

	No. of different subjects
1868	22
1873	24
1883	26
1893	27
1903	46
1913	63
1923	106
1933	144

SOURCE: Indianapolis Public Schools, *Survey Findings: Senior High School Division Secondary Schools* (Indianapolis: Indianapolis Board of School Commissioners, 1934), 14.

ARSENAL TECHNICAL SCHOOLS

Including the Technical High School and the Vocational Schools
Indianapolis, Indiana
DeWitt S. Morgan, Principal

The chart below sets forth the subjects offered in the Arsenal Technical Schools by years and semesters. The upper part of the chart lists subjects in the Technical High School from which pupils who wish general education, both cultural and practical, may make elections. The lower part of the chart lists subjects in the vocational schools for pupils whose abilities, interests, and circumstances call for training for specific skill in established industrial processes.

THE TECHNICAL HIGH SCHOOL

(For pupils wishing a general education, both academic and technical courses are offered)

Subjects are listed below in perpendicular columns according to the year and the semester in which they may first be taken, as determined by the grade of English. In the ninth year pupils elect subjects according to instructions as set forth in the bulletin for Junior High Schools. (q.v.) Above the ninth year, each pupil shall select four full credit subjects to which one half-credit subject may be added. Deviation from this amount of work requires special permission; conditions under which this is permitted are set forth in the Description of Courses of Study. Symbols used in the chart are explained in the footnote.

ACADEMIC COURSES

SPECIFIC REQUIREMENTS FOR GRADUATION	Ninth Year		Tenth Year		Eleventh Year		Twelfth Year	
	First Semester	Second Semester	First Semester	Second Semester	First Semester	Second Semester	First Semester	Second Semester
ENGLISH	ENGLISH I	ENGLISH II *Physical Education II*	ENGLISH III	ENGLISH IV	ENGLISH V *AMERICAN HISTORY I HYGIENE (Girls) or PHYSIOLOGY (Boys and Girls)*	ENGLISH VI *AMERICAN HISTORY II*		
	Physical Education I					In addition to the required subjects specifically listed here, pupils must elect as follows: One year of mathematics (see below); One year of laboratory science, (see below); and one additional year of social studies (see below).		
			ENGLISH III *(LIBRARY PRACTICE)*	ENGLISH IV *(LIBRARY PRACTICE) II*	ENGLISH V *(LIBRARY PRACTICE) III ADVERTISING I JOURNALISM*	ENGLISH VI *(LIBRARY PRACTICE) IV EXPRESSION I* PUBLIC SPEAKING I* *German Practice*	ENGLISH VII* ENGLISH VIII* ENGLISH VIIC* EXPRESSION II* PUBLIC SPEAKING II* *German Practice*	ENGLISH VIIC* ENGLISH VIIIC* ENGLISH VIIC* EXPRESSION III* PUBLIC SPEAKING III* *German Practice*
MATHEMATICS	GENERAL MATHEMATICS I ALGEBRA I	GENERAL MATHEMATICS II* ALGEBRA II	GEOMETRY I	GEOMETRY II*	ALGEBRA III* ARITHMETIC*	*SOLID GEOMETRY*	*TRIGONOMETRY* COLLEGE ALGEBRA*	*SURVEYING*
FOREIGN LANGUAGE	LATIN I FRENCH I GERMAN I SPANISH I	LATIN II* FRENCH II GERMAN II SPANISH II	LATIN III FRENCH III GERMAN III SPANISH III	LATIN IV FRENCH IV GERMAN IV SPANISH IV	LATIN V FRENCH V GERMAN V SPANISH V	LATIN VI* FRENCH VI* GERMAN VI* SPANISH VI*	LATIN VII FRENCH VII GERMAN VII SPANISH VII	LATIN VIII* FRENCH VIII* GERMAN VIII* SPANISH VIII*
SOCIAL STUDIES	SOCIAL STUDIES I	SOCIAL STUDIES II*	ECONOMIC GEOGRAPHY I (J) EUROPEAN HISTORY I	ECONOMIC GEOGRAPHY II* (J) EUROPEAN HISTORY II	AMERICAN HISTORY I EUROPEAN HISTORY III INDUSTRIAL HISTORY I (J)	AMERICAN HISTORY II* EUROPEAN HISTORY IV* INDUSTRIAL HISTORY II* (J)	AMERICAN GOVERNMENT*	GOVERNMENT PROBLEMS*
SCIENCE			*BOTANY I PHYSIOGRAPHY I* ZOOLOGY*	*BOTANY II PHYSIOGRAPHY II* ZOOLOGY II*	*CHEMISTRY I* *PHYSICS I*	*CHEMISTRY II* *PHYSICS II*	*CHEMISTRY III* *PHYSICS III*	*CHEMISTRY IV* *PHYSICS IV*

For ... requirement is waived for vocational shop pupils.

PRACTICAL AND TECHNICAL COURSES

INDUSTRIAL ARTS (f)	†GENERAL SHOP IB / ‡GENERAL SHOP IM / (PRINTING IM*) (Ninth year only)	†GENERAL SHOP IIB / ‡GENERAL SHOP IIM / PRINTING II*	†GENERAL SHOP IIB or General Mathematics II† / ‡GARDENING	†MILL WORK I / ‡RADIO I / ‡LANDSCAPING*	†MILL WORK II* / ‡RADIO II*	‡MILL WORK III / ‡RADIO III	‡MILL WORK IV* / ‡RADIO IV*
				For Radio and Mill Work, Physics I and II and Chemistry I and II are required just as for Advanced Shop Practice.			
DRAFTING (g)	Mechanical Drawing I*	Mechanical Drawing II*	Mechanical Drawing III	Mechanical Drawing IV*	‡MACHINE DRAFTING I (Pupils must have at least a B in Mechanical Drawing IV. They must have taken or must start certain requirements is waived for vocational shop pupils.) / ‡ARCHITECTURAL DRAFTING I* (h)	‡MACHINE DRAFTING II* / ‡ARCHITECTURAL DRAFTING II*	‡MACHINE DRAFTING III (Pupils electing this course must start Physics and Advanced Shop Practice in Machine Shop.) / ‡ARCHITECTURAL DRAFTING III (h)	‡MACHINE DRAFTING IV* / ‡ARCHITECTURAL DRAFTING IV*
FINE ART (h)	†ART I	†ART .... II* / Arts and Credits I* — II*	‡CRAFTS I* / †ART IV*	‡CRAFTS II* / †ART III	†ART APPRECIATION I* / †ADVANCED DRAWING I* / †DECORATIVE ART I* (One year of shop work also when pupil eligible) / †ART V* (h)	†ART APPRECIATION II* / †ADVANCED DRAWING II* / †DECORATIVE ART II* / †ART VI* (h)	‡ADVANCED DRAWING III / †ADVANCED DRAWING IV* / †DECORATIVE ART III / ‡STAGE COSTUME I*	†ADVANCED DRAWING IV* / †DECORATIVE ART IV* / ‡STAGE COSTUME II*
GRAPHIC ART (i)	‡GRAPHIC ART I (One year of Mechanical Drawing, or four semesters of Print Design also make pupils eligible.)	‡GRAPHIC ART II*	‡COMMERCIAL ART I	‡COMMERCIAL ART II*	‡COMMERCIAL ART III / ‡LAYOUT I	‡COMMERCIAL ART IV* / ‡LAYOUT II*		
COMMERCE (j)	JUNIOR BUSINESS I (Ninth year pupils only)	JUNIOR BUSINESS II*	‡BOOKKEEPING I / STENOGRAPHY I (Prerequisite: B in English, Typewriting I or II must be taken with Stenography.) / Typewriting I / Typing may be taken one year without stenography	‡BOOKKEEPING II / STENOGRAPHY II / Typewriting II	‡BOOKKEEPING III / STENOGRAPHY III / Typewriting III	‡BOOKKEEPING IV* / STENOGRAPHY IV* / Typewriting IV* / Open before English IV to pupils 16 years of age.	BUSINESS ORGANIZATION I (d) / ‡OFFICE PRACTICE I* / ‡MACHINE CALCULATING* / FILING* / SALESMANSHIP I*	BUSINESS ORGANIZATION II (d) / ‡OFFICE PRACTICE II*
HOME ECONOMICS (k)	Social Practice I / HOME ECONOMICS I (Open to ninth year girls only)	Social Practice II* / HOME ECONOMICS II*	‡FOODS I* / ‡CLOTHING I* (Dressmaking I, II, III, Millinery II, III =Foods, III, IIIB. IV and IVB require supplementary units. See "Description of Courses.")	‡FOODS II* / ‡DRESSMAKING I* / ‡CLOTHING II* / ‡FOODS III* / ‡MILLINERY I*	‡FOODS IV* / ‡DRESSMAKING II* / ‡CLOTHING IV* / ‡FOODS III* / ‡TEXTILES* / ‡MILLINERY II*	‡DRESSMAKING III* / ‡FOODS III* / ‡MILLINERY III*	‡FOODS IVB*	
MUSIC (l)	Chorus IB / Chorus VIB* / Orchestra I / Band I / Instrumental Music I	Chorus IIB* / Chorus VII* / Orchestra II / Band II / Instrumental Music II*	Chorus VII / Orchestra III / Band III / HARMONY I / HARMONY II (Pupils taking any instrumental music take private music lessons; for conditions see "Description of Courses.") / VOCATIONAL MUSIC I	Chorus VII / Chorus VIII / Orchestra IV / Band IV / HARMONY III / HARMONY IV / MUSIC APPRECIATION I / VOCATIONAL MUSIC II (C F G B)	Chorus VII / Chorus VIII / Orchestra V / Band V / HARMONY IV / MUSIC APPRECIATION II / VOCATIONAL MUSIC III / C—Choral directing / F—Piano accompanying	Orchestra V / Band V / VOCATIONAL MUSIC IV / C—Choral directing / G—Orchestra directing / B—Band directing	Orchestra VI* / Band VI*
HEALTH EDUCATION, PHYSICAL TRAINING, MILITARY TRAINING (m)	Physical Education IB* / Physical Education IG*	Physical Education IIB* / Physical Education IIG*	Military Training I / Physical Education I?G* / HYGIENE (girls) / PHYSIOLOGY	Military Training II* / Physical Education I?G* / NURSING I	Military Training III* / NURSING I	Military Training IV	Military Training V	Military Training VI*

A **major** consists of six credits; a **minor** consists of four credits. For graduation, a pupil must select his work so that he has at least two majors and two minors in distinct subject fields. The separate subject fields are listed at the left of the chart and are designated by letters. The vocational shops are considered as belonging in the same field as Industrial Arts (f). Fine Art (h) and Graphic Art (i) cannot be offered as separate majors or minors. Certain subjects listed on this chart are followed by a letter in parenthesis: e. g., Business Organization II (d). A subject so designated may count toward majors or minors either in the field in which it is listed on the chart or in the field designated by the letter in parenthesis: i. e., Business Organization may count toward majors or minors either in Commerce or Social Studies.

*Not more than two credits earned in half credits may be counted, in this group, toward majors and minors.

(continued)

THE VOCATIONAL SCHOOLS
(For pupils wishing definite trade training)

A pupil who elects a vocational school takes all subjects exactly as listed in the school chosen. At the completion of the two years of work as provided in any vocational school, a certificate is granted. If upon the completion of the work a vocational school, a pupil wishes to continue in high school, all credits earned in high school may be applied toward graduation, from The Technical High School. Vocational certificates are granted in the 14 groups below and may also be earned in certain of the subject groups above: Drafting, Graphic Art, Home Economics, Music, Radio, Mill Work.

TWO YEAR VOCATIONAL SCHOOLS

	Ninth Year — First Semester	Ninth Year — Second Semester	Tenth Year — First Semester	Tenth Year — Second Semester
	1AGRICULTURE I / ENGLISH I / ELECTIVE	1AGRICULTURE II / ENGLISH II / ELECTIVE	1AGRICULTURE III / ENGLISH III / ELECTIVE	1AGRICULTURE IV / ENGLISH IV / ELECTIVE
	1PRINTING I (VOC.) / Print Design I / PRINT MATHEMATICS I / ENGLISH I	1PRINTING II / Print Design II / PRINT MATHEMATICS II* / ENGLISH II	1PRINTING III / Print Design III / ENGLISH III / ELECTIVE	1PRINTING IV* / Print Design IV* / ENGLISH IV* / ELECTIVE
	1GEN. SHOP IE (VOC.) / Related Work I / Mechanical Drawing I / ENGLISH I OR OTHER / ACADEMIC ELECTIVE	1ELECTRICAL SHOP II / Related Work II / Mechanical Drawing II / ENGLISH II OR OTHER / ACADEMIC ELECTIVE	1ELECTRICAL SHOP III / Related Work III / Mechanical Drawing III / ENGLISH III OR OTHER / ACADEMIC ELECTIVE	1ELECTRICAL SHOP IV* / Related Work IV* / Mechanical Drawing IV* / ENGLISH OR OTHER / ACADEMIC ELECTIVE
Building Crafts Group	1CABINET MAKING II / Related Work II* / Mechanical Drawing II* / ENGLISH OR OTHER / ACADEMIC ELECTIVE	1CABINET MAKING III / Related Work III* / Mechanical Drawing III* / ENGLISH OR OTHER / ACADEMIC ELECTIVE	1CABINET MAKING IV* / Related Work IV* / Mechanical Drawing IV* / ENGLISH OR OTHER / ACADEMIC ELECTIVE	
	1CARPENTRY II / Related Work II / Mechanical Drawing II* / ENGLISH OR OTHER / ACADEMIC ELECTIVE	1CARPENTRY III / Related Work III / Mechanical Drawing III / ENGLISH OR OTHER / ACADEMIC ELECTIVE	1CARPENTRY IV* / Related Work IV* / Mechanical Drawing IV* / ENGLISH OR OTHER / ACADEMIC ELECTIVE	
	1CEMENT WORK II / Related Work II / Mechanical Drawing II / ENGLISH OR OTHER / ACADEMIC ELECTIVE	1CEMENT WORK III / Related Work III / Mechanical Drawing III / ENGLISH OR OTHER / ACADEMIC ELECTIVE	1CEMENT WORK IV* / Related Work IV* / Mechanical Drawing IV* / ENGLISH OR OTHER / ACADEMIC ELECTIVE	
1GENERAL SHOP IB / VOCATIONAL / Related Work I / Mechanical Drawing I / ENGLISH I OR OTHER / ACADEMIC ELECTIVE	1PLUMBING II / Related Work II / Mechanical Drawing II / ENGLISH OR OTHER / ACADEMIC ELECTIVE	1PLUMBING III / Related Work III / Mechanical Drawing III / ENGLISH OR OTHER / ACADEMIC ELECTIVE	1PLUMBING IV* / Related Work IV* / Mechanical Drawing IV* / ENGLISH OR OTHER / ACADEMIC ELECTIVE	
	1PAINTING AND	1PAINTING AND	1PAINTING AND	

Advanced Technical courses are open to pupils completing two years of vocational shop with an average grade of B. Certain pupils with less than two years of vocational shop training may be given special permission to enter an advanced technical course providing there is evidence of sufficient industrial background and educational need, on account of the advanced technical nature of these courses, Physics and Chemistry are both taken with the Advanced Shop Practice as indicated in the chart at the right. The Advanced Shop Practice does not need to be in the same shop as the one in which the pupil has done the two years of vocational work...

ADVANCED TECHNICAL AND VOCATIONAL COURSES

	Eleventh Year — First Semester	Eleventh Year — Second Semester	Twelfth Year — First Semester	Twelfth Year — Second Semester
	1ADVANCED SHOP PRACTICE I PE / with / PHYSICS I	1ADVANCED SHOP PRACTICE II PK* / with / PHYSICS II	1ADVANCED SHOP PRACTICE III PE / with / CHEMISTRY I	1ADVANCED SHOP PRACTICE IV* / with / CHEMISTRY II
	1ADVANCED SHOP PRACTICE IE / with / PHYSICS I	1ADVANCED SHOP PRACTICE IIE / with / PHYSICS II*	1ADVANCED SHOP PRACTICE IIIE / with / CHEMISTRY I	1ADVANCED SHOP PRACTICE IV* / with / CHEMISTRY II
	1ADVANCED SHOP PRACTICE I	1ADVANCED SHOP PRACTICE II*	1ADVANCED SHOP PRACTICE III	1ADVANCED SHOP PRACTICE IV*
	I CM = CABINET MAKING / CR = CARPENTRY / PL = PLUMBING / PD = PAINTING AND DECORATING	II CM* / II CR* / II PL* / II PD*	III CM / III CR / III PL / III PD	IV CM* / IV CR* / IV PL* / IV PD*
	2GROUND MECHANICS I	2GROUND MECHANICS II*	2GROUND MECHANICS III	2GROUND MECHANICS IV*

Pupils I and II (see group (a), Science, above) must be elected with these advanced shop practice courses.

Chemistry I and II (see group (b), Science, above) must be elected with these advanced shop practice courses.

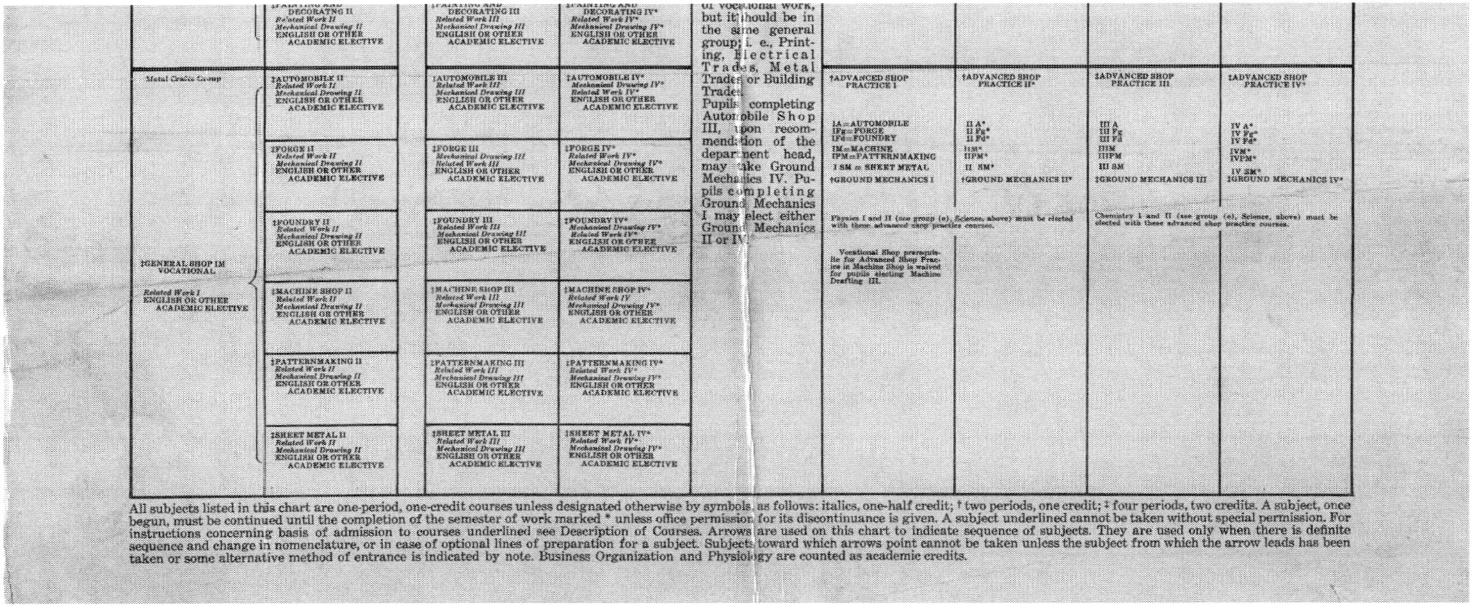

FIG. 3.1 Chart of courses offered at Arsenal Technical High School, circa 1935. (Courtesy of Indianapolis Public Schools and Indianapolis Public Library Digital Collections.)

All subjects listed in this chart are one-period, one-credit courses unless designated otherwise by symbols as follows: italics, one-half credit; † two periods, one credit; ‡ four periods, two credits. A subject, once begun, must be continued until the completion of the semester of work marked * unless office permission for its discontinuance is given. A subject underlined cannot be taken without special permission. For instructions concerning basis of admission to courses underlined see Description of Courses. Arrows are used on this chart to indicate sequence of subjects. They are used only when there is definite sequence and change in nomenclature, or in case of optional lines of preparation for a subject. Subjects toward which arrows point cannot be taken unless the subject from which the arrow leads has been taken or some alternative method of entrance is indicated by note. Business Organization and Physiology are counted as academic credits.

from a modest 22 courses. By 1903, as the city quickly industrialized, that number more than doubled to 46, in large part as a result of the opening of Manual Training High in 1895 and its expansive curriculum for the so-called hand-minded. In 1923, five years after the release of the *Cardinal Principles* report, the number of courses had more than doubled *again* to 106, and in 1933, four years into the economic woes of the Depression, the city's school leaders had added dozens more, bringing the total to an astounding 144 courses. In the span of three decades, the number of options available to high schoolers had increased more than 300 percent.[18]

An analysis of the individual courses Indianapolis offered by the 1930s reveals that Angus and Mirel are correct in defining the custodial mission, insofar as it related to the curriculum, as an instructional pivot to the "immediate and clearly relevant problems of youth."[19] Before the Depression, each Indianapolis high school's respective history department offered only six courses: US History, Ancient History, Medieval History, Modern History, English History, and Civics. By the 1930s, however, the History Department had been completely supplanted by the more broadly conceived Social Studies Department. The course offerings had expanded to fifteen, then featuring the less academic (and often ambiguously titled) Indiana History, Vocations, Economic Geography, Industrial History, Community Civics, and Sociology.[20]

A similar pattern emerged in the Home Economics Department. Though always a bastion of sexist and decidedly gendered courses aimed at preparing young women for their roles as wives and mothers as opposed to breadwinners, the number of courses offered in "Home Ec" grew from a mere three in 1913 (Sewing, Cooking, and Home Nursing) to thirteen in 1933. At that point, female high school students (and *only* female students, judging from enrollment data) could receive instruction in courses as diverse as Social Practice, Hygiene, Dressmaking, Decorative Art, Cooking, and Home Living.[21] While turn-of-the-century teachers would have expected that young women learn to be hygienic or stylish at home, by the 1930s many embraced these lessons as central to their work.

From the 1930s on, therefore, students in Indianapolis were bombarded with both academic and less-than-academic options. The traditional academic subjects did not disappear from the high school—they never would, in fact—but they were reimagined by Depression-era administrators in frequently watered-down forms. Outside of social studies and home economics, for instance, courses on Shakespeare were joined in the English Department by Grammar Practice, Public Speaking, and Play Producing. Courses in the Science Department on chemistry and astronomy were joined by General Science, Agriculture, and Household Science. And courses in the Art Department, which offered only lessons in drawing at the turn of the century, soon included Home Industry, Art Appreciation, and Book Illustration.[22] Options abounded, yet the

FIG. 3.2 Arsenal Technical High School, 1935. (Courtesy of Indiana Historical Society, P0469.)

courses administrators added to the curriculum signaled a shift from the academic to the "practical."

Over that same period of curricular expansion, enrollments in the city's secondary schools increased markedly, and graduation rates, an indicator of how long students spent in the high school, more than kept pace. Between 1923 and 1933, total secondary school enrollments leapt from 9,140 to 16,017, an increase of more than 50 percent. Similarly, the total number of high school graduates grew steadily from 1,293 in 1923 to 2,431 in 1933 (see table 3.2). By the middle of the decade, the graduating classes at Tech had become so large—reaching well over 1,000 students—that administrators chose to spread the commencement ceremony over two days. Seniors with last names beginning with *A* through *K* would receive their diplomas on a Tuesday evening, and their *L*-through-*Z* classmates would follow on a Thursday evening. The two groups, the "A–K Division" and the "L–Z Division," as they were known, had their own valedictorians, salutatorians, and scholarship medal winners. All told, the events lasted more than eight hours.[23]

To school leaders in Indianapolis and elsewhere, the simultaneous growth of the student population and the less academic (and purposefully less challenging) subject matter were both natural and vital. As they made clear in a mid-1930s report titled *The Senior High School*, Indianapolis, like its urban

Table 3.2
High School Enrollment and Graduates, 1923–1938

	Total HS enrollment	No. of graduates
1923	9,140	1,293
1933	16,017	2,431
1938	17,662	2,819

SOURCES: For 1923 and 1933, see Indianapolis Public Schools, *Survey Findings*, 7. For 1938, see Indianapolis Public Schools, *High School Enrollment, 1920–1938* (Indianapolis: Board of School Commissioners, 1938), 25.

peers, had entered a new era in secondary education, one brought on by the Depression, that was driven by the responsibility to educate more children than ever before and the wholesale embrace of the custodial mission. To that end, "Our High Schools," they wrote, "serve two distinct types of pupils," those "preparing for higher training in college," and those "preparing... for immediate participation, after leaving school, either through employment or otherwise, in the industrial and civic life of the community."[24] By this logic, the high school was just a stepping-stone to college for some of the city's adolescents, but it was also a crucial educational, social, and cultural endpoint for most.

Accordingly, the first group, which was relatively small and elite, required only a one-sentence description of what it was owed. It was "*the obligation* of the high school," school leaders reasoned, "to give training... that will most effectively contribute to ... success in whatever higher institution [these pupils] may enter." Whether the destination was Butler, Michigan, or Yale, the path ahead—the "college prep" path—was straightforward. The second group of students, however, was much larger (and growing from year to year), so it required multiple pages of explanation, since "the methods and procedures for meeting *the obligation* are necessarily more varied and complex." The schools would need to teach non-college-bound high schoolers not only about participation in likely avenues of employment but also how to function "in the home, the church, [and] the community."[25] The boundaries of this obligation were expansive, to say the least, for the city's administrators.

From this perspective, the high school had to embed into the evolving curriculum—in new courses like Household Science, and Public Speaking, and Home Living—a whole host of lessons. Specifically, administrators hoped to provide training to address the pupil's total development, including his or her attributes "of personality (physical, spiritual, mental, and cultural)," contributions "to the life of government and industry," growth "of moral attitudes and convictions (which are the basis of character)," and maturation "of personal skill and efficiency (which will make ... definite service to the community)."[26] While the public high school had always concerned itself with the students' "character" and "moral development," that concern moved into a position of prominence during the Depression. And the move, in both its ambitiousness and its zeal, would be permanent.

It was no coincidence, then, that *The Senior High School* contained a detailed explanation of the school system's precarious financial position, for weak budgets continually threatened to imperil the grand goals of the institution. Compared with seventy other cities with total populations over one hundred thousand, Indianapolis spent "less, in a year, for each pupil ... than the average amount spent in ... the [urban] United States." While urban districts on the whole allotted $120.87 per student, the report alleged that Indianapolis spent only $102.81.[27] Derived from a tax rate that grew from $0.58 per $100.00 of taxable property in 1909, to $0.70 per $100.00 in 1919, to $0.96 per $100.00 in 1940, the operating budget still fell during the Depression.[28] As a result, school leaders in Indianapolis (and nationally) found it paramount to describe their fiscal limitations because, from their point of view, they had never been asked to do so much for so many students with so little money.[29]

Even in hard times, however, the school budget favored the city's all-white schools over Crispus Attucks. In 1931, the board reported spending, on a line item called "Teachers' and Assistants' Salaries," roughly forty dollars per pupil at Manual, Tech, and Shortridge. Meanwhile, at Attucks, that figure was nearly halved, at twenty-three dollars per pupil.[30] The schools' respective libraries, in 1934, told a similar story. Manual, the board noted, held nearly seven thousand books and 40 magazine subscriptions; Tech boasted an astounding sixteen thousand books and 128 magazine subscriptions; and Shortridge, although roughly half the size of Tech, offered its students thirteen thousand books and 70 magazine subscriptions. Attucks, according to board records, did not have an on-campus library.[31]

Despite the board's racial biases in funding, the custodial mission nevertheless required more courses, especially of the nonacademic variety, but in its reach, it would require much more. In terms of their infrastructure alone, high schools in the Depression and thereafter were obliged to house and care for thousands more young people. They needed more space, more lockers, more custodians, more cooks, more nurses, and more attendance officers. In turn, administrators, whose positions now resembled those of chief executives more than those of educators, needed more rules and procedures, not to mention more teachers and textbooks.

If high schools by the 1910s and 1920s sought to be "comprehensive" in offering a broad range of courses, then high schools by the 1930s sought additionally to be all-inclusive: to offer a complete social and cultural experience for every pupil. The custodial mission, in that way, attempted to blur the line between a student's personal life and academic life. By the 1930s, teachers and administrators felt increasingly comfortable weighing in on both, or at least obligated to do so.

Further, if secondary schools hoped to shape their pupils' "character," "moral attitudes," and "physical, spiritual, mental, and cultural" personality, they would need to develop a culture of their own, and instill that culture both in the curriculum *and* in extracurricular activities. By successfully expanding the size and scope of clubs and activities in the 1930s, administrators in Indianapolis, helped by surging enrollments, moved the high school to the center of the city's adolescent experience. Along the way, they advanced a school culture of their own design, one that stressed obedience to authority and that was rooted in the norms of the nation's mainstream, white, middle-class values.

The High School at the Center of the Adolescent Experience: Administrators and the Cultivation of Cultural Homogeneity

It was during the Depression that student handbooks became a fixture in each of the city's high schools. The mounting size and complexity of these in-house guides to life in large urban secondary schools demonstrate that administrators had become leaders of thousands of teenagers, managers of scores of teachers and staff members, and figureheads of important educational and cultural institutions. They saw their responsibilities broaden as enrollments boomed during the nation's economic collapse. While they had once imagined their work as primarily academic (in terms of curriculum and instruction), they now had to focus on safety, order, and compliance. Creating a homogeneous student culture became their top priority.

Since Tech was the city's largest high school, it was fitting that its student handbook followed suit. It expanded year by year, and its 1938 edition, *The Tech Way*, was 150 pages long. It included a map of Tech's massive campus, multiple pages of rules and procedures, an exhaustive glossary of terms, and an index in the back for students looking to access information quickly (it was even printed as "pocket-sized"). On its first page, Tech principal Hanson Anderson welcomed his students, and he assured them that "the information contained within [the guide's] pages, boys and girls, if carefully studied, will familiarize you with the organization and workings of the school." Indeed, considerable "time and thought has been spent in preparation of this little volume," he continued, "[so] preserve it carefully, for its true value lies in frequent reference."[32] If high school–going was becoming a religion at Tech by the 1930s, then this would be its bible.

Above all, *The Tech Way*, like every other student handbook in the city, stressed teenage obedience to authority, often with remarkable specificity.

While the so-called standards of the school included predictable rules such as observing "order, quiet, and punctuality" in the halls and in classrooms, other rules seemed derived from ongoing behavioral challenges unique to the school. For example, the guide noted, "No snow-balling is permitted anywhere on the grounds," "Smoking is not permitted on the campus or in the range of vision of *anyone* on the campus," and, most perplexingly, "Room 5 is entered at the door leading to the basement at the west side of the Arsenal."[33] While it is unclear what could possibly go wrong if Room 5 were entered improperly, perhaps from the east side, one can imagine that adolescent mischief was part of the equation. Exercising administrative power was the real goal.

What made the rules and procedures even more striking, especially as markers of the custodial mission in action, was that they attempted to control the behavior of students *beyond* the school and school-related activities. On the one hand, it seemed reasonable that *The Tech Way* included a section on behavior "at athletic contests," because student-athletes and their supporters were then acting as high school pupils, and they were likely even dressed in their school's letters and colors. On the other hand, it demonstrated the depth of control administrators sought that the section also stated, "At all times the student body shall be *vigorously* and *enthusiastically* for the Tech teams."[34] What if a student wanted to observe an athletic contest casually or even passively? What if, for any number of reasons, a student was indifferent about the outcome of the contest? In the heyday of custodialism, it seemed, the tone and zest of one's cheering were subject to administrative influence.

The Tech Way also included extensive sections on how to behave "in public," stating up front that "each student shall act as to reflect upon the training of his home and of this school." That meant, somewhat naturally and innocuously, that students should "avoid rude, boisterous actions," and "respect the property of others," and "scorn cheating, cutting, and lying," but it could mean much more. In fact, the guide also demanded that students "speak only *good* of the school, [and] censure false statements concerning . . . faculty," and that they must "be conscious constantly of the responsibility of serving as a personal representative of Tech."[35] Critical thinking, individualism, and a healthy skepticism of authority, according to the handbook, were subordinate to the school's reputation. By extension, a student was a "Techite" first, and an individual second.

Noticeably, Tech's administrators omitted the punishments for breaking the handbook's rules (they were presumably handled on a case-by-case basis), but the potential rewards were quite clear. Each year, teachers could nominate 10 to 20 percent of their students for a much-celebrated "Personal Merit Citation," which reflected one's commitment to dozens of classified "traits," all of which were published in the student handbook. "Type 1" traits included, among others, helpfulness, fair-mindedness, and democratic spirit; "Type 2" included affability, neatness in dress, and cordiality; and "Type 3" included steadfastness, thrift, and—perhaps most importantly—obedience.[36] In this system, therefore, students who adopted a "pro-school" attitude and "community of practice," as scholars have defined it, were rewarded handsomely beginning in the Depression-era secondary school.[37] In an age of rising enrollments, it was "the Tech way" or the highway.

While Tech's student handbook was the largest, it was by no means unique. By the late 1930s, Manual Training High, for example, changed the name of its guide to *Facts for Freshmen*, demonstrating that it was the high school's newcomers who had the most to learn. Its opening pages reveal that the rhythms of the modern (and increasingly complicated) high school, which were developing year by year, necessitated detailed explanations. It was during the 1930s, for example, that most urban high schools installed intricate bell-signal and clock systems, so freshman at Manual needed to know that "the first bell is the warning bell," "the second is the dismissal bell," and "the third is the class bell." As important, the handbook advised, "You have four minutes between classes and therefore ought not to be late!"[38] The slavish deference to efficiency, speed, and punctuality that Charlie Chaplin famously lampooned in the film *Modern Times* (1936) was part of the fabric of the high school, too.[39]

In the same vein, Indianapolis added thousands of individual lockers to its high schools in the Depression, so new students at Manual needed to know that "a combination padlock is furnished for which the pupil makes a fifty-cent deposit."[40] If they rode their bike to school, they had to take it to the basement Bicycle Room. If they needed extra school supplies or were looking for the lost and found, they headed to the Sales Room. If they were sick or got hurt while on campus, they should see "the school nurse, Miss Mertz, in room 123."[41] Information that decades before had been passed on informally, and issues that had been resolved on an ad hoc basis, now had rules and predictability.

At the all-black Crispus Attucks High, administrators took care to orient freshmen to the school's academic rigors and lofty goals, as well as providing information about how they, as students, might meet the challenge before them. The school's handbook, *The Viewpoint*, began with a section titled "Aims of Attucks High," which included phrases such as, "to foster the highest ideals of citizenship," and "to promote culture through and appreciation of literature, science, history, and the fine arts," and "to stress the social, economic, and moral advantages of good homes."[42] Recall that African Americans in Indianapolis demanded that Attucks, after its contentious founding in 1927, stand as a symbol of community pride and high achievement. And these "aims," down to the word, reflected that pressure.

In a special section for Attucks's incoming freshmen, *The Viewpoint* contained advice about "how to do school work successfully," and, even more exactly, "how to study." The latter section was a full three pages long, and it was filled with paragraphs of specific information. Among its painstakingly detailed tips were, "Plan out every day," and "Get eight or nine hours of sleep," and "If possible, have a quiet place in which to study, the best light you can get, and a desk or table away from the rest of the family."[43] When it came to studiousness and scholarly success, the principal and vice principals at Attucks were not leaving anything to the freshman's imagination.

For administrators at Attucks and every other high school in the city, patrolling and regulating the lunch hour, as well as arrival and dismissal, were the cause of great concern. As late as the 1920s, high school students in Indianapolis were free to leave campus at lunchtime; many did, traveling home or to local establishments for a midday meal. Indeed, the city's school newspapers in the 1910s and 1920s were crammed with advertisements for lunch destinations near the respective schools. For Northsiders, Stokes Pharmacy, which offered "fountain service" and its famed "Toastwich," was a popular destination. For teenagers on the South Side, Saffell's, just "one-half square from [Manual]," was known for ice cream so good that "The More You Eat, The More You Want."[44] And Attucks's pupils, of course, frequented the Walker Drug Store (located in the renowned Walker Theatre Building), which, in an era of segregation and threats of race-based violence, described itself as "A Safe Place to Go," with "Home Cooked Food" and "The Best Ice Cream in the City."[45]

Before the Depression, on-site high school cafeterias were forced to advertise in school newspapers alongside their neighborhood's more exciting cafés and lunch counters. Likely in hopes of not overpromising, the ads for the Shortridge cafeteria stated simply, "Shortridge Cafeteria: Clean Cooking at Prices You Wish to Pay."[46] With abundant and desirable alternatives nearby, many students understandably preferred to leave their buildings for lunch.

By the mid-1930s, however, every Indianapolis high school demanded that students stay on the property for lunch, a decision consistent with the custodial mission. Judging from their handbooks, school leaders were preoccupied with preventing pupils from leaving campus for *any* reason without permission. At Attucks, students could leave only if they had permission from the principal, and the principal alone.[47] At Manual, students could apply through a byzantine process for a "lunch pass," but only if they lived "within walking distance of the school" and promised to walk home and eat there without classmates.[48] And at Tech, its dogged principal, Milo Stuart, had even convinced the financially strapped school board to pay for fencing around the perimeter of its seventy-six-acre campus.[49] Between the prohibitions, policies, and protected perimeters, the message to students was clear: there is nothing you need—not socializing, not personal development, not even food—that you cannot find at your high school.

Faculty

FACULTY SUPERVISION IN THE LUNCH ROOM

Twenty-four chairs have been broken up in the Tech Lunch Room or carried outside and broken during the fall semester.

One-third of the spoons have been carried away. (These are difficult to replace. In fact, by April 1, it will be necessary for people eating in the Tech Lunch Room to bring their own service at the present rate of loss.)

Dishes and milk bottles are carelessly broken or carried away. The growing tendency towards vandalism; the tendency to forget conventional refinement and ethics; and the difficulty in securing lunch room help who are accustomed to dealing with children, presents an opportunity for the teachers of Tech to render a real service to the school.

The plan is to have a teacher spend one period per day in the lunch room for a total time of two weeks. This will not make an excess burden on any one teacher.

The duty of the teachers will be limited to dealing with pupils only and assisting the women and student traffic officers.

The following things are suggested to be on the alert for:

1. Running in the lunch room
2. Loud yelling and talking
3. Cutting into the lunch line
4. Pushing and shoving in the lunch line
5. Carrying things from the lunch room (food, silver, dishes, chairs, etc.)
6. Playing with the drinking fountains
7. Failure of pupils to get into line at once and who wish to roam about over the lunch room and visit
8. Pupils leaning back on two legs of their chairs or who fail to push chairs under the tables when finished eating.
9. Pupils who leave milk bottles and trays with dishes on the tables
10. Pupils who cause trouble at the steam table over rationing, or slipping candy bars or food in their pockets until after passing the cashier.
11. Wearing hats or caps in the lunch room
12. Any other things which come up which are not proper lunch room etiquette.

SUGGESTIONS ON HANDLING DISCIPLINE

1. All cases of running, cutting into line, or pushing or crowding in order to get ahead of other pupils at lunch time should be turned in to Mrs. Cloud on a 3 x 5 giving pupil's name, period, offense, and teacher's name.

2. All minor cases should be handled by the teacher by talking to the pupil and getting a promise of cooperation. Remember that pupils who are not known to the teacher will not hesitate to repeat their activities the following day. A cure for this is taking the pupil's name and making a notation of the case. A pupil's name placed in a little black book works wonders.

3. Cases of refusal of cooperation, of willful destruction or repeated misdemeanors should be turned in to Mr. Gorman or Mr. Kettery or Miss Thuemler.

4. Mr. Lancaster will be glad to advise with you about any difficult problems which arise.

Respectfully,

HANSON H. ANDERSON, Principal

FIG. 3.3 Arsenal Tech High School "Faculty Supervision in the Lunch Room" notes, circa 1940. (Courtesy of Indianapolis Public Schools and Indianapolis Public Library Digital Collections.)

Because of these closed-campus policies, high school cafeterias were handed a monopoly on the American teenage lunch, for bringing food from home was the only other (and always less popular) option. And the sheer quantity of food that high school cooks were obliged to produce was staggering.[50] In 1933, the *Arsenal Cannon*, the Tech newspaper, reported with awe that its cafeteria had prepared nearly eighty-six thousand individual lunches in the month of April alone. That meant students had consumed hundreds of bushels of potatoes, hundreds of pounds of butter, and roughly fifty thousand cookies. In a single school day in April 1933, the students of Tech ate and drank "roughly 2,600 to 3,100 sandwiches, 600 to 700 bottles of milk, 11 dozen frankfurters, 50 to 60 gallons of ice cream, and 110 gallons of chili." Indicative of the high school cafeteria's lackluster culinary reputation—one that would stick, unfortunately—the student-editors titled the article, "Not to Be Read before Lunch."[51]

Aside from increasingly elaborate rules, procedures, and demands for obedience, Depression-era administrators drastically expanded extracurricular activities to build school pride and cultivate cultural homogeneity. While clubs and student organizations were as old as the high school itself, they increased in number and variety in Indianapolis in the decades after 1900, from an average of about sixteen per school in 1915, to about twenty-three in 1925, to nearly forty-five in 1935 (see table 3.3). A close reading of student yearbooks and school handbooks (which often listed and described each club and activity), moreover, displays that school leaders sought not only to meet as many of their students' interests as possible but also to supplant informal teenage gatherings with school-sponsored events and activities. Creating an all-inclusive high school experience, one that filled the whole of the teenager's day, appeared to be their unstated goal.

Then as today, the heart of the high school's extracurricular activities was the organization of interscholastic athletics. After the citywide ban on boys' sports was lifted in 1920, they remained wildly popular throughout the first half of the twentieth century. Conversely, girls' sports changed drastically in the Depression, and the change indicated the schools' commitment to fostering a patriarchal culture. For example, each high school in the city offered at least one varsity sport to young women in 1915 (typically basketball), but only Shortridge maintained this practice through the 1930s.[52] In place of varsity athletics, school leaders implemented Girls' Physical Training Clubs, which claimed to "promote physical efficiency, foster loyalty to the school, [and] exalt school standards and traditions at all times."[53]

While young men won "letters" for their "varsity sweaters" by practicing robust leadership, fierce competition, and committed teamwork, young women, in contrast, earned dainty "school pins" by earning a fixed number of "points," as determined by their female instructors. If they practiced "healthy habits," for example, they earned ten points; if they volunteered at school, they earned twenty-five

Table 3.3

Extracurricular Activities in the Indianapolis High Schools, 1915–1945

	Shortridge	Manual	Arsenal	Attucks	Average tot.
1915					
Arts	7	2	2	Founded 1927	
Academ./Service	11	3	4		
Boys' Sports	5	4	3		
Girls' Sports	3	1	2		
Total	26	10	11	—	15.7
1925					
Arts	7	5	6	Founded 1927	
Academ./Service	13	10	9		
Boys' Sports	5	5	3		
Girls' Sports	4	0	1		
Total	29	20	19	—	22.7
1935					
Arts	9	5	12	10	
Academ./Service	27	17	39	34	
Boys' Sports	6	4	5	3	
Girls' Sports	4	0	0	1	
Total	46	26	56	48	44.8
1945					
Arts	8	10	7	9	
Academ./Service	24	33	13	16	
Boys' Sports	5	4	6	3	
Girls' Sports	3	0	0	0	
Total	40	47	26	28	35.3

SOURCES: Drawn from the yearbooks of Shortridge, Manual, Tech, and Attucks from 1915, 1925, 1935, and 1945. They are all available in the Education Section of the Digital Indy Archive, which is part of the Indianapolis Public Library, http://www.digitalindy.org/cdm/ (accessed December 2016).

points; and if they possessed desirable "individual traits," they earned fifty points.[54] Young men received their letters, win or lose, but the performance of high school femininity was made formal and measurable during the Depression.

Working in unison with the Girls' Physical Training Club were dozens of other new clubs that taught young women to be wives, mothers, and consumers in a male-dominated, heteronormative society.[55] While the Home Economics Club had operated since the mid-1910s in Indianapolis, the Modes et Manteaux Club, founded in 1936, allowed for "the study of manners and dress" to "create and instill interest in the study of trends."[56] Assuming that freshman girls could learn to be "respectable young women" from older female students, each school formed its own Freshman Girls Club. At Attucks, it was described as "a guidance program for freshmen girls planned by a committee of teachers,

[and] carried out by a sisterly group of upperclass advisers."[57] At Manual, it was organized "for the purpose of developing scholarship, service, and character."[58] These peer mentoring groups were often overseen by the school's full-time "Dean of Girls," a position that, quite revealingly, had no male counterpart in Indianapolis. Perhaps girls were more prone to misbehavior. Or perhaps monitoring and shaping—ultimately controlling—female bodies and behavior was more important culturally.

Further, as several scholars have explained, high school dances were brimming with traditions and pageantry that reinforced not only society's commitment to patriarchy but also—in their strictly boy-girl arrangement—steadfast heteronormativity.[59] Usually in concert with the school-sponsored and adult-supervised dances, several of the city's schools elected young men and women annually (typically seniors) who best represented their institutions' ideals, meaning they had won the admiration of their teachers and peers by mastering and performing the hallmarks of a traditional, middle-class culture.

At Shortridge that meant revered students were given the titles "Bluebelle," for the young women, and "Uglyman," for the young men, the latter implying that young men should downplay the importance of their appearance (publicly, at least). Established in 1931 and 1932, respectively, the pair were voted on by the entire student body and crowned, as one would expect, at the Bluebelle and

FIG. 3.4 Shortridge High School dance, circa 1939. (Courtesy of Indiana Historical Society, M0482.)

Uglyman Hop, held in the fall of each year. Although prom and homecoming, with their separate "queens" and "kings," would become the standard high school social event after World War II, both locally and nationally, school-specific dances ruled the day during the Depression, and administrators organized them frequently, maintaining full control. As a male Shortridge student recalled, "I remember the All-School Dances in the gym . . . that beloved Miss Mary Pratt [a teacher] sponsored—where admission was 10 cents, and you could buy your date a Coca-Cola after the dance and walk her home, and have a whale of a big time for a total outlay of 30 cents!"[60] For high schoolers, it was a chance to have a good time with friends; for teachers and administrators, it was a chance to chaperone teenage socializing and encourage appropriate heterosexual courtship.[61]

In line with the school-sponsored dance's emphasis on wholesomeness and deportment were the prevalent "Hi-Y" clubs, or the official high school branch of the city's Young Men's and Young Women's Christian Associations.[62] Though the public school system refrained from sponsoring a religion, at least formally, references to a Christian god were common in school newspapers, yearbooks, and even official school reports, especially at Thanksgiving and Christmas. In a front-page article titled "A Thanksgiving Prayer for Renewed Faith," for example, the student editors of Tech's *Arsenal Cannon* wrote, with the permission of their sponsors, "Our dear heavenly Father, we humbly bow before Thee in this season of Thanksgiving." They continued, "We have so many things for which to be thankful, dear God, but too often we are prone to forget Thee whose power grants our wishes and has given use life itself."[63]

As such, the Hi-Y club often bridged the gap between Christianity and Christian morals, on one end, and acceptable behavior and success in the high school, on the other. In the Shortridge student newspaper, the Christian Hi-Y club advertised as promoting "clean speech, clean scholarship, clean sports, and clean living." At the club's meetings, one could engage in "inspirational discussions of life problems."[64] In the Attucks annual yearbook, the description of the club was even more overtly Christian. In 1938, it stated, "The Hi-Y club, under the sponsorship of Mr. Radcliffe, has given the school some of its most popular leaders," and "its purpose is to develop Christian character."[65] Within the walls of the public high school, popularity and outward displays of Christianity paired nicely.

While the student clubs and activities in Indianapolis, including Hi-Y, were remarkably similar from school to school, only the all-black Attucks High, unsurprisingly, demonstrated any form of cultural diversity or racial sensitivity. In 1935, the school started a Negro Literature Club, as well as a Negro Music Club. The annual yearbook described the music club as "spending the activities this period listening to songs by Negro composers as well as those carrying Negro themes."[66] By 1938, Attucks had a Negro History Club. Though the school also offered an unclassified History Club (like the city's all-white schools), students interested in African and African American history had "the able guidance of Dr. Joseph Carroll [who also taught a course in black history], an authority, as their sponsor. Much interesting research has been accomplished by them."[67] One such research report, titled "The Contribution of the Negro to American Civilization," adeptly wove together narratives about African-born slaves and notable African Americans, including Phyllis Wheatley, Richard Allen, Booker T. Washington, and George Washington Carver. "The Negro's contribution to culture in this country has been marked," the student-author, Mary Louise Harry, concluded succinctly.[68]

Though some were quite meaningful, most of the myriad clubs that administrators added during the Depression proved that they desired, perhaps above all, to occupy as much of their pupils' time as possible. While a young person's curiosity in collecting stamps, or playing chess, or volunteering would have in the past been cultivated informally or at home, by the 1930s these interests were facilitated in the high school's Stamp Club, Chess Club, and Service Club.[69] Similarly nonspecific, the Nature Study Club was for students "interested in *any* outdoor activity." Somewhat redundantly, the Sportsman Club catered to those "interested in fishing, hunting, archery, golf, tennis, and other outdoor *and* indoor sports."[70] One could even join the Informal Discussion Club, which, perhaps most curiously of all, was an opportunity for those with an interest in "one aspect or another . . . to meet and discuss these subjects."[71] Ten years earlier, high schoolers (and all other people, for that matter) would have called this "sitting around and talking." By the 1930s, however, it warranted a full-fledged, school-sponsored activity, with its own president, bylaws, teacher-sponsor, and weekly meetings. One wonders how informal the informal discussions actually were.[72]

Within the extracurricular activities and the regular school day, high schoolers, shepherded by their administrators, participated in a nearly all-inclusive world, one that offered them a culturally cohesive environment in which they could study, exercise, and socialize. It was no surprise, therefore, that students in Indianapolis wrote increasingly about the importance of their high schools in their lives. As one Tech student put it in 1938, "Beyond the burning candle lies the Tech Town, where we 'live' for four wonderful years. Tall and stately, with the wise look which belongs only to the very old, the Arsenal still stands guard over the seventy-six wooded acres that make up the campus—acres that have felt the buoyant steps of happy youth."[73] Tech, like all the city's high schools, was not simply school—it was a "town." And its students, like all the city's students, did not attend school there—they "lived" there. For pupils who accepted the high school's broadening mission, custodialism could be quite beautiful.

What made the custodial mission even more powerful and lasting was that administrators skillfully enlisted many high school students to their cause. As secondary school attendance skyrocketed, the student culture associated with it became more and more palpable, for, without question, the institution was moving to the center of the American adolescent experience. However, by incorporating a school-sponsored, adult-approved student culture into their administrative plans, school leaders allowed young people to police themselves and pursue cultural homogeneity collectively. In the form of student newspapers, yearbooks, and social events, high schoolers in Indianapolis often marched lockstep—culturally and regarding conformity—with their teachers, administrators, and parents.

School-Sponsored Youth Culture: Students' Voices and the Conservation of Cultural Homogeneity

It has been challenging for historians to capture the student perspective on the American high school, in large part because young people left fewer records than their adult counterparts. What makes Indianapolis unique, however, is that each of its high schools maintained vibrant student newspapers in the first half of the twentieth century. Recall that Shortridge (with an on-campus press) printed a *daily* newspaper, the first and longest running of its kind in the nation. The preservation of these papers, in combination with annual yearbooks, provides a unique opportunity to investigate the student culture in the city's high schools, in particular as it was mediated by adults with the custodial mission in mind.

That is, the students who were permitted to write for school papers, or who were highlighted in yearbooks, had necessarily embraced the culture of the school and had adopted a "pro-school" attitude.[74] Though they operated apart from their teachers and administrators, and sometimes playfully feigned rebelliousness, they maintained a remarkably similar perspective: students should support their school; everyone should follow the rules; and new students (freshmen, especially) should respect and heed the advice of upperclassmen. As such, the student culture that emerges from these documents is remarkably conformist. And while there were obviously teenagers who bucked their administrators' wishes and resisted the institution's predominant culture (just as today), their voices were systematically excluded from official student documents. They were purposefully denied a school-sanctioned platform.[75]

By the 1930s, moreover, student newspapers, judging from their sales figures, had proved a powerful medium. At Tech, as one example, the *Arsenal Cannon* rose in popularity during the Depression from 991 subscribers in the fall of 1932 to nearly 2,500 in the spring of 1937.[76] At Shortridge, the *Echo* staff bragged on the front page about its subscription numbers, which hovered between 1,500 and 2,000 in the 1930s, or about half of the student population.[77] The Manual paper, the *Booster*, placed a student-representative in every first-period "home room" to sell papers, for either five cents each or fifty cents for the semester. Similarly, Tech's paper-selling "*Cannon* agents" numbered a considerable 150 in 1939.[78] Beyond official sales, one could imagine that the pass-along readership, in a tight-knit high school community no less, was substantial.

In tens of thousands of student newspaper articles in Indianapolis, the most common subject by far—rivaled only by the coverage of boys' sports—was the call for better student behavior. In issue after issue, student-reporters and their editors complained that the hallways were too chaotic, that too many students broke the rules, and that the sum of these transgressions offended them personally and embarrassed the school. In an emblematic article titled "Tech's Public Enemies" in the *Arsenal Cannon*, the author fumed about "the student who goes up the DOWN stairs," "the half-starved student who breaks in the lunch line," "the hat-snatcher," and, perhaps worst of all, "the person who put an ice cream dish on the stack of dirty potato dishes."[79] At Manual, the student paper printed a recurring section called "Our Pet Peeves," which called out "the confirmed 'borrower'—all the way from pencils to your favorite compact," not to mention "he who tells the world in general and particular how clever he is."[80] Offenders of common decency, as well as the schools' rules, lurked around every corner.

In countless editions of the Shortridge *Echo*, students wrote earnestly about how dangerous the hallways were during passing period. "Let us crouch against the wall . . . for the glorification of education," one brave field reporter wrote, and hope that "we will be spared with only three limbs broken and four teeth eradicated, cuts and bruises (or desired combination) and see what some . . . of the horde are doing on their way to classes."[81] On other occasions, students referred to the halls as "like being on an old ship crashing about the waves," or "like you were a spectator of the route of General Braddock's army."[82] In November 1932, a particularly distraught student abandoned the hyperbole, choosing instead to philosophize on the subject. "Shortridge is life," the author began. "There are those who lead, [and] those who almost, but not quite, make the grade," but "we have definite rules to follow; well-constituted authority to obey." While in school, "we are not laying the foundation for life, we are living. Look around. Even in our lunch room we have government, leaders, and followers. Arouse me out of dreaming in my lunch room chair, that I may earn for myself a place in the world."[83] Sure, the hallways could be dangerous physically, but the chaos, to this author (beyond his or her years), portended something far more troubling.

In maintaining the schools' cultural norms, student editorials often singled out the behavior of young women. No facet of acceptable or unacceptable femininity was off limits, including the use of makeup. "Her cheeks flamed in a perpetual blush," a female student of Tech wrote mockingly about one of her classmates, adding, "Her lips were covered with a coating of lipstick which looked as if it had been applied with a trowel." Like many out-of-control "flaming youth" and "flappers" of the 1920s perhaps, the student described by the author lacked "self-analysis," that "valuable guide to the solution to any problem," which "no less applies to the art of make-up."[84] Along those lines, a student in the Manual paper penned a poem titled "Reasons Why (You Should Vote for the May Queen)," which made plain that a young woman's appearance was the most important determinant of her high school popularity. The author mused,

> If gentlemen prefer blondes, Deloris'll get them in her bonds
> Jeanette is such a lovely girl, Brown eyes and hair that really curls.[85]

Next to the poem was a ballot that students could cut out and drop off at their polling stations. The May Queen process—from the nominees, to their pertinent qualifications, to voting—was complete.

While gender norms mattered, freshmen, more than any other group, were attacked for their lack of awareness, their all too frequent faux pas, and their misplaced confidence. In a recurring column in the Shortridge *Echo* named "Freshmen's Diary," a fictional first-year student demonstrated his stupidity and naïveté from week to week. "Der Diery," he wrote in a 1932 installment, "I am so ecksited I don't know what to do. I got all Bees on my card so mom sez she'll give me an ackstra kuarter to go to the game Wednesday. Gee, I wuz scared that I wouldn't get to go, cause I reely eckspected a C in Latin."[86] It was plausible to the reader, one can assume, that even the most clueless freshman took Latin at the prestigious Shortridge.

For all his inexperience, the fictional freshman from the pages of the *Echo* still knew what fitting in socially at the North Side high school required. "Well, diery, since I got all Bees, I get to go to the game [against Tech], and got a date with my espeechial girlfriend . . . and then I'll tell you all about the game and also the girl, casue I know you'll be interested."[87] In what could have been a companion piece, an *Arsenal Cannon* article entitled "Our Tiny Freshman" began insensitively, "It is a well-known fact that each year the incoming freshman are becoming more and more like the pigmy race."[88] At Manual, the newspaper mocked freshmen with that age-old fake advice: "Tickets to the roof garden may be bought in room 450, and coupons for the use of the elevator may be obtained from your home room teacher."[89] Even if first-year students were in on the jokes (and they likely were), the implications were clear.

While freshmen were always a favorite target of derision in student newspapers, upperclassmen also regularly reminded them that there was hope. In essence, the message went, if they atoned for their sins of ignorance and embraced what the high school had to offer, then they, too, could transition from lowly freshmen to true high schoolers. They needed to learn the rules (spoken and unspoken), join clubs, do well in their courses, and, above all, pledge allegiance to their institution and its culture. Reflecting on his time at Attucks, for example, the senior commencement speaker in 1943 stated, "In September, 1939, there entered into the portals of Attucks some two hundred freshmen. They were just like all other high school freshmen. They thought they knew everything, but they soon found they *did* not. After a few weeks of hurry-scurry, they settled down to work. [Soon] a year passed by, and we found these 'know-it-all' freshmen were then sophisticated sophomores."[90] At Tech, the message to freshmen was framed as a list of "dos and don'ts" in the newspaper at the start of the school year. "Don't loiter in the halls," "Don't try to make a new path across a grass plot," "Support Tech's teams," "Be a sport at all times," and, of course, "Subscribe to the *Arsenal Cannon*."[91] In the Manual *Booster*, one student took a less playful tone. "As to you, Freshman, I am not going to preach. I am just going to tell you to take advantage of your opportunities." The author continued, "Don't forget that it is easy to be a good student if you are only willing to work. Go out for athletics, play in the band, join school organizations, and make the most of your time here." In hundreds of articles from Indianapolis's student newspapers, older students implored freshmen to adopt a "pro-school" attitude. Whether through jokes or heartfelt advice, they framed it as the only avenue to social and educational success.

If administrators demanded obedience to their authority, upperclassmen demanded the same of freshmen. It was merely a different rung of the same ladder of power and social conformity, and all of it served the pursuit of compliance and cultural homogeneity. During the 1930s, as the high school moved to the center of the adolescent experience, the students themselves—aided by the reach of their schools' abundant resources—policed one another's behaviors with frequency and vigor. Administrators added more courses, more rules, and more activities and clubs, all in the name of the custodial mission. But students, for their part, fabricated a youth culture that sought similar ends.

They spoke for themselves, but in doing so, they preached deference over rebellion. They at times preferred a playful tone, but they wielded significant power by establishing the norms of high school–going. When students stepped outside those cultural norms—which were largely middle class, white, and patriarchal—they were likely derided by their peers and shut out of the institution's power structure. It would be more than a decade before movies like *Blackboard Jungle* and *Rebel without a Cause* (both from 1955) captivated audiences by bringing the "antischool" perspective to life. The appetite for pushback, however, was years in the making.[92]

While the nation moved from economic depression to war, as the next chapter explains, Indianapolis's commitment to a racist school system once again moved to the fore. In 1949, after years of petitioning and lobbying by civil rights leaders, the state government officially banned school segregation, permitting black secondary school students, for the first time in twenty-two years, to apply to any school in the city. While the 1949 law banning segregation had little effect on the racial disparities in Indianapolis's classrooms, the broader movement for racial integration did prompt the state athletic association to allow the Attucks High boys' team (and those of other all-black schools) to participate in the state basketball tournament, from which it had been excluded throughout its history. When Attucks made a series of deep runs in the state tournament in the 1950s, it became for a time the toast of the town, among both whites and blacks. It did not, though, solve the problem of racism or racial segregation in the local school system.

4

An End to De Jure School Segregation, Crispus Attucks Basketball Success, and the Limits of Racial Equality, 1941–1955

•••••••••••••••••••••

> I believe that If others can succeed,
> so can I and that if I will, I can—
> "All men are created equal."
> —"A Student's Creed," Crispus Attucks
> High School 1946 student handbook

As in the city and the nation at large, World War II had gripped Indianapolis's high schools by the end of 1941. Within months after the attack on Pearl Harbor, school leaders organized the High School Victory Corps, which encouraged young people to sign an official document pledging allegiance "to perform any community war services within the limits of [their] ability and experience," and "to prepare [themselves] for future service whether in the armed forces, in war production, or in essential civilian occupations." The corps and its mission were immensely popular and eventually attracted thousands of students. Superintendent DeWitt S. Morgan even proclaimed in 1942, "In the mind of every high school pupil is this serious question: 'How can I do my part in this time when my country is at war?'" As Morgan knew, "This war is different than any in history." Without question, "it has been called a 'total war.'"[1] Morgan's high school students wholeheartedly agreed.

By 1942, students at Tech were encouraged daily to buy "their War Bonds and Stamps" alongside their "tickets for athletic games" at the school's Financial Office.[2] In 1944, the all-black Attucks High devoted its entire yearbook to the war effort, naming the volume *The American Way*. The introduction's author described the role of the student in the following way: "It is my duty to serve my country well, to cherish, and protect it from its enemies within or without, and serve under arms when called in an emergency, sacrificing my life and property if need be that this nation might live."[3] Similarly, the Manual yearbook in 1943 was dedicated "To Our Soldiers, To Our Sailors, To Our Marines." The inside cover featured a drawing of a young woman sitting in front of a framed picture of a serviceperson (her special someone, one would presume) as she composed a letter to him. "From Beth to Bill," she wrote. "When I leave school, whether I become a steno, a college girl, or a Rosie the Riveter at Allison's, I'll always visualize the fun I've had at Manual, especially during my senior year."[4] The all-inclusive high school experience had been magnificent, the fictional and remarkably stereotyped Beth implied, but the real world and its real problems awaited her after commencement.

Meanwhile, at the prestigious Shortridge, the city's wealthiest and most privileged students, no doubt buoyed by their parents' money, raised an astounding $1,302,224 in a three-week "Buy-a-Plane" drive. Equal to more than $18 million in today's dollars, this outpaced even the wildest expectations. It was enough to purchase two Flying Fortress bombers, as well as a pursuit plane, the latter being the original and more modest goal. One of the bombers purchased was even christened the *Shortridge Blue Devil*. The *Echo* proudly reported that it was sent to Japan in 1945 "to pay Shortridge's 'respects' to Tokyo."[5] It was a "total war," indeed.

Aside from inspiring extreme patriotism and fund-raising in the city's high schools, the war, as many scholars have explained, also prompted more intense calls for civil rights for African Americans. After fighting for freedom from oppression in Europe and the Pacific (where more than one million served), African American soldiers returned, much to their dismay, to the realities of a Jim Crow society filled with hate and governed by the norms of white supremacy. While the Servicemen's Readjustment Act of 1944, or GI Bill, provided white veterans with unprecedented access to higher education and low-interest mortgages, African Americans were typically denied both. And though the General Motors Allison plant in Speedway and the Naval Avionics facility in Warren Township provided thousands of well-paying jobs for the people of Indianapolis, African Americans were rarely given fair access to employment.

In an era of seemingly boundless prosperity, the racial divide in Indianapolis and elsewhere felt as palpable as ever.[6]

In response, civil rights leaders articulated and pursued the Double V campaign, which sought "a Victory over racism at home as well as Victory abroad." The Congress on Racial Equality, known for its nonviolent resistance, was founded in 1942 in Chicago and would be a major force for decades; and the National Association for the Advancement of Colored People (NAACP) experienced a tenfold increase in size during the war, adding scores of local chapters and reaching half a million members in 1945. As Swedish economist Gunnar Myrdal wrote in his famous study on race, *An American Dilemma: The Negro Problem and Modern Democracy* (1944), "Not since reconstruction ha[s] there been more reason to anticipate fundamental changes in American race relations . . . there is bound to be a redefinition of the Negro's status as a result of this War."[7]

The mobilization for civil rights, while broad in its quest, eventually ran headlong into the high school system in Indianapolis. As was customary nationwide, the city's public high schools were tasked with playing a significant role in educating returning servicemen, of all races, and attempting to prepare them for a peacetime economy. As early as 1943, for example, each high school began offering classes in a variety of trade and technical fields, as well as resources for pupils interested in passing the recently developed General Education Development test.[8] However, because the classes (like the K–12 schools) were racially segregated, African American veterans only had access to those taught at Crispus Attucks. The Attucks program for veterans was well funded and relatively expansive, but it was necessarily limited. Since it simply did not have the equipment and teachers available at Shortridge, Manual, and Tech (from which white veterans could freely choose), it was demonstrably unequal.[9]

As a result, returning African American veterans viewed racial inequality in the schools as an attack not only on their children but also on their own futures. As historian Richard Pierce writes, "No longer was the action of the school board only pertinent to children; its reach now extended to the economic world of men."[10] In response, Jay T. Smith, a black veteran and official spokesperson of the Veterans Civil Rights Committee, presented a petition to the school board in December 1946. Signed by nearly fifty thousand of the committee's members, it called for the end of segregation in Indianapolis, not only because they believed it was an inherent good but also because it would lead to better programs, services, and jobs (as teachers) for the city's black people. "A fully integrated system," the petition stated, "with fair protection of Negro teachers and administrators should be retained, and no teacher or administrator should be dismissed as a result of this change."[11]

Soon, Smith and his committee's protests were joined by a chorus of others, all calling for an end to segregation. By 1947, for example, civil rights leaders ran candidates for the school board, which meant taking on the wealthy and elite Citizens' School Committee (CSC), an organization that nominated successful candidates to the board every four years and had maintained a lock on local education politics in the 1930s and 1940s. Avoiding overt racism, the CSC board claimed to protect the "status quo" in the schools, which in the 1940s meant preserving segregated schools, even in the face of a quickly growing postwar city (from 386,927 people in 1940 to 476,000 in 1960) that was increasingly African American (13 percent in 1940 and 20 percent in 1960). In many respects, Willard Ransom, the Harvard-educated lawyer and son of Freeman Ransom, led the charge to unseat the incumbents. Though ultimately unsuccessful, the campaign gained the support of both black and white antisegregationists and helped to articulate a vision of a more equal school system for Indianapolis's black children.

Blocked by the school board, civil rights leaders shifted their focus to the courts and the Indiana General Assembly. Coordinating with Thurgood Marshall of the national NAACP, two groups of African American parents planned a lawsuit against the school district for denying their children access to their neighborhood school, which was all-white. Just as the suit was developing—gaining traction in the city and winning endorsements from the major local newspapers—a new Democratic governor and majority in the legislature was elected into office in the fall of 1948. The new administration, whose campaign platform included ending segregation in the entire state, organized with local civil rights leaders and key politicians in the house and senate to pass a bill ending segregation in public education. Although a major victory for civil rights, House Bill 242, signed into law in March 1949, produced few real changes in the city's schools. Not only would the Indianapolis board and superintendent's office slow its implementation, but housing segregation and gerrymandered school boundary lines also made the bill's efforts elusive. True integration remained a goal on the horizon.

Complicating race relations in the city, the all-black Crispus Attucks boys' basketball team became a perennial power in the annual state tournament in the 1950s, nearly winning Hoosier Hysteria, as it was known, in 1951 and 1954, and winning it all in 1955 and 1956. As with House Bill 242, however, the team's victories, which earned it the right to be called "Indianapolis' Team," often appeared more symbolic than substantive. In the years surrounding the Supreme Court's historic *Brown* decision in 1954, which ended school segregation from coast to coast, the basketball players and the community that supported them soon understood the limited ability of sports to transform society. The young men of Attucks were legends on the hardwood, but not regarded as neighbors, co-workers, partners, or spouses in a racially integrated society. Basketball was Indianapolis's most treasured pastime, but in the end, it was just a game.[12]

Local Politics, School Board Intransigence, and the Maintenance of a Racist "Status Quo"

Soon after the New Year in 1946, the all-black elementary school PS 63 burned to the ground. While local police and fire authorities never determined the cause of the blaze, the building, which suffered $50,000 worth of damage, was rendered inadequate to house the 335 students who would soon return from their holiday break. When it became clear that school leaders would be forced to find a new school (or combination of schools) for the children, several civil rights leaders saw a perfect opportunity to challenge the public system's segregation policy, which had always been defended as somehow "cost-effective" and "logical."[13] While there had been a steady stream of moderate opposition to the apartheid schools for decades, the size and character of this protest marked a turning point, one that matched the postwar call for racial equality heard nationwide.[14]

Within days, several of Indianapolis's most prominent civil rights groups, both white and black, met on the city's northwest side at the Senate Avenue YMCA, which had been built in 1913 with funds secured by Booker T. Washington in a gesture of accommodationism. In attendance were leaders of the all-black YMCA (led by charismatic executive director Faburn DeFrantz), the League of Women Voters, the local NAACP (led by President Lowell Trice), the all-white YWCA, the all-white YMCA, the American Legion, and the Madame C. J. Walker Company (led by Freeman Ransom). The meeting, apart from being a showing of interracial solidarity, led to the formation of the Citizens' Committee to Abolish Segregated Schools.[15]

As a sign of its immediate power and standing in the community, the committee convinced three white elementary school principals near PS 63 to accept the displaced students, a move that would solve the problem and integrate three schools in the process. As Pierce notes, "The solution was . . . simple and cost-effective."[16] When they presented the plan to the school board in February, however, it was rejected outright. The board submitted a plan of its own, doubling down on its intransigence: to bus most of PS 63's children ten miles away to a then-abandoned building and to send the rest to PS 26, a nearby all-black elementary school. To make space at PS 26, the board proposed allocating money for a ten-room addition at the school, which was already overcrowded and the largest elementary school in Indianapolis.[17]

Over the next several months, the interracial committee and the all-white board went back and forth over the issue. At one meeting, DeFrantz attempted to sway school leaders with his gift for oratory, reading prepared remarks that "invoked the spirit and name of Abraham Lincoln." That same night, Walter Frisbie, the state secretary of the Congress of Industrial Organizations, "challenged . . . [them] to take the necessary steps needed to create a truly democratic and fully integrated system."[18] In addition, a group of male students from Crispus Attucks in October 1946 reiterated to the board that busing black students to maintain segregation caused educational and emotional harm for secondary pupils as well. One of the students even penned a humorous, albeit poignant, poem to capture the crowded and unpredictable nature of their transportation. He wrote, "The school bus passed me again—That's why I'm here at noon!"[19] At a press conference organized the following morning by the NAACP's Education Committee, the young men from Attucks explained that letting them attend the high schools nearest their homes would solve the problem of forced segregation instantly.[20] This group of teenagers may have loved Attucks, but they recognized that racial separation was an affront to their citizenship.

The board listened to its critics but remained steadfast in its defense of school segregation. As in the 1920s, it highlighted the benefits of racial separation for African Americans. Carl Brandt, for example, who was president of the board in 1946, claimed that parents from PS 63 actually wanted the school's children to stay together at all costs, and he read aloud one parent's letter that said, "As it is well known that #63 is one big happy family[,] we are happy that faculty and children are still together." What Brandt concealed, however, was that the letter was only one of several the board received, and that it also called for an improved building and better services for the school's children.[21] While it pointed out that PS 63 was surrounded by a tight-knit community, as one might expect, the parent's letter was principally a challenge to discrimination. In any case, the board was unmoved, and the policy of segregation remained intact.

As historian Emma Lou Thornbrough has noted, Brandt and his colleagues owed their seats on the school board to the backing of the powerful, nearly all-white CSC.[22] Formed in 1929, the CSC was responsible in its first year of existence for ousting the Ku Klux Klan–backed "United Protestant School Ticket" from office, a fact it celebrated during its reelection campaigns every four years. Thornbrough observes that the CSC was "a somewhat shadowy, self-perpetuating group" of about two hundred prominent citizens. It disbanded after each election and formed again in four years' time to raise money for its candidates, who were generally elected.[23]

Though the CSC's candidates avoided outward displays of racism, Thornbrough finds that "there was never any mention of views on educational philosophy or policies . . . or suggestions for reform or changes," proving that "the [real] object . . . was to preserve the status quo."[24] John Niblack, for example, a local lawyer who influenced the group more than any other individual in the 1930s and 1940s, claimed that the candidates did "not represent any particular class, race, creed or special interest, but . . . are pledged to administer the affairs of the school city . . . and taxpayers of the city."[25] Similarly vague, the five candidates the CSC chose (typically four men and one woman), according to the

Indianapolis Times, "were usually cut from the same civic cloth—honest, sensible and durable, but without a great deal of variety."[26] By 1942, the CSC had drafted its usual, ostensibly innocuous platform, to which its candidates were required to subscribe. It stated that they vowed "to maintain the present high standards of our schools . . . [while observing] the strictest economy consistent with the best possible administration of school affairs."[27] The platform, as was often the case, aimed to offend few and promise very little.

Between 1929 and 1946, therefore, the school board in Indianapolis was run entirely by prominent white men and women, nearly all of whom had secured the backing of the CSC. Time and again, they claimed to represent the "entire city," but they overwhelmingly lived on the well-to-do North Side (or wealthy enclaves on the East Side). They seldom lived on the South or West Side and were never African American. Accordingly, if they had children in high school, the students likely attended Shortridge, maybe attended Tech, probably did not attend Manual, and absolutely did not attend Attucks. And though they wrapped their commitment to the school system in "nonpartisan" and "good government" language, they were devoted to the "status quo" above all.[28] The system was working well for them and their children, after all.

In Indianapolis in the 1940s, the "status quo" meant segregated schools. In their attempts to avoid conversations about racial equality, the CSC-backed board gained a reputation for "isolat[ing] themselves . . . [and] spen[ding] most of their time inspecting and approving reports on . . . financial matters, plans for buildings, appointment of teachers, and salaries."[29] According to Pierce, most civically active whites "avoided confrontation because they . . . [wanted to protect] the fact that Indianapolis had a national reputation for civility and order."[30] While they preferred passivity to hate, their actions—or lack thereof—maintained a racist, segregated system, one that benefited their children most.

The race- and class-based advantages of this approach extended well beyond education. Enshrined in "residential security maps," which were produced by the Home Owner's Loan Corporation (HOLC) between 1935 and 1940, white homeowners and developers in cities across the country were financially incentivized by the federal government (as well the local real estate market) to live in and maintain segregated neighborhoods that were served by segregated schools. The HOLC's agents surveyed hundreds of American cities and, with the aid of local lenders, appraisers, and developers, assigned neighborhoods individual grades based on their "mortgage security." Neighborhoods given the grade of A were colored green on the maps and deemed "best," while D neighborhoods were colored red and considered "hazardous." The so-called redlined neighborhoods were almost always black, racially mixed, or low income. As a result, Americans who were not both white and affluent had a far harder time gaining access to homeownership. For many, especially African Americans, it was impossible.[31]

Indianapolis's HOLC map was representative of this process. The areas around Crispus Attucks High, for example, were all redlined. The HOLC agents wrote in their descriptive notes that they were "blighted area[s]"; that their "detrimental influences" were "age," "almost solid negro," and "industrial"; and that their "favorable influences" were "none." A similar pattern emerged around Manual High. Though some of the nearby neighborhoods were graded with a B ("still desirable") or C ("definitely declining"), the great majority were redlined. Just south of Manual, in D17, the HOLC found "very old" homes near "numerous factories," homes that were occupied by "native white—Laboring and Mechanic classes." As a result, the area was considered "hazardous." By contrast, on the North Side, just north of Shortridge, was an A neighborhood, one inhabited by "native white; executive and other white-collar type" people, "where such families with good incomes desire their children to attend . . . schools."[32] Race, class, housing, and education were inexorably bound, documented in this case by the federal government. People on the North Side of Indianapolis could more easily accumulate wealth because of where they lived and where their children attended school.

Meanwhile, by the summer of 1947, a handful of members of the CSC had tried to broaden the list of potential candidates for the school board. Four of its roughly two hundred members were influential African American members of the community, and each one was devoted to ending segregation. They included lawyer and Republican state senator Robert Lee Brokenburr (serving from 1940 to 1948 and 1952 to 1964), Harvard-educated lawyer Willard Ransom, chairman of the local NAACP Education Committee Carrie Jacobs, and prominent physician Sumner Furniss. Although Brokenburr and Furniss were usually more conservative in attitude and style compared with the reportedly "impatient" and "forceful" young Ransom, the group deftly worked together to get three black community members on the 150-person list of potential CSC-sponsored candidates. It was a small step, but an accomplishment nonetheless.[33]

In July, the CSC held its quadrennial luncheon meeting to announce its candidates for the upcoming school board election. As an indication of how perfunctory the process had become, only twenty-five or so of its members bothered to attend, and only one newspaper "of general circulation sent a reporter." John Niblack, who chaired the meeting, rose to the podium, banged a metal knife to call the group to order (he had misplaced the gavel, apparently), and announced the candidates' names—and none of them were among the three supported by Brokenburr, Ransom, Jacobs, and Furniss.[34]

Niblack expected the usual unanimous approval of the slate of candidates, so he was shocked when the young Ransom shot to his feet and demanded an explanation. When pressed on where the CSC's all-white candidates stood on segregation, Niblack dodged the question, replying, "I think we have . . . picked

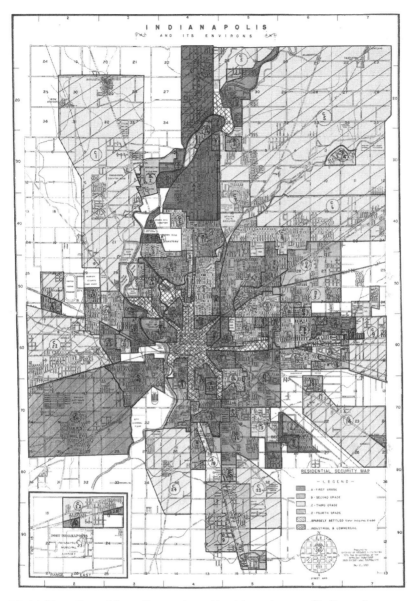

FIG. 4.1 Home Owner's Loan Corporation residential security map of Indianapolis, 1937. (Sourced from Robert K. Nelson, LaDale Winling, Richard Marciano, Nathan Connolly, et al., "Mapping Inequality," *American Panorama*.)

out some mighty fine citizens . . . [and] as to their stand on segregation, you'll have to ask them. I don't know what it is." Even some more moderate white liberals in attendance were dismayed, including Rabbi Morris Feverlicht. The rabbi, a leader in the Jewish community and on the CSC, stated that board members should not be chosen merely because of their race (black or white) but thought it was time for the CSC to take a stance on the issue. "If you're referring to a case where a Negro child who lives in a predominantly non-Negro neighborhood must go to another section to attend school," he stated, "then I'll help you fight that."[35]

Overwhelmed and frustrated, Niblack was replaced at the podium by Thomas Sheerin, who led the CSC's candidate selection subcommittee. In a more measured tone, he explained to Ransom and others that the subcommittee believed it was politically imprudent to address segregation head on. Furthermore, he explained, while the three black candidates *had* been considered, "the time was not ready." He continued, "We thought we'd have a measure of difficulty carrying the candidates [to victory] on the ticket."[36] Sheerin went on to state that African Americans in Indianapolis should be pleased that the CSC's slate was free of outright racists, made up instead of people who were at least indifferent about segregation. As Pierce notes, Sheerin believed he was appeasing civil rights leaders by claiming confidently, "We have given you no extremists." While the debate continued for some time, the nominees that Niblack originally presented—including current board president Carl Brandt— were approved by a majority of those in attendance.[37]

Ransom left the meeting ready to challenge the CSC slate in the general election. Within days, he formed a small organization (called the People's Committee), and he and his group promptly chose two highly qualified people to support: Reverend R. T. Andrews, who led the large and influential Mount Zion Baptist Church, and Charles Preston, who was known for being "the only white reporter on the *Recorder*."[38] While Andrews and Preston campaigned vigorously and raised a relatively large amount of money, they were soundly defeated. Emblematic of the local politics of race, the CSC won all five seats on the school board.[39]

By the fall of 1947, despite considerable mobilization at the local level, civil rights leaders shifted their focus to the courts and to the statehouse. During the next two years, owing to persistent efforts in both arenas, they found success in the form of House Bill 242, which finally ended segregation in the Indianapolis public schools. It was an important victory but proved to be more symbolic than substantive. De facto segregation and the maintenance of white privilege continued, ensuring that educational and social equality remained elusive.

State Politics, Court Challenges, and an End to School Segregation

While the attempt to wrestle school board seats away from the "status quo" CSC was unfolding, several members of the Indiana General Assembly tried to end school segregation through action at the state level. In some respects, this effort was inspired by the savvy Robert Brokenburr's success in passing a 1946 law prohibiting persons or organizations from circulating "malicious hatred by reason of race, color, or religion." At the passage of the so-called hate speech law, Brokenburr was the only black member of the state senate. He was a leader in the black wing of the Republican Party, which was losing members to the Democrats at unprecedented rates, a postwar phenomenon nationally.[40]

Soon after, two Republican state representatives from Marion County, William Fortune (who was white) and Wilbur Grant (a former NAACP leader), wrote and sponsored a bill that addressed school segregation directly. Drawing from the anger of their constituents, many of whom had children in the Indianapolis public schools, the bill stated that Indiana had an inherent responsibility "to provide equal educational opportunities and facilities for all, regardless of race, creed, or color" (see table 4.1 for changes to the African American population). Therefore, local school leaders, despite their relative autonomy, should be barred from "establish[ing], maintain[ing], continu[ing], or permit[ting] any separation of public schools or public school departments or divisions, on the basis of the race or color of attending pupils." The bill, which was referred to the Committee on Education for review, gave localities two years to dismantle their segregated systems.[41]

Proponents and opponents of segregation in Indianapolis—where the Fortune-Grant bill would have the most profound effect—instantly went to

Table 4.1
African American Population of Indianapolis, 1930–1960

	Population of Indianapolis	African American population	% African American	% African Am. growth over prev. decade
1930	364,161	43,967	12.1	26.8
1940	386,927	51,142	13.2	16.3
1950	427,173	63,867	15.0	24.9
1960	476,258	98,049	20.6	53.5

SOURCES: Population statistics for 1930: Department of Commerce, Bureau of the Census, *Fifteenth Census of the United States: Population, Volume II* (Washington, DC: Government Printing Office, 1933), 69; for 1940, 1950, and 1960: Campbell Gibson and Kay Jung, "Table 15. Indiana: Race and Hispanic Origin for Selected Large Cities and Other Places: Earliest Census to 1990," in "Historical Census Statistics on Population Totals by Race, 1790 to 1990, and by Hispanic Origin, 1970 to 1990, Cities and Other Urban Places in the United States" (Working Paper No. 76, US Census Bureau, Washington, DC, 2005).

work making their respective cases.[42] The most vocal champion of the bill was the large and interracial Church Federation, which included several members who had helped Fortune and Grant draft its language. At a public hearing in 1947, the federation was joined by the NAACP, the Congress of Industrial Organizations, and numerous church organizations. Henry Richardson, a local lawyer, public school parent, active Democrat, and key player in the Church Federation, succinctly stated the group's case. He explained that Indianapolis in 1947 was "the only large northern city with a [legally] segregated school system." Furthermore, Richardson stressed that its maintenance was not only embarrassing but also "expensive, unfair, undemocratic, unreasonable, and immoral."[43]

Meanwhile, the bill's opponents found their most forceful voice in the form of Indianapolis school superintendent Virgil Stinebaugh, who had led the school system since 1944. He cited the bill's potential social ramifications and its undue stress on the city's educational institutions. He stated that segregation "cannot be considered wisely without reference to . . . local practices in race relations in business and industrial life, in religious and fraternal organizations, recreational and character building agencies, and in neighborhood agencies."[44] As one historian concluded, Stinebaugh was suggesting that in Indianapolis "the whole apple was rotten," so asking the public schools alone to desegregate was unfair and unwise. The schools, the logic went, merely followed the city's lead.[45]

Stinebaugh and his supporters further argued that school desegregation would eliminate many middle-class jobs for black teachers, implying there was little or no support to allow African Americans to teach in all-white or mixed-race classrooms. This tactic of intimidation was common in the 1930s and 1940s in the urban North, but several historians of Indianapolis have pointed out that it was quickly losing traction in the postwar era.[46] In a survey of nearly three hundred local black teachers, "80 percent favored the outright abolition of segregated teaching staffs."[47] Black educators recognized that ending segregation put their own jobs on the line.

While the debate raged on, the Committee on Education, back in the statehouse, was dragging its feet on the Fortune-Grant bill. Worried that it would "die in committee," an African American representative from East Chicago, James Hunter, moved that it be brought to the floor for a vote "with or without a recommendation." It was an unorthodox move, but Hunter sensed it was his only play. "Right here in Indianapolis," he stated in making the case, "the school board pays out [thousands of dollars] annually to prevent Negro pupils from attending schools that are located just around the corner from where they live." Despite his efforts, the house of representatives (in a vote of forty-six to twenty-five) tabled Hunter's motion. As he predicted, the bill expired in the Committee on Education.[48]

In the wake of the Fortune-Grant bill's demoralizing defeat, a handful of Indianapolis's civil rights leaders returned their focus to challenging segregation in the courts, long the preferred method of the NAACP.[49] In 1947, Henry Richardson and his wife, Roselyn, were among the first to act. Henry was born in Huntsville, Alabama, but moved to the city as a child and had attended an integrated Shortridge as a teenager. He and his wife lived on the wealthier North Side of the city on North Meridian Street, although the home, owing to restrictive covenants, had to be purchased by a white friend acting on their behalf. In any case, they wanted their children to attend the elementary school in their neighborhood, and—just as importantly—they were interested in taking the school board to court over the matter.[50]

The Richardsons were joined by Clarence Nelson, a local minister and former president of the Minneapolis NAACP. Together, the two respectably middle-class families attempted to enroll their children at the wealthy, all-white PS 43. As expected, their request was rejected by the school's principal and superintendent, Stinebaugh. A letter from the assistant superintendent informed the families that their children (two Richardson boys and the twin Nelson girls) had to attend an all-black school, a school that was not only overcrowded but also nearly twenty blocks from their homes.[51]

Incensed though unsurprised, Nelson and the Richardsons, along with Ransom (then the leading local NAACP lawyer) and Jacobs, visited the school board to appeal. When the board held firm, saying that "important financial and administrative factors must be considered" first, Nelson announced that he would file a joint suit with the NAACP. Indeed, a series of letters between Ransom and Thurgood Marshall, who led the NAACP's national Legal Defense Fund, reveal that the two had been formulating a strategy for months. Essentially, their argument went, the public schools in Indianapolis needed to be integrated or made completely equal in terms of their funding and amenities: truly "separate but equal," as the *Plessy* (1896) decision mandated. They knew that the latter option would cost millions of dollars, and that the board would choose, or be forced to accept, the former.[52]

While the local and national NAACP coordinated its case, Ransom continued to put pressure on the school board, insisting that African American community members attend their meetings and be heard. In one prophetic exchange, local NAACP president William Ray spoke to the board about the deleterious psychological effects of segregation, evidence that would be instrumental in legal challenges in the *Brown* decision in a few years.[53] In response, a seemingly naïve board member replied, "I thought that when Crispus Attucks was built we solved that problem." Without skipping a beat, Ray retorted, "That only started the problem."[54]

By the fall of 1948, the school board, for the first time in decades, appeared to be wavering. In an unprecedented move, it ordered more than one hundred

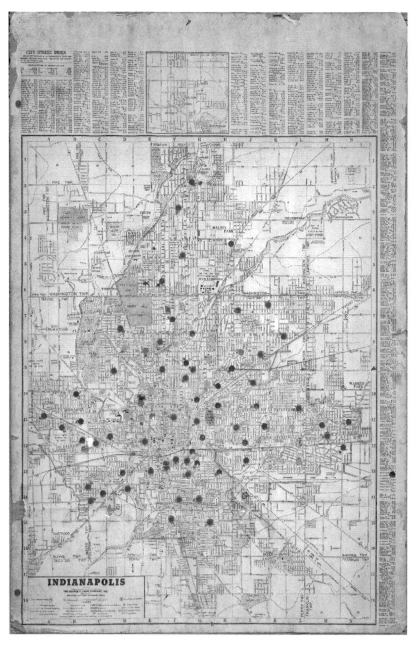

FIG. 4.2 Henry Richardson's segregation map, 1948. Richardson created this map as part of his efforts to end segregation in the public schools. (Courtesy of Indianapolis Recorder Collection, Indiana Historical Society.)

black elementary school students to relocate from an overcrowded all-black school to PS 32, an all-white school in a working-class neighborhood on the West Side. While historians have found little evidence that PS 32's white parents objected to integration per se, they did object to being the only school chosen by the board. Further, they argued that classism was at the root of the plan, an argument difficult to dismiss since the mostly well-heeled board was ready to go to court to keep PS 43 (on the wealthy North Side) completely white. At a board meeting, one white parent summed up the class-based animosity perfectly, stating, "It's just that we don't like being pushed around by those Northside swells." Later that night, PS 32's parents announced that they would boycott their school until the black children were removed or the entire city was integrated. They refused to be a "laboratory," they said.[55]

As the board attempted to weather the boycott, three other changes marked the beginning of the end of segregation in the Indianapolis schools. First, the bipartisan Indianapolis Community Relations Council released a conclusive report, authored by Max Wolff, that condemned the board's actions outright. Wolff, a respected member of the community, concluded that black children had "to travel excessive distances to reach inadequate schools," and that "whatever conditions may have ... justified ... a segregated school system ... no longer hold true."[56] Second, the influential *Indianapolis Star*, which had given nearly unqualified support to the school board and the CSC for decades, changed its position. Not only did the editors of the *Star* encourage wide discussion of Wolff's report, but they also took a firmly antisegregationist stance, one that appealed to the city's moral and financial sensibilities. "The mixing of races in our schools is the just and economical way to run our schools," they concluded.[57]

And third, in the November 1948 state election, Democrats—who campaigned on "work[ing] unceasingly to end all discrimination based on account of race"—won the governor's office and elected a decisive number of representatives from Marion County. In many respects, the victory was the result of the growing preference among the white working class and African Americans for the Democratic Party, as well as of the city's steady increase in black residents relative to the total population.[58] After the election, Ransom, reading the political winds in the city and in the statehouse, wrote to Marshall to tell him that he believed the time was right for another run at a state law banning school segregation. Marshall advised against the plan, citing their case's strong chance of success, but Ransom refused to yield. With time, Marshall wished him well and began looking elsewhere for suitable test cases.[59]

What Ransom knew and Marshall may not have fully appreciated was that his ally Henry Richardson had the new governor, Henry Schricker's ear. By working to keep the Dixiecrat Strom Thurmond off the ticket in the state of Indiana, Richardson had bolstered Schricker's chances of victory significantly.

And when the governor asked what he wanted in return, Richardson was unequivocal: a state law ending school segregation—nothing more and nothing less. As Richardson's wife, Roselyn, later recalled, Henry was willing to wait on other civil rights legislation (including the Fair Employment Practices Commission) and wanted to focus on the schools "because he knew all those tricks." Mrs. Richardson continued, "You get three or four [civil rights bills] going and then nothing happens."[60] Henry Richardson knew that it would take singular focus.

It was no small feat, but the governor delivered on his promise. Through his persistent efforts, skillful lobbying in the house by James Hunter, vote whipping in the senate by Richardson and Robert Brokenburr, and a steady flow of antisegregationist editorials in key Indianapolis newspapers (the *Star*, *Times*, and *Recorder*), House Bill 242 passed in March 1949. Nearly all the city's papers printed laudatory accounts, but the *Recorder*'s was the most authentic and beautiful. "A solid front of all Negro groups, with the help of liberal white organizations, was credited with bringing about the most unprecedented reversal of action" by the state. "Never before in Indiana's history," it continued, "had Negro political leaders of various parties shown such unity on a legislative measure." For his efforts, Ransom won the Cable Award in 1949 for "outstanding work in race relations."[61]

Symbolically, the bill was a triumph, without question, but the road to racial integration, to say nothing of educational equity, was just beginning. While the 1949 bill ended the city's official program of segregation, little changed in the city's classrooms, especially at the high school level. Soon after the bill's passage, for example, the school board approved a plan for integration put forward by Superintendent Stinebaugh, one that favored a remarkably gradual approach. To begin with, elementary school students would be reassigned to their new schools at the kindergarten level only, so that the level of integration would increase only slightly from year to year. At the high school level, the plan stipulated that students would continue to enroll at the secondary school their elementary school had fed before 1949. Furthermore, only students who lived more than two miles from any school could appeal to the school board for a reassignment.[62]

On the one hand, therefore, the burden to integrate the city's high schools was presumably placed on aggrieved black families, in particular those who had been forced for years to send their children across town to attend Attucks. On the other hand, Stinebaugh's policy ensured that no white children would attend Attucks, even if it was the school closest to their homes (which, owing to housing segregation, it rarely was). And the plan, to that end, was incredibly effective: the first white student to enroll at the historically black school did so in 1968. As Pierce rightly notes, "Having a law to end segregation was far different than actual integration."[63]

While the politics of gradualism took hold and the spirit of House Bill 242 was thwarted, the all-black Attucks boys' basketball team became a statewide powerhouse. Along the way, its success complicated race relations in Indianapolis. By the 1950s, the basketball team and Attucks as a school—conceived by de jure segregation and maintained by de facto segregation—became a source of pride for everyone in the city. However, after finally winning the state championship in 1955, a year after the historic *Brown* decision, it was clear that the limits of racial understanding that sports can engender were significant. Whites in Indianapolis mostly cared about Attucks's young men only as they existed between the painted lines of the court. Beyond those lines, African Americans were lesser citizens, and they would have to fight for equality—in schools, in the labor market, in housing, and beyond—in other arenas. Even in basketball-obsessed Indiana, racism and white supremacy reigned supreme.

Becoming "Indianapolis's Team": Attucks Boys' Basketball, 1941–1951

As with House Bill 242, it took years of lobbying for Crispus Attucks High School, as well as Indiana's other all-black high schools, to gain access to the annual state basketball tournament. The event, known informally as Hoosier Hysteria, was controlled by the Indiana High School Athletic Association (IHSAA), was held each March in Indianapolis, and was arguably the most important state-specific occasion of the year. In its famed 1929 report on high school athletics nationwide, for example, the Carnegie Foundation listed only a few public school systems by name, and most of them in the Hoosier State, noting, "Some cases of 'high schools built around basketball courts,' may be found in Indiana."[64] After the report's authors visited thousands of schools, it seemed, the state's obsession with high school basketball loomed large in their minds. The doctor and educator James Naismith may have invented the game of basketball in Massachusetts in 1891, but Indiana was its adopted home.[65]

Despite its significance, black high schools had been barred from participating in the state tournament since it was first organized in 1911. Recall that the Attucks team, from the school's founding in 1927, had been forced to travel long distances, often across state lines, to play other all-black high schools. Trips as far as Louisville, Kentucky; St. Louis, Missouri; Dayton, Ohio; Evansville, Indiana; and Chicago, Illinois, were common in the 1930s and early 1940s. One player, Harry Petrie, who graduated in 1931, remembered that the team often "stayed in YMCAs . . . [or] stayed in flop houses [where they endured] roaches and chinches, and all that kind of pollution." "Sometimes," he continued, "we slept in [the opposing teams'] gyms."[66]

All-black schools and antisegregationists alike were encouraged in 1941 when the state senate drafted Senate Bill 181, which sought to "ban segregation in

IHSAA tournaments." After the bill failed to make it through the house of representatives, civil rights leaders turned up the pressure on Arthur "King" Trester, the IHSAA's powerful secretary, who had denied both black and Catholic schools access to the tournament throughout his more than twenty-year czar-like reign. By the end of 1941, Trester finally conceded, announcing that for the 1942–1943 academic year, "[all] public, private, parochial, colored, and institutional high schools" could compete.[67]

By the mid- to late 1940s, the Attucks boys' team had gained a reputation for moderate success, though it never made it deep into the state tournament. Much of the team's steady improvement was attributable to its demanding coach, Fitzhugh Lyons, who had been at the helm for more than a decade. The style of play that Lyons preached was rooted in the game's fundamentals, but it was often rigid, emotionless, and slow moving. One historian calls it "a passive non-confrontational approach," while another describes it as a list of "don'ts: don't leave your feet, don't fluster your opponent with physical defense, don't improvise, and don't anger a white official ... with a complaint."[68] To a large extent, Lyons's teams reflected what the school's principal, Russell Lane (1930–1957), wanted for Attucks as a whole. Sure, Lane and his basketball coach hoped that the team would win, but putting their pupils in any sort of race-based conflict, where they could be at potential risk, was to be avoided at all costs.[69] Lyons believed that modesty, discipline, and safety should trump winning.

Attucks's reputation—for a passive style of play and only modest on-court success—changed quickly when Lyons announced his retirement in 1950 and was replaced by Ray Crowe, a thirty-five-year-old former collegiate multisport star from rural Whitefield, Indiana. Known for his composure, his intense stare, and his immaculate suits, Crowe, who also taught math and physical education, turned Attucks into a perennial basketball power during his seven-year tenure. Like Lyons before him, Crowe stressed sportsmanship, demanded respect, and was known for visiting players' homes unannounced to discuss discipline problems. Unlike Lyons, however, he preferred a more relaxed, open-ended style of play. Before being named coach, Crowe had served as coordinator of an afterschool basketball program at Indianapolis's Lockefield Gardens, a segregated federal housing project built with New Deal money in 1935. As coordinator, Crowe had witnessed on the Lockefield courts (the famous "Dust Bowl," as they were collectively known) a form of basketball that, as one historian puts it, "emphasized showmanship, athleticism, and improvisation." Like the world-famous Indianapolis jazz that reverberated up and down the neighborhoods along Indiana Avenue, "it was a style that was distinctly black."[70]

In his first season, Crowe expertly wove together the two styles of play, making use of the old (personified by Attucks center Bob Jewell) and the new (personified by forwards Hallie Bryant and Willie "Dill" Gardner, as well as guard Bailey "Flap" Robertson). As his team took the court that winter, they were met with mixed reactions, many positive, but some negative, too. Using only thinly veiled racist language, for example, a reporter for the *Indianapolis Star* claimed the game should not allow the "jumping-jack legs" that the players often sported. Furthermore, even some of the faculty at Attucks questioned the stylistic and tactical changes. Later in life, Crowe told an interviewer, "Some of the older teachers [like Lyons] still believed that the best way to improve the perception of blacks was to avoid being aggressive." He continued defiantly, "I needed to make them understand that the worst disgrace [our players] could bring to our school was to lose when they had the chance to win."[71] After all, Attucks was founded on and stood for success.

And win they did. After sailing through the regular season in Crowe's first year with only one loss, the young men of Attucks entered the 1951 playoffs as likely contenders for the state title. Along the way, the Attucks student cheering section gained a reputation for its favorite chant, "The Crazy Song" (written by student Edwena Bell in the early 1940s), which they sang in unison during the contests' most intense moments. Dressed in their green and gold school colors, the Tigers' cheerleaders and fans sang (to the tune of Cab Calloway's 1931 "Minnie the Moocher"), "They can beat everybody, / But they can't beat us!" By March 1951, the team had, win after win, reached the state semifinals, and "The Crazy Song" filled the rafters of Butler University's Hinkle Fieldhouse on Indianapolis's North Side, the tournament's host and, with its fifteen thousand seats, the biggest shrine to basketball in the state.[72]

In the semifinal, Attucks faced Anderson High School, an all-white team from Madison County with a tradition of winning. Many spectators claimed that the game's officiating was dreadfully one-sided in Anderson's favor that night, an all too common experience for Attucks, an all-black team that only played under the supervision of white referees (the IHSAA still forbade African American officials). "By the end of the game," Attucks assistant coach Al Spurlock later noted, "it seemed as if Anderson had seven players on the court— two with striped uniforms."[73]

Nonetheless, with only seconds left in the game, Attucks possessed the ball, trailing by one. In a soon-to-be-famous moment, sophomore guard Bailey Robertson "grabbed the ball, shot, and prayed," he told a reporter afterward. When the ball fell through the net, he, as one historian explained, "became immortal." The Attucks student section inside the fieldhouse erupted, of course, but so did Indiana Avenue over on the northwest side of town. "You could hear car horns honking . . . and people cheering in their homes" up and down the neighborhood's streets, one observer said. A local news reporter, caught up in the excitement, claimed it was, "without a doubt, one of the most thrilling high school basketball games ever played in Indiana—or the world." Robertson, sixteen at the time, remarked, "People [later] told me their relatives died of heart attacks" when he made the shot. "One lady," he continued, "told me that when the ball went through the hoop, she started to go into labor."[74]

In the coming days, the importance of Attucks's reaching the finals generated enthusiasm across the city, in white and black neighborhoods, for no team from Indianapolis had ever won a state championship in basketball. In a column in the *Indianapolis Star*, for example, a white sportswriter wrote excitedly that a group of young black men could end the city's championship drought, and in doing so the writer referenced the lyrics of "The Crazy Song," a fact that would not have been lost on the paper's readers. "For Indianapolis, after 40 years of frustration," he wrote, "[we have the chance] to face the rest of Indiana on Saturday and say, 'You can beat everybody, but you can't beat us!'" In that moment—a moment set in motion when the all-black school was forced on the black community—"us" implied that Attucks and the city as a whole were one and the same. From then on, as several historians have observed, the basketball team was known in newspapers and private conversations as "Indianapolis Attucks" as opposed to "Crispus Attucks." In its athletic triumphs, Indianapolis was happy to adopt the school.[75]

Praise also came from the city's school leaders, despite the fact that they had lost the battle to maintain a segregated system two years earlier. Superintendent Herman Shibler, who had replaced Virgil Stinebaugh in 1950 and publicly favored integration, saw the moment as an opportunity for greater racial understanding among whites. He stated, "That basketball team accomplished more for race relations in one season than you could accomplish in ten years of forums and discussions." He went on, "The white people here have a completely new impression of the colored race. It's marvelous." Even the all-white school board paid tribute to the team and its accomplishments in an official proclamation. "Whereas the basketball team of Crispus Attucks," it announced, has "reflected great credit upon the Indianapolis Public Schools," and "whereas . . . [they] have shown great skill, determination, and sportsmanship," "be it resolved by . . . [the board] that it express its deep appreciation."[76]

As the title game against Evansville Reitz High School neared, both Coach Crowe and Principal Lane recognized its larger significance. They knew that the eyes of the state were on them, their beloved school, and—most of all—the young men on the basketball team. Observers who were white supremacists, or opposed to integration in general, would have been happy to see Attucks lose the game, but even happier to see them lose their composure. The double standard was palpable. As was his custom, therefore, Lane visited the team's locker room shortly before tip-off. His message was always the same, but on that night in 1951, the players could sense an added level of seriousness in his voice. As one of them later recalled, Lane calmly told them, "You are representing much more than your school. You *are* black Indianapolis. This time the whole state is watching. More important than winning is good sportsmanship. Be gentlemen."[77] They were merely high schoolers in tank tops, shorts, and sneakers, but in that moment, they were being asked to be much more.

In the end, it was a relatively close game, but Evansville Reitz edged out Attucks sixty-six to fifty-nine. Heartbroken, Crowe took the blame, always seeking to protect his young players. "We were not ready, and that was my fault," he explained, but "I made up my mind right then that we would be back, and the next time we would be ready." As it turned out, Crowe was absolutely right. In the meantime, however, the city's black press used the moment to explore the intersection of sports and society, as well as the irony that Indianapolis, a city teeming with racism, had seemingly fallen in love with an all-black high school basketball team; a team, let alone a school, that would not exist if not for segregation.

An editorial in the *Recorder*, for example, stated, "Where the appeals of religion, reason, and education [for equality] seem to have fallen on deaf ears, the spectacle of brilliant basketball has turned the trick." When it came to any form of racial understanding, "in deep humility, we observe that God does move in mysterious ways." Days later, in an apropos article titled "Attucks Tigers and Hoosier Democracy," the *Recorder*'s author pondered, "We know that Bob Jewell [the team's center] can get the rebounds, but what we are wondering is whether he can get into college." Furthermore, the author continued, "It is very fine to give Hallie Bryant a hand, but how about giving him a job when the time comes?" And, "Will 'Dill' Gardner be able to move about in Indianapolis as he moves about on the basketball court?" or could Gardner "eat in all the restaurants where his achievements are providing dinner"? The columnist knew that the answer to these questions was almost certainly no. They needed to be asked all the same, rhetorically, while the memory of the tournament—and Attucks's exciting and vital role in it—was still fresh in the minds of Indianapolis's citizens.[78]

After bitter losses in the 1952 and 1953 seasons, Attucks returned to the state tournament's final four again in 1954 and 1955, in both cases led by Flap Robertson's younger brother Oscar. He was on his way to becoming the most celebrated high school basketball player in state history, an all-American at the University of Cincinnati, and a hall-of-fame professional in the National Basketball Association. As Robertson's and Attucks's athletic star continued to rise, however, both championship runs—their loss in 1954 and their win in 1955—revealed that racism was too powerful of a force for basketball alone to overcome. Attucks could become "Indianapolis's team," but the benefits of that distinction were always circumscribed. Through hard work and skill, they finally gave the city its first state title in 1955, but—in the era of the *Brown* decision, the Montgomery Bus Boycott, and the murder of Emmett Till— educational and social equality remained elusive.

Basketball Heroes, but Unequal beyond the Court:
Attucks Boys' Basketball, 1951–1955

When Oscar Robertson returned from summer vacation as a sophomore in 1953, he was seven inches taller and no longer looked like a lean and lanky teen-ager. He had spent the three previous months on a farm outside Charlotte, Tennessee, where he was born and where his extended family still lived. After a summer of tough manual labor, "pick[ing] tobacco . . . put[ting] up hay [and] shuck[ing] corn," he had, in his words, "put some breadth in my chest and some meat on my arms."[79] Young for his grade, he was only fourteen years old at the time, but that winter, back in Indianapolis, he promptly asserted himself as the best Attucks Tiger and the most promising basketball player the city had ever seen.

With Robertson quietly and confidently leading the way, Attucks once again reached the state tournament's semifinal game in 1954, this time against an all-white team from the tiny town of Milan, Indiana: home to family farms, a single-stoplight downtown, and only 1,100 residents, none of whom were African American. Milan had boasted a strong basketball program for several years (despite its size) but its matchup against Attucks, an all-black school from the state's biggest city, promptly drew comparisons to the Bible's David and Goliath. It also provoked a considerable amount of race-based tension, the expression of which was more measured in some cases than in others.[80]

Milan's star player, Bobby Plump, for example, vividly remembered the racism that many fans attached to the game in the days prior. "When we went out to dinner [the night before in Indianapolis], an unusual number of people followed us around." Several of them, he continued, told Plump and his teammates, "C'mon Milan, beat those niggers. People were saying it everywhere."[81] In the *Recorder*, columnist Andrew Ramsey, with infinitely more grace, attempted to capture the African American community's perspective on the game. "To the Negro fans," he wrote, "the game was a sort of vicarious struggle against . . . second class citizenship." Those who "daily take a beating from the whole white race in industry, in business, in religion, and in their living conditions were jubilant" to potentially see "a symbol of white supremacy bite the dust."[82] Again, the basketball players shouldered far more than the pressure of dribbling, shooting, winning, and losing.

While tensions rose off the court, the game proved to be far less exciting than expected, with Milan winning comfortably, sixty-five to fifty-two. In the tournament's final game, Milan went on to beat Muncie Central in dramatic fashion, thirty-two to thirty, and was crowned state champion (which would later be the subject of the critically acclaimed 1986 film *Hoosiers*). After the team collected its trophy, it was loaded onto a fire truck and paraded around Indianapolis, stopping at Monument Circle for photographs and revelry, as the tournament's champions had done for years. Afterward, they and their supporters drove the eighty miles back to Milan, and along the way, it has been reported, their bus was stopped multiple times by women with celebratory fresh-baked pies for the team. The fete in Milan the next day, emblematic of the victory's broad appeal throughout rural Indiana, was attended by more than twenty thousand people.[83] The symbolism was unmistakable: though they were merely students from a small school in a small farming community, the all-white Milan had beaten the state's biggest schools, and all-black schools. They were named champions of the state's most beloved game in Butler University's Hinkle Fieldhouse, home to the game's most venerated court.

When Attucks won the state tournament the following year, in 1955, the team and its fans were treated remarkably differently, and racism marked the change. This was despite the fact that the Attucks championship was claimed and honored by a number of different groups, both black and white. The *Chicago Defender*, for example, covered the game extensively, placing it side by side with the University of San Francisco's National Collegiate Athletic Association men's basketball championship, which occurred on the very same day. Given that San Francisco was the first collegiate team to start three black players (including the incomparable Bill Russell), a columnist in the *Defender* wrote, "I'm firmly convinced that March [1955] was the greatest month of achievements in the history of Negro athletics."[84] Back in Indianapolis, moreover, the city's newspapers printed scores of articles praising the team and its achievements, each more hyperbolic than the last. Even the city's mayor, Alex Clark, proclaimed, "This was not alone an Attucks victory, but a victory for every one of the 450,000 people here in Indianapolis."[85]

Despite all the praise, backslapping, and political opportunism, Attucks and the community it served were denied the chance to celebrate fully, as other teams and their fans had done for decades. As the final games approached in 1955, Attucks's principal Russell Lane was called to the superintendent's office to talk about his basketball team. He recalled, "When we were about to win that championship, the week before they called me down to the school office. The superintendent did, Dr. Shibler." When Lane arrived, he said, Shibler "had the fire chief down there and the police chief, and representatives of businessmen downtown, sitting around the table." He "called me in, said to me, 'Mr. Lane, it looks like your team's going to win the championship next Saturday night . . . [and] the merchants downtown are frightened that after you win that championship, colored people will come downtown and tear up the downtown." They were worried, and felt physically afraid, that African Americans might "break out the windows and knock out the streetlights, and all that." Lane, who was offended, replied firmly, "I . . . [don't] believe they would do one thing."[86] Flanked by the city's most powerful white leaders, Shibler ignored

FIG. 4.3 Crispus Attucks High School basketball team, state champions, 1955. (Courtesy of Indianapolis Recorder Collection, Indiana Historical Society.)

Lane's assurances. He insisted that the festivities take place near Attucks High School, in the city's predominantly black neighborhood.

Therefore, while the state tournament's winning teams had for decades stopped and celebrated at Monument Circle, in the heart of downtown, the Attucks parade would only be allowed to make a quick lap. There would be no stopping for pictures. There would be no stopping for hugs. And apart from its clear-cut racism, the decision was ironic, given that the all-white Shortridge and Manual high school football teams used to meet at the Circle for an annual fistfight following their Thanksgiving Day game. Perhaps Shibler, the police chief, the fire chief, and the city's business community did not know that history. Perhaps they had forgotten it. Perhaps, because those students were white, they did not care about it.

Later in life, Oscar Robertson wrote about his team's rerouted parade, the details of which they were unaware of at the time; it appears Lane, hoping to protect their spirits, did not have the heart to tell them beforehand. Robertson remembered, "The motorcade completed the [lap around Monument Circle] and headed up along Indiana [Avenue], and then north on West Street. Something was wrong. I knew the traditional parade route. I'd seen other champions . . . [stop in] the heart of the city. Instead, we were moving

FIG. 4.4 Celebratory bonfire after Crispus Attucks High School basketball team state championship, 1955. (Courtesy of Indianapolis Recorder Collection, Indiana Historical Society.)

into territory I knew all too well. Into the heart of Naptown. Past the brick walls of Crispus Attucks."[87] There, on the city's northwest side before a bonfire, Robertson remembered, "the sea of what seemed like thousands of people cheering as our truck stopped, the friends who embraced us as we climbed down, the familiar faces all around us, ecstatic."[88]

The memory, for Robertson at least, recalled the questions that had long perplexed the city's African American community and civil rights leaders. Should they pursue integration as the only path to true equality, even if it meant attending schools or gathering freely in spaces where they were seemingly unwanted? Or, given the realities of racism, should they rally around their own institutions, such as the beloved Crispus Attucks, which they could govern with their own interests in mind? Robertson's teammate and friend Bill Swatts, for example, remembered the night as wholly joyous. "There was no place I would have rather been that night," he explained, "no people I would have rather been with." Robertson, however, could not shake the pain of the inequity, the sting of the exclusion. "On that chilly night," he later wrote, "I stood and stared at the bonfire and all the celebrating faces, all black, and I could not help but think about little Milan High." While those white high school students, just teenagers, "hadn't even been from the city... their team got to... [celebrate] downtown. Why was that honor denied us?"[89] To Robertson, they had done everything that was asked of them. They worked hard at a segregated school, and they had proved themselves on the basketball court. But it still was not enough. The game of basketball and the game of life were played in separate arenas, with separate rules.

To that end, Robertson noted in his biography, "I've always thought that a wonderful thing about sports is that they give everyone a chance." Even more optimistically, he continued, "That's one of the wonderful things about America as well. The country promises everyone a chance. It is a promise that has not always been kept," he acknowledged, "but the promise has always been there, a shining beacon down the road."[90] As the next chapter explains, the road to equality, as it related to the Indianapolis high school system, proved long and winding. And the shining beacon, though lit, remained off in the distance in the late 1950s and 1960s. Through a continued diversification and broadening of the curriculum, a persistent effort to keep the schools racially segregated, and an acceleration of suburbanization, the city's high schools continued to be divided and unjust. For all that would change, much remained the same.

5

"Life Adjustment" Education, Suburbanization, Unigov, and an Unjust System by a New Name, 1955–1971

•••••••••••••••••••••

As we look ahead, there is one thing that can be said for certain about the school system's second 100 years. It is that the system's success will be governed largely by the interest, cooperation, and support that the public gives it.
—Superintendent Herman Shibler in 1953, upon the Indianapolis Public Schools' Centennial

On April 25, 1954, the Indianapolis public school system concluded its centennial. To celebrate the occasion, Superintendent Herman Shibler, in concert with the school board, published a souvenir booklet titled *Living and Learning in the Indianapolis Public Schools*. It included an extensive history of the school system, from its "tuition-school" beginnings in "a log cabin, 20 by 20 feet," in 1821, to the founding of the city's first free public high school (eventually named Shortridge) in 1864, to the opening of the industrial-minded Manual High in 1895, to the establishment of the comprehensive Arsenal Tech

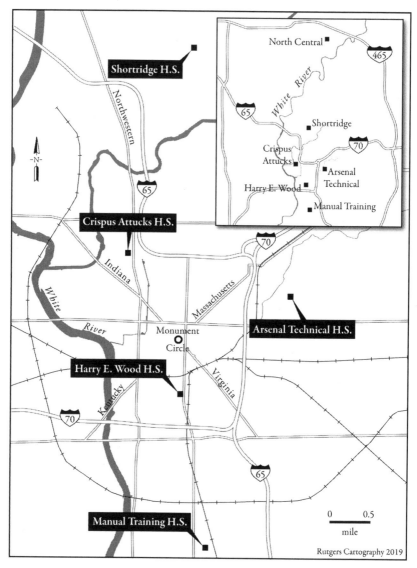

FIG. 5.1 Map of selected Indianapolis area high schools, 1971

High in 1912, to the construction of the racially segregated Crispus Attucks in 1927. But "these events provide only the barest plot of the drama," said the school leaders. That, they reasoned, "was acted out daily in the classrooms of our city, where teachers and pupils working together sought to acquire the best of our great traditions and knowledge."[1]

The booklet also detailed the "year-long observance" of the system's longevity and accomplishments. The board had worked closely with the local chamber of commerce, as well as the nine-person Citizens Centennial Committee, to plan a "kick-off parade" downtown, reportedly attended by "an estimated 175,000 persons." In the following days and months, school leaders drew out the festivities, placing a commemorative plaque at "the site of the first schoolhouse in the city," overseeing "the all-city vocal music festival," and enjoying "a football jamboree in the Butler Bowl in which all public high school teams and bands took part." Indeed, it was a year of well-deserved praise and "of reviewing the past," the booklet explained, but also a year "in which the city gave much thought to the future of its public schools."[2] Some celebrating was fine, but some reflection—in moments like these—was necessary.

In the introduction to *Living and Learning*, Shibler took time to do just that. In plain language, he told his constituents what would make the Indianapolis public school system "great" for another century. "There is one thing that can be said for certain about the . . . system's second 100 years," he wrote. "It is that the system's success will be governed largely by the interest, cooperation, and support that the public gives it." If "this support is forthcoming, and we hope that it will be," Shibler continued almost nervously, then "progress during the second 100 years will be even more fruitful than during the first 100."[3] Local school systems reflected their communities' most powerful voices, the shrewd Shibler knew.

As the coming years revealed, Shibler's words, however vague, were prophetic, for Indianapolis and its public high schools were transformed—through the curriculum, through shifts in demographics, and through a new form of municipal government—in the years between 1955 and 1971. The school board and administration once again broadened the curriculum by introducing a range of new courses and certificates in "life adjustment" education, which was developed at the national level by longtime vocational education advocate and lobbyist Charles Prosser, among others. Promising to prepare the high schools' weakest students for "life," as opposed to high-skill work or college, life adjustment education flourished from coast to coast in the years after 1950. When it came to Indianapolis, however, it was pushed by school leaders most forcefully on the city's more working-class, and increasingly African American, South Side. Housed in a brand-new Manual High School (completed in 1954) and a newly devised Harry E. Wood High School (which took over the old Manual), children south of downtown's Monument Circle were offered an abundance of courses described as more "practical" than "academic," just as they had been since 1895. Tracking, from building to building and classroom to classroom, was as pronounced as ever. "Life adjustment" education, accordingly, was just a new label for a decades-old trend.

While Manual High and Wood High continued to offer forms of education "for the mind and hand and heart" on the South Side, Shortridge continued to stand out academically in the 1950s. It won multiple prizes, churned out droves of college-bound graduates, and most strikingly was named one of the best high schools in the country by *Time*, *Newsweek*, and several other publications in 1957. Despite its success, suburbanization in Indianapolis—"white flight" from the central city, in particular—transformed Shortridge almost overnight. By 1964, the student population was 60 percent black, and the school's remaining white parents (aided by its powerful alumni base) demanded that the board take action to "save Shortridge."

To slow the process of integration and attract affluent white families back to the North Side school, the school board passed the Shortridge Plan in 1965, which declared it the city's true "academic high school" and instituted an admissions examination for entry. Though it failed to stem the tide of suburbanization and was scrapped by 1969, the Shortridge Plan, spearheaded by Shortridge alumnus, board member, and future mayor and US senator Richard Lugar, proved how far school leaders would go to maintain the prestige of the "blue and white."

By the late 1960s, after years of petitioning by local civil rights groups, the Justice Department sued the Indianapolis public schools for failing to adequately integrate. When the case was finally heard, in 1971, the department's lawyers, aided by the National Association for the Advancement of Colored People (NAACP), articulated clearly and forcefully what the people of Indianapolis already knew: that the school system—through its placement of new buildings, its zoning, and its transfer policies for "crowded schools"—had endeavored to make a racially divided and unjust system for generations. Indeed, from 1949 (when legal segregation was ended in Indiana) to 1968, school leaders had shifted the schools' boundary lines 360 times, none of which, the prosecution demonstrated, made the schools less segregated. Gerrymandering for the sake of racial separation—at a pace of almost twenty times per school year—had habitually been near the center of the administration's action plan.

In August 1971, United States district judge Samuel Hugh Dillin ruled in agreement with the Justice Department, charging the Indianapolis public schools with de jure segregation and eventually mandating that they implement a race-based busing program. Owing to numerous appeals and vociferous opposition, another ten years passed before that plan would take effect. Even then, as was typical nationally, it only sent black children from the city to surrounding suburban districts in small numbers. It was a symbolic victory for local civil rights leaders, but, as was often the case in the decades after the *Brown* decision, it did little to challenge the pooling of resources and academic prestige among affluent (and mostly white) families in Indianapolis.

Meanwhile, as the Justice Department's legal battle was beginning, Mayor Lugar skillfully negotiated the passage of the so-called Unified Government (Unigov), a measure that united most of the city's and county's governmental services and legislative bodies. When it took effect in 1970, it helped to widen the ailing city's tax base, but it simultaneously made Indianapolis a more unjust place, both politically and educationally. On the one hand, it significantly weakened the voting power of the city's increasingly African American, low-income, and Democratic population, for it added a quarter of a million suburban voters, many of whom were white and conservative, to the democratic process. On the other hand, Unigov most notably did not include the city and county school districts within its plan for consolidation. As Lugar later admitted, to include the school systems in Unigov would have made it impossible to pass.

White families had moved to the suburbs, just like white families had moved to the North Side of Indianapolis fifty years earlier, to form affluent, mostly white neighborhoods. And they demanded that those neighborhoods be served by affluent, mostly white schools. Unigov, therefore, was simply an unjust educational system by a new name.

The Life Adjustment Movement and Postwar Vocationalism: Manual High and the New Harry E. Wood High

By the late 1940s, school leaders in Indianapolis and across the nation began to worry quite publicly that having only two paths to graduation—the vocational and the college preparatory—would be insufficient in the postwar age. With the economy booming, high school attendance on the rise, and the so-called dropout problem regularly in the news, many educators believed (as their predecessors had for decades) that most of the era's students needed courses and subject matter that were less challenging and more practical than ever before. Indeed, it was an old story being told in a new way: the ideas and educational impulses that had created manual and industrial high schools at the turn of the century, vocationalism and comprehensive high schools in the 1910s, and the "custodial mission" and all-inclusive high schools in the 1930s were once more ascendant.[4]

At the national level, the Division of Vocational Education, which operated as a wing of the federal Office of Education, met in 1947 in Washington, DC, to address the issue. Leading educators from all over the country attended and gave their perspectives. In the conference's closing days, Charles Prosser delivered his prepared remarks and, after a series of debates, won over his colleagues decisively. While this was a new crusade for him, Prosser had been associated with vocationalism since the early 1900s: he had been the executive secretary of the National Society for the Promotion of Industrial Education (1912–1915), head of the Federal Board of Vocational Education (1917–1919), and president of the Minneapolis-area Dunwoody Industrial Institute (1915–1945). He had spent his career trying to bring more industrial and vocational courses into secondary schools.[5]

By the late 1940s, as several historians have documented, Prosser argued that only 20 percent of the nation's high school pupils could benefit from high-level vocational training on their way to "desirable skilled occupations." Another 20 percent, he believed, were suited for traditional academic subjects on their way to colleges and universities. The remaining 60 percent, Prosser claimed, were being left behind and needed instead a "life adjustment education," or a high school experience that would provide "guidance and education in citizenship, home and family life[,] . . . health, tools of learning, [and] work experience and occupational adjustment." Without this form of instruction, he warned, most young adults would fail to "receive the life adjustment training they need and to which they are entitled as American citizens."[6]

The Prosser Resolution, as it was eventually called, was passed unanimously by the conference.[7] And in its popularity and widespread adoption in the coming years (largely driven by the National Commission on Life Adjustment Education for Youth, which operated from 1950 to 1954), it not only broadened what the American high school sought to accomplish but also changed how educators talked about courses and teaching at the secondary level. As historians David Angus and Jeffrey Mirel have written, "For at least the next 30 years, virtually all youth problems—unemployment, teenage pregnancy, drug use—and even some major national problems—the Cold War, international economic competition—would be debated on the national level as if they were *curricular* problems."[8] As Prosser knew, there was little that "life adjustment" failed to capture. The coming years would reveal, moreover, that almost any high school course—from physical education, to driver's education, to civics—could conceivably further its aims. Just like the *Cardinal Principles* report of 1918, which was in many respects its ideological forebear, the life adjustment movement's vagueness and malleability were often its strengths.[9]

As it had for decades, Indianapolis, like most of its urban peers, looked to adopt the recommendations handed down by the nation's educational luminaries. When it came to the life adjustment movement, the city's school leaders quickly resolved to modify and broaden the curriculum in their existing secondary schools and to initiate plans for a new, separate high school, one distinctly suited for the postwar age. Aside from the curricular changes, the inclusion of life adjustment was also part and parcel of the school system's ambitious new building plan, which since its start in 1946 had spent roughly $16 million to add nearly four hundred new classrooms citywide. While a "problem of the schools today is that of meeting the individual needs of pupils," Superintendent Shibler announced in the early 1950s, life adjustment and the building program meant that "the schools of today are meeting these needs better than ever before, providing a variety of special courses in addition to the traditional courses which have been a part of the school system since it began."[10]

Geographically speaking, the focus of Shibler's life adjustment plan was, as one might expect, on the city's South Side, still home to many of Indianapolis's industrial zones and working-class neighborhoods, some of which were

FIG. 5.2 The new Manual High School, 1957. (Courtesy of Indiana Historical Society, P0569.)

becoming increasingly African American.[11] Though school leaders did not openly connect social class or race and the need for additional nonacademic courses in the 1950s and 1960s, their actions indicated a very clear relationship between the two. That is, the hallmarks of Prosser's movement were evident at every secondary school in the city to one degree or another, but—in the form of a new home for Manual High and the newly conceived Harry E. Wood High—they were most obvious south of the Circle.

The school board, backed by Shibler, voted to build an entirely new Manual Training High School early in 1950.[12] Furthermore, among its first announcements on the subject was that the school would be located on twenty-one acres at Pleasant Run Boulevard and Madison Avenue, more than two miles south of Manual's original home, which made it the city's southernmost high school by a wide margin. Though the project faced several financial hurdles and construction setbacks (costing over $40 million in today's dollars), the modern, multibuilding campus was formally dedicated on May 21, 1954. The ever-perceptive Shibler, along with his supporters, used the occasion to confirm the school system's commitment to an abundance of nonacademic choices for the city's high schoolers—whether they be vocational or in life adjustment.[13]

At the dedication ceremony, Shibler beamed that, "symbolic of the school's longstanding work [in the building trades], a striking mosaic design has been worked into the terrazzo floor at the foot of the main entrance stairway . . . where indirect lighting sets off the contents of twin display cases," all designed and installed by Manual alumni. Perhaps more to the point, board president Joseph Guidone used his time at the podium to announce, "At the beginning of a new century of public education in our city, it is especially fitting that the new . . . Manual Training High School be dedicated to its pupils, its community, and to the thousands of future citizens who will receive their training [here]." It would be training "in the Manual tradition of mind and hand and heart."[14] It may have been a "new century," Shibler and the board president knew, but Manual would still stand for "red and white," and "working class," and "South Side."

To herald the new Manual's arrival, the school board distributed hundreds of copies of a nearly fifty-page booklet, *For a New Century, a New School*. It featured dozens of pictures of smiling students at work in their state-of-the-art classrooms and demonstrated the easy dovetailing of vocationalism (which Manual had offered since 1895) and the life adjustment movement. It was no coincidence, of course, that the national Division of Vocational Education had developed it. One page, for instance, explained that "machine shop boys . . . produce jigs, and fixtures of various kinds, [and] become accustomed to working with the types of machines used in industry." In the same vein, students "in industrial arts classes, who helped install much of their new equipment, have a real application in their department."[15]

Another page, by contrast, explained, "Manual's home economics classes . . . [provide] a solid foundation on which to build a satisfying family life." Perfectly in line with Prosser's thinking, therefore, Manual's intricate models of residential kitchens and living rooms allowed "student cooks to learn to go from menu planning through mopping up" and, just as important, enabled "good [home furnishing] arrangement to become more than a theory as pupils arrange and re-arrange . . . furniture."[16] In the minds of school leaders, courses like these—some in preparation for work in industry and some in preparation for "living"—paired nicely and were worth the considerable price tag. The course offerings had broadened once more, but the school's motto and southernmost location had stayed the same.

Further suggestive of the life adjustment movement's popularity, as well as its foothold on the South Side, school leaders decided to make use of the old Manual High by opening the Harry E. Wood High School on its vacated campus in 1954. Completely unique in its course offerings compared with the rest of the city's high schools, Wood High, according to the board, was able to provide options for "normal, mentally retarded, and socially maladjusted children" all within one building. Put another way, Shibler stated in 1955, "Each [high school] pupil needs a custom-job of training; but we deal in such large numbers that we cannot hand-craft each pupil's training; we have to use a mass production method."[17] To Shibler, Wood High—with its pared-down academic options and terminal certificate programs in auto body repairing, barbering, beauty culture, dry cleaning, commercial food preparation, and shoe building, among others—was merely one more set of tracks in his ever-expanding system.[18] It was, by the mid-1950s, an essential feature of "mass production" education.

According to school leaders, Wood provided "exceptional training opportunities to pupils who have completed the eighth grade and wish to train for certain types of jobs," and although "a high school diploma is not required by law for employment in these occupations, it is highly recommended."[19] Despite the recommendation, the young people who enrolled at Wood would have known the real reason they were there, regardless of whether they finished with a diploma or not. The young female students who chose to pursue the beauty culture track, for example, received a license from the Indiana State Board of Beauty Culture Examiners; the young male students who completed the auto body repair track were automatically certified by the Indianapolis Automobile Trade Association; and the male and female students who enrolled in the commercial food preparation track met the standards of the city's Hotel Managers Association.[20] The private sector, more so than the public school system, dictated the curriculum and instruction at Wood High.

Wood's students may have earned a high school diploma from the school system along the way, therefore, but these privately mediated, job-specific certificates, which helped them secure a place in the workforce, were their actual educational endpoints. And by 1959, as a result, only 2 percent of Wood High's graduates planned to attend college or university. Even more damning of the school's mission and clear-cut ties to the life adjustment movement, Wood's administrators reported an annual dropout rate of roughly 80 percent in the late 1950s, a staggering figure and by far the highest in Indianapolis.[21] It was ironic, given that both Wood High and life adjustment were supposed to prevent students from dropping out. Perhaps the irony was lost on Wood High's first principal, Dick Emery (known to students as "Big Daddy"), who once bragged that he presided over a staff at Wood who could manage to "love the unlovely."[22]

Even though eight out of every ten students chose to leave Wood before graduating, school leaders still attempted to persuade those who stayed that they were important educational pioneers, blazing a trail for the nonacademic, but job-minded, students of tomorrow. Its 1957 yearbook, the *Wood Log*, proclaimed that "the pioneers of the past pushed farther and farther to the west," and "as they struggled on, they were resourceful and courageous in meeting the problems of new frontiers." "The fortitude of these pioneers," it continued, "lives again in the faculty and students of Wood High School." Their "frontiers are in education, and consist of classes fitted to the individual needs and interests

FIG. 5.3 Harry E. Wood High School dry cleaning class, 1955. (Courtesy of Indiana Historical Society, P0569.)

of special groups."[23] The comparison implied that Wood's students were brave, but that they were making some sort of sacrifice. It also ignored the reality that not every trip to the American West was successful, let alone a good idea.

While the high dropout rate may have alarmed some, citizens and school leaders alike could have found justification for their heavily tracked system nearly everywhere they looked in the 1950s. Besides Prosser and the National Commission on Life Adjustment Education for Youth, tracking was espoused by James Conant, president emeritus of Harvard, former ambassador to Germany, and then-director of the influential Study of the American High School. Conant toured the country extensively in the late 1950s to describe his research, in which he suggested that more forceful tracking and curricular diversification were what students and school systems needed most. His straightforward, sobering argument convinced many, and his impressive academic and diplomatic background gave significant intellectual authority to a way of thinking about the high school that his opponents often called "anti-intellectual."[24]

In his stop in Indianapolis in May 1958, Conant told a large crowd at the downtown Murat Temple, "Of one thing I am absolutely certain, namely, that in the high schools of the United States it is impossible to have all pupils studying advanced mathematics, chemistry, physics, and foreign languages." Echoing Prosser almost verbatim, he stated, "I recommended [rigorous college preparatory tracks] only for the academically talented pupils, some 15 percent of the usual high school class."[25] As one historian notes of Conant's work, his "recommendations were hardly revolutionary but seemed to confirm local practices."[26]

As the reimagined Manual High and new Wood High demonstrated, life adjustment education was here to stay, and with so many new tracks to choose from, navigating the public high school system was as complicated as ever. In response, the school board began publishing a guidebook called *Educational Opportunities in the Indianapolis Public Schools* in the mid-1950s, which they distributed to every eighth-grade graduate. Shibler wrote in the introduction, "One of your first duties is to . . . make wise choices in terms of your purposes," for "you may choose to prepare for college . . . [or] prepare for your future career . . . [or] develop special interests and abilities." No matter the case, the superintendent warned the reader, "when you fill out an enrollment card for the high school you will attend, you should be ready to write down your choice of subjects with confidence, knowing that you are off to a good start on a successful career."[27] At thirteen or fourteen years old, therefore, these students and their families were making a decision that would have a lifetime of consequences. Tracking in the public high school, whether in Indianapolis or elsewhere, demanded decisiveness.

While the guidebook for eighth graders indicated that options abounded, in reality, it explained that "pupils are expected to attend the high school in their [residential] district," and that appeals for "permission to attend another high school should be made through the elementary school principal." Recall from chapter 4 that ending open enrollment in the high schools was a way to maintain racial segregation after 1949. By this system, therefore, class-based residential segregation, as well as racial segregation, reigned supreme. As a result, it was clear that Shortridge, located on the wealthier North Side, was still the city's undisputed academic powerhouse throughout the 1950s, a distinction it had celebrated since its founding. In fact, a close reading of the guidebook indicated that only Shortridge's freshmen could enroll in rigorous and presumably college-preparatory electives such as Physiography, Ancient History, and Music Appreciation, among several others. Every freshman in the city, by rule, had to take English and physical education, but the similarities between the schools, by tradition, often ended there.[28]

Nonetheless, it was clear by the early 1960s that suburbanization, particularly the exodus of middle-class and wealthy white families from the city's school system, was changing Shortridge's racial and socioeconomic makeup. Paired with the gradual movement of African American families to the neighborhoods just west of the school (which had previously been all-white), many of Indianapolis's more elite citizens began talking about the school's racial "tipping point" and bemoaning how much their beloved Shortridge was "changing."

To maintain Shortridge's academic reputation and, just as importantly, retain its affluent white students, the school board—led by Richard Lugar—passed the Shortridge Plan in 1965. Though it was discarded just a few years later, the plan was designed to keep Shortridge as the city's premier "academic" school by introducing an entrance examination, one that would presumably weed out low-income and black students. Despite its collapse in 1969, the Shortridge Plan codified the board's long-held intentions when it came to its high schools: the maintenance of a divided and unjust system.

Debates over Shortridge's Elite Academic Reputation: Suburbanization, Racial Diversity, and the Shortridge Plan

In 1957, Robert Marschner, an educator and former school board president from the southwest suburbs of Chicago, conducted a survey to determine the best high schools in the United States. In October of that year, Marschner sent a letter to Shortridge's principal, Joel Hadley, to inform him that his school had been chosen as one of the top thirty-eight nationwide. Marschner stated that his "compilation" of prestigious institutions "was based on the community, the school, teachers, pupils, administration, curriculum, counseling, board of education, and attitudes."[29] While Shortridge's reputation was unquestionable within Indianapolis, the honor confirmed that the city's first high school was relatively well known throughout the region and even country, and that it could hold its own among both public *and* private secondary schools.

As the *Indianapolis Star* reported soon after, "Six [of the thirty-eight schools] are in the New York area[,] ... three are near Chicago[,] ... [and] the remainder are scattered throughout the Northeast, Midwest, Far West, and South." "Five of the schools," the *Star* enthused, "select their pupils, three are private, and three are boys' schools."[30] Magnifying the effect of Marschner's survey considerably, several national publications chose to cover it, ostensibly confirming the results. By the end of 1957, therefore, *Time, Newsweek, Ladies' Home Journal,* and the *Wall Street Journal* (as well as a handful of lesser-known publications) had crowned Shortridge among the best of the best.[31] All told, the publicity cemented the notion that in the late 1950s, Shortridge still stood for "blue and white," "North Side," and "elite." Little had changed in the last ninety years.

The simple fact was that Shortridge—because it drew its students from the wealthiest neighborhoods, because it was founded and maintained as *the* "academic" high school, and because it was habitually given preferential treatment by the school board—truly outperformed its rivals in Indianapolis in the fifteen years after World War II. By design, the markers of academic excellence were nearly ubiquitous. For example, when the National Merit Scholarship tests were first administered in 1955, Shortridge claimed seven of the winners, an impressive number that had climbed to thirteen winners by 1957. In both years, that was the most from any single school statewide. In 1956, Shortridge was among the first schools nationally to participate in the American Field Service program, which "undertook to promote international understanding" by "placing students [from other countries] in American high schools . . . [and in the care of] carefully selected American families."[32]

Furthermore, in 1959, three Shortridge students, all of whom wrote for the *Echo*, came in first, second, and fifth in "the annual creative writing contest" held by the *Atlantic Monthly*. They had competed against "419 of the nation's top high school writers," the city's newspapers reported, but were singled out by the magazine's editors for their unique talent and undeniably superb training.[33] The editors noted of the winning essay, written by senior Kirk Harker, "This is a really impressive piece of writing, based on wide reading and expressing the conclusions of the writer clearly and with conviction."[34] It was a triumph for Shortridge—rooted in serious literary criticism and top-notch composition—that had been decades in the making. A finely tuned college-preparatory curriculum and daily student newspaper had their benefits.

The opportunities afforded Shortridge students simply confirmed how heavily resourced the school was relative to its peers. In the mid-1950s, for instance, the powerful Shortridge PTA raised thousands of dollars, in concert with the school board, to purchase an FM transmitter from a radio station in nearby Lafayette, Indiana (recall that the school had also received an on-campus printing press in 1899). On October 1, 1954, WIAN, as the school's station was named, went on the air for the first time. A few years later, in 1958, WIAN's signal strength was increased from 120 watts to an astounding 890 watts, so that its programming could be broadcast in every classroom in the city. And while the other high schools sent their interested students to Shortridge to work on the station, it was, as one former student suggested, "essentially operated by . . . Shortridgers." It was placed in *their* building on the North Side, after all. It was *their* PTA that could afford to raise the funds. It was *their* parents who had the influence to lobby the board to subsidize the project.[35]

Shortridge's reputation for success, opportunity, and preferential treatment was so glaring, in fact, that the rest of the city's students often found it necessary to comment on the imbalance. Indeed, one former student recalled, only Shortridge's athletics teams were summarily booed when they stepped onto the football field, basketball court, or baseball diamond. "This did not happen to any other high school" in the city, another student remembered. By the mid-1950s, students at Manual, Tech, Attucks, and elsewhere (in a rare gesture of interschool solidarity) had adopted a fitting anti-Shortridge chant, one that captured their feelings toward the North Side school and its Merit Scholarship winners, award-winning essayists, FM radio hosts, and mostly college-bound seniors. "Shortridge, Shortridge, you think you're it!" they yelled. "S-H for Shortridge, I-T for it!"[36] Adults within earshot—parents, administrators, and

Table 5.1
African American Student Population
(as percentage) at Shortridge, 1949-1966

	% African American
1949	—
1953	13
1957	32
1964	60
1966	75

SOURCE: Laura Sheerin Gaus, *Shortridge High School,*
1864–1981, in Retrospect (Indianapolis: Indiana
Historical Society, 1985), 223, 224, 239, 247.

community members alike—almost certainly detested the chant, but its
sentiment was crystal clear. The city's interscholastic rivalries had been wrapped
in class- and race-based animosity for decades.

While academic prestige had defined Shortridge in the 1950s, suburbanization and demographic shifts within city limits changed the racial makeup of the
North Side school swiftly, moving the student population from 100 percent
white (by law) in 1949, to 87 percent white in 1953, to 40 percent white in 1964,
to just 25 percent white in 1966 (see table 5.1). In large part, this change was
driven by the exodus of white families from the city to new neighborhoods farther and farther north. Prodded by post–World War II low-interest-rate mortgages (for white servicemen) and increased federal and local funding for highway
construction (allowing breadwinners to commute to the city for work), more
than one hundred thousand new housing units were built in Marion County in
the two decades after 1950. The first phase of the I-465 "outer loop" highway,
which would eventually encircle the city, opened in 1962. With time, developers
turned farmland in Washington Township, roughly ten miles north of the Circle, into the Westlane, Greenbriar, and Delaware Trails subdivisions.[37]

As a result, Washington Township, one of several northern suburbs that
sprang to life, grew from 42,978 people in 1940 to 97,861 in 1960. By 1954, the
population boom had necessitated the construction of two new junior highs
and a palatial new secondary school, named North Central High School. Shortridge's more status-conscious students looked on intently, a few writing in the
Echo that the steeply rising enrollment was "the problem facing J. Everett Light,
superintendent of the schools in Washington Township," and, in some jealousy-
tinged journalism, that "the new pupils will reportedly name their new
school!"[38] As one former Shortridge student explained, the process was alarm-
ing because Washington Township's North Central High became a rival and
posed a threat to its dominance almost overnight; it "was immediately filled

with [affluent white] students who, prior to the movement to the suburb, would have gone to . . . Shortridge."[39] While white families of means had moved to the North Side of Indianapolis to escape the smoke and noise of the South Side at the turn of the century, they were moving even farther north, out of the city altogether, in the 1950s and 1960s. The same phenomenon that had created Shortridge's prestige was now calling it into question.

Cathedral High School, the city's largest and most celebrated Catholic secondary school, was also altered significantly by the demographic change. Recall from chapter 2 that the all-male Cathedral, founded in 1918, raised more than $1 million in the mid-1920s for a new building at Fourteenth Street and Meridian, comfortably on the North Side and not too far from Shortridge. By the mid-1950s, "Cathedral was overflowing," prompting the diocese to open three other schools: Scecina Memorial to the east, Bishop Chatard on Kessler Boulevard, and Cardinal Ritter to the west. Nonetheless, by the late 1960s, the movement of white families—in this case families who had an interest in a Catholic secondary school and the means to afford the tuition—caused Cathedral's enrollments to drop quickly. By the early 1970s, the diocese announced that the school would close; it ultimately took the efforts of Robert Welch, a real estate developer and alumnus, to save the school. To make it viable, however, Cathedral's new board decided to make it coeducational for the first time in its history and, perhaps more importantly, to move even farther north, just miles from North Central High.[40]

As suburbanization unfolded, forever changing once-vaunted schools, more and more black families moved into the neighborhoods that surrounded Shortridge, in particular the roughly 120 city blocks known as Butler-Tarkington, an area sandwiched between Butler University to the north, State Highway 431 to the east, and the Crown Hill Cemetery to the west. Although a group of white homeowners organized the Fairmap Realty Company to block African Americans from moving into the neighborhood (by buying up available homes and land), their efforts were ultimately unsuccessful. Emblematic of their determination to achieve homeownership, many black families, as one historian has written, purchased or built homes with "financing from [an African American–owned] Louisville insurance company when local institutions rejected their applications."[41] At a time when most people of color were denied access to this facet of the so-called American Dream, this group boldly found a way.[42]

By the late 1960s, the Butler-Tarkington Neighborhood Association, an interracial organization that favored residential integration, noted that the once all-white "area has been faced over the last 15 years with a gradual increase of all-Negro blocks, one by one, from south to north across the neighborhood." Further, it explained, "About 60% of the households in the total area are now Negro," meaning that "the basic problem at this time is to make the rate of white move-ins greater than the rate of Negro move-ins."[43] For the sake of maintaining property values and racial integration, the association knew, the imbalance had to be addressed. It was clear that access to previously all-white neighborhoods in Indianapolis, as difficult to achieve as it had been for African Americans, was only the first step toward achieving legitimate residential integration.

Indeed, similar conversations were taking place with respect to Shortridge, where concerned white parents talked increasingly about the school's purported racial "tipping point" and expressed fears that it would eventually become an all-black school. As early as 1959, the Shortridge PTA met in the school's gymnasium to discuss what it was then calling the "Shortridge problem." After hours of heated deliberation, the PTA decided to form a committee to present its opinions to the school board, and its assessment was unequivocal. The "PROBLEM," they wrote, was that "the percentage of Negro students at Shortridge continues to rise. Because of the high proportion of economically and culturally disadvantaged young people in this group, the existence of Shortridge as a fine academic high school is threatened unless measures are taken to preserve it." As such, the "GOAL," they reasoned, should be "an academic and integrated Shortridge. The city's investment in Shortridge's physical plant and the gradual achievement of its national reputation will soon be irrevocably lost unless—50 percent Negro is the crucial point. Beyond that Shortridge cannot maintain itself."[44] Never had the city's well-to-do and North Side parents been so clear about what they thought had made Shortridge so great for so many years. While they were not outright segregationists—they were fine with *some* integration, obviously—their logic was straightforward and plainly discriminatory. Without a critical mass of affluent white students, 50 percent at a minimum, they believed, "economically and culturally disadvantaged" students of color would ruin the school's hard-won "national reputation." It was a form of racial bias, rooted in the fabricated value of whiteness and maintaining one's privilege at all costs, that would be lasting.

Always quick to appease the well-connected Shortridge PTA, the board adjusted the school's boundary lines repeatedly over the next five years—gerrymandering for the sake of its reputation—but Shortridge continued to become more African American and less white. There were simply too few white families left in Shortridge's vicinity to maintain racial balance through the board's "neighborhood school" model, no matter how creatively it divided up the city. By the mid-1960s, with the black student population eclipsing 60 percent, the board concluded that it needed a new strategy. Arguments over integration and Shortridge's academic reputation aside, "racial tension [among the pupils]," one former student explained, "was a cause of concern. Fights [in the early 1960s] were not as frequent as they were rumored to be, but they did occur."[45]

In 1964, the Shortridge PTA gained an especially talented, energetic, and charismatic champion on the school board in the form of thirty-two-year-old Richard Lugar. Lugar was destined to become mayor of Indianapolis (1968–1976) and Indiana's six-term United States senator (1976–2012), but even at thirty-two, he was no ordinary school board member. After graduating as valedictorian of the Shortridge class of 1950 (where he played multiple sports and wrote for the *Echo*), he graduated Phi Beta Kappa and (again) valedictorian from Denison University in Ohio, going on to study public policy, philosophy, and economics at Oxford as Denison's first Rhodes scholar. Following Oxford, Lugar spent three years in the navy, after which he returned to his hometown to run the family business. "His age belied the experience he brought to the job," one commentator explained. He was "a local son" with ambition, community connections, and a deep love for the Shortridge of yesteryear.[46]

With the help of Lugar's political brilliance, the school board, voting six to one, passed the measure that would be known as the Shortridge Plan in August 1965. When it took effect in the fall of 1966, it promised to "make Shortridge an academic school . . . [by] requir[ing] entrance examinations for all incoming freshmen," who were invited to take the exam no matter where they lived.[47] In its subtle discrimination—the implication was that most low-income black students would not be able to pass the test—Don Baker of the *Indianapolis Times* reported, it proved that many "old grads [of Shortridge] have been too busy pointing to the pride of past achievements to face the problems of the present." While "whites moved [to northern suburbs]," he continued, "Shortridge remained in their mind and hearts. It nagged at the conscience of conservatives."[48]

Essentially turning Shortridge into what Americans would soon call a "magnet school," the board's measure was applauded by the PTA and initially praised by some news outlets, most of which claimed that it made the school population "more intelligent" and helped to stabilize property values on the North Side.[49] Early in the school year in 1966, for example, the *Christian Science Monitor* reported that "of 500 applicants for the freshman class, 272 with a median IQ of 110 were selected" and that the "Negro percentage of the new class has dropped to a more balanced" level. Exploring the connection between the perception of "good public schools" and real estate prices, the *Indianapolis Star* interviewed realtor Thomas Osborne (a general sales manager for A.H.M. Graves), who "said he believes racial patterns have stabilized" near Shortridge and that "property values are on the rise." To Osborne, who studied the city's housing market for a living, "white buyers don't mind living in an integrated neighborhood if they feel like they are not going to be overwhelmed."[50] They would tolerate *some* black neighbors. They would allow their children to attend school with *some* black children, so long as they were screened by an admissions exam first.

The broader movement for civil rights, as one would expect, saw the board's actions for their racial implications. Andrew Ramsey, the outspoken columnist for the *Indianapolis Recorder*, wrote about the issue at length. In an emblematic article titled "Shortridge Uber Alles [above all]," he explained that "to attempt to cure the Indianapolis public schools of *de facto* segregation by treating one of some one hundred twenty-odd public schools is like treating pneumonia by rubbing salve on one big toe of the patient." "The plan," he continued, "beautifully ignores the real cause of the racial imbalance in the public schools and by subtly implying that the cause of the Shortridge situation is the great influx of Negroes who have run the whites out, it puts the shoe on the wrong foot." The force driving segregation at Shortridge was "the white man's preoccupation with racism. Residential segregation is, of course, at the bottom of the whole thing."[51] To attempt to "fix" the schools while ignoring the complexities of systemic racism was a fool's errand. To Ramsey, it asked too much of the school system at best and papered over Indianapolis's history of discrimination at worst.

With time, the NAACP weighed in on the matter, and its tone and conclusions matched Ramsey's. Donald Davidson, a member of the NAACP's national Education Committee, noted that "efforts to eliminate *de facto* segregation in the local system should begin [not at Shortridge but] at [the still all-black] Attucks. Seventy-seven per cent of the students at Shortridge are Negroes." He further suggested that "the board construct an addition to Attucks for classes for gifted pupils with intelligence quotients of 125 or more," estimating that "more than 1,500 pupils would qualify." "The Shortridge plan," Davidson made plain, was a "farce to save the Shortridge image."[52]

Nonetheless, a number of high school students—some white, some black—favored the Shortridge Plan and saw it as a way to integrate the school system. Of note, the Human Relations Council, led by a group of Shortridge students, formed in 1964, and in its first year of existence more than two hundred of its members marched outside a meeting of the school board in favor of the plan. While others found their arguments contradictory, the council claimed to want to "save Shortridge," provide support for their school, and see integrated education.[53] While one might take the organization's intentions as sincere, to many commentators, to "save Shortridge," to keep it as it once was, was to avoid true integration. The two goals were incompatible.

For his part, Lugar agreed with the Human Relations Council. In an interview near the end of his life, he indicated that he remembered the Shortridge Plan not as an effort to make his alma mater more white and less black but instead as an effort to desegregate the high schools in the city. He noted, "We had had some success [in changing the racial composition of Shortridge] with the Shortridge Plan." In the mid-1960s, "if you were coming in as a freshman, you could go to Shortridge from anywhere in the city. The bars were down low.

Classes were about 50% black, 50% white. Now, it had been prior to that time, 90% black, 10% white." Recalling the praise he received in making the change, he explained, "Educational journals said it's like water going uphill. But it didn't last." Most of Lugar's white fellow board members, by contrast, expressed dismay, hoping to ignore school segregation altogether. He recalled them saying, "Lugar, you're too interested in sociology and race and what have you; we're just interested in education."[54] What Lugar failed to appreciate, despite his willingness to talk about race, was that changing the racial composition at Shortridge, in particular at the request of affluent parents, did nothing to address larger racial segregation concerns.

Meanwhile, the Shortridge Plan was being reviewed far less favorably at Manual, Tech, Wood, Attucks, and elsewhere, where each neighborhood's stakeholders assessed its implications. As historian Laura Sheerin Gaus found, "The resentment that the other high other schools had long felt . . . came to an angry boil," for if Shortridge was now officially "*the* academic school, what were they?" Did their school leaders not have "academic" hopes for them? Indianapolis's civil rights leaders and African American community were divided on the issue (some black Shortridge families favored it, for example), but the faculty and students at Crispus Attucks were "outraged," Gaus has written. At its core, they saw it as an effort to steal talented black students. Attucks had been "established by law as a totally segregated institution . . . [but over] the years they had made it into a good school." While it was still all-black in the mid-1960s, despite House Bill 242, Gaus explains that its leaders detested that "now all its better students were being encouraged to go to Shortridge, while weaker students who could not pass the entrance exam would, for the most part, be shunted into Attucks" or to their less challenging neighborhood high school.[55] For many, the board's bold-faced preference for Shortridge was a step too far.

As the debates continued, the 1966 school board election affirmed the city's feelings, as three Shortridge Plan supporters were supplanted by three new members who opposed it. With the backing of Superintendent George Ostheimer (Shibler had resigned in 1959), the new board phased out the admissions exam at Shortridge before the end of the decade, ending its controversial run once and for all. For the time being, Lugar retained his seat (he was not up for reelection until 1968), but the new board members also worked in concert to neutralize his influence. "From that time on," Lugar would later say, "I would have had trouble so much as entering a comma in a [school board] document."[56]

Feeling disaffected by the board's new direction, Lugar chose to step down from the post in 1967, but his role in the school system's development was just beginning. As civil rights leaders and the Justice Department mounted a legal battle against the public school's inadequately integrated system, Lugar, who transitioned seamlessly into the mayor's office in 1968, orchestrated a complex plan to merge the city and county governments' primary functions. When it went into effect in 1970, Unigov effectively expanded Indianapolis from 82 to 402 square miles, from 480,000 to 740,000 people, and from 293,000 to 406,000 registered voters. Its supporters claimed that it would fortify the city's dwindling tax coffers while saving money by cutting redundancies in city-county services. In an era of suburbanization, it was a win-win for voters, Lugar promised.

Crucially, however, Unigov barred a merger between the Indianapolis public schools and Marion County's numerous township school districts, meaning suburbanization would continue to drain the city system of its families of means, most of whom were white. While Unigov proved to be an unqualified victory for Lugar in the coming years—and an important stepping-stone near the beginning of his very long career in politics—it was a decisive blow to the city's already struggling schools. Decades of dwindling enrollments, racial segregation, and a largely unsuccessful busing program were on the horizon.

Stalled Integration, Federal Intervention, and Unigov: An Unjust System by a New Name

By the early 1960s, federal government officials, prodded by local civil rights leaders, had taken note of Indianapolis's efforts to stall in desegregating its schools. While administrators and the school board had claimed that integration was a "success" and "complete" as early as 1953, enrollment figures from the city's high schools told a much different story (see table 5.2). In 1955, for example, black children constituted roughly one-third of the student population, but their school-to-school distribution, owing to the system's "neighborhood school" model, was wildly unequal. At Manual, only 25 of its 1,653 students were black; at Tech, only 611 of its more than 4,000 students were black; and at Broad Ripple, a North Side school the city had annexed decades earlier, there

Table 5.2
Racial Composition of the Indianapolis High Schools, 1955

School	White students	African American students	Total students	% African American
Tech	3,646	611	4,257	14.4
Shortridge	1,341	649	1,990	32.6
Manual	1,628	25	1,653	1.5
Broad Ripple	1,790	1	1,791	0.1
Attucks	0	1,588	1,588	100.0
Wood	718	163	881	18.5

SOURCE: Ted Green, dir., *Attucks: The School That Opened a City* (Indianapolis: WFYI Public Television, 2016).

was only *one* black student in 1955. Perhaps most telling of all, Crispus Attucks had remained completely black since it first opened its doors in 1927.

Official school publications, including yearbooks and student newspapers, were almost universally reticent on race relations within the schools, but anecdotal evidence from black students themselves suggests that the integration that did take place in the 1960s could be painful. In her memoir, Janet Cheatham Bell, who grew up on the South Side, described her time at Manual as follows: "Like I was entering an alien land. Like I had been abandoned in some far away place and had no chance of rescue. That's how I felt." While many of her white classmates simply ignored her, she said, "I remember a few of them wanting to touch my skin, to see if it felt like theirs." Bell also believed her teachers and administrators saw her as less capable because she was black, and that they routinely tried to guide her to less challenging classes, despite her protests. At one point, she explained, her guidance counselor pushed her to pursue a "home economics path," so that she could learn to be "a maid" or housekeeper for a wealthy family. "The lack of social interaction with my white classmates," she wrote, "plus being excluded from most school activities because of my *race*, left me with no emotional attachments to Manual, no school spirit. Manual wasn't part of my real life, my Negro life."[57]

At Shortridge, where integration had taken place most significantly, there were a number of racially charged incidents in the 1960s, despite the actions of the student-led (and pro–Shortridge Plan) Human Relations Council. Aside from periodic race-related fistfights, a group of black students at the school, backed by local leaders, organized a protest against the textbook used in the course in ancient history. While the course's teacher claimed that she taught her students that "the book had its shortcomings," it nonetheless argued in its pages that "the Negro and Mongol" people "occupy an important place in the modern world, but they have played no part in the rise of civilization."[58] Months later, a vice principal confronted Otto Breeding, a black student, in the cafeteria for "violating the school's unwritten dress code" by "wearing mirrored sunglasses and a t-shirt bearing a clenched black fist." When Breeding refused to change, he was suspended. When he refused to leave the school's property that day, he was arrested and expelled, which prompted days of protests and a petition asking for his reinstatement.[59]

The combination of events like these, in tandem with subtle gestures of racial bias on a day-to-day basis, gave many black students a clear message regarding their status at Shortridge. As Patricia Payne, a black graduate from the 1960s, later explained, "I can't remember any blatant experiences of racism [against me personally] . . . at Shortridge. It was just the environment itself. It was the feeling you got. You don't have to be called a nigger to . . . feel you weren't wanted. Let me put it like that."[60] Some black students enjoyed their time at Shortridge, but to Payne and many of her fellow black classmates, the gulfs between segregation and integration and between integration and acceptance were wide.

Given, then, that the city's schools were only marginally integrated and that race relations remained poor, it came as no surprise when the United States Civil Rights Commission reported in 1963 that Indianapolis's efforts to desegregate had been "minimal." Vested with no real authority to effect change at the time, however, the commission's words fell on deaf ears among the city's educational elites. When asked to comment on the allegations, Superintendent Ostheimer simply defended the "neighborhood school" model, just as he, his colleagues, and their predecessors had done for over a decade. There was only so much that public schools could reasonably fix, he argued. The board could not "control where people live."[61]

Not until 1968, in fact—after the landmark Civil Rights Act of 1964, after scores of race riots across urban America, and after the assassination of Martin Luther King Jr.—did the Justice Department officially act against the Indianapolis public schools. On April 23, 1968 (three weeks after King was killed), Assistant Attorney General Stephen Pollack sent a letter to the board president, Mark Gray, informing him that the Civil Rights Division of the Department of Justice had received a complaint from an African American parent, and that it had conducted a follow-up investigation. The investigation revealed, Pollack wrote, that "the school system's practices . . . denied Negro students in Indianapolis the equal protection of the laws, in violation of the Fourteenth Amendment to the Constitution."[62] The Justice Department claimed that the city assigned "faculty members on the basis of race" and perpetuated "segregated elementary and secondary schools" through gerrymandered boundary lines. This letter, therefore, was their "opportunity to take appropriate steps to eliminate voluntarily the racially discriminatory practices."[63]

Once more, the board held firm, touting not only its efforts to successfully end segregation but also its innocence in carrying out a "neighborhood school" assignment plan. "Indianapolis has been in the forefront of progress in achieving equal treatment of all races in our schools," the board wrote adamantly in its response. In addition, the board flatly rejected both of the Justice Department's claims, arguing that "there was no hint of segregation in assigning pupils or teachers," and that its long-held "neighborhood concept" was "sound and would remain board policy." If an elementary school happened to be all-black, for example, it was "the result of neighborhood characteristics," and when it came to Crispus Attucks, the student body was the result of "the composition of the neighborhood surrounding the school." Above all, the board's attorneys claimed that the Justice Department had no authority to meddle in the business of local school agencies, citing a portion of the Civil Rights Act of 1964. "Nothing herein shall empower any official or court of the United States," they quoted, "to issue any order seeking to achieve a racial balance by requiring the transportation of pupils or students from one school to another or one school district to another in order to achieve such racial balance."[64] The board, it seemed, was prepared for a long fight.

As the Justice Department stepped back to build its case, Mayor Richard Lugar was meeting privately with the local Republican power brokers to iron out the details of Unigov. While some of the Unigov deliberations were made public, most of the meetings between Lugar and his Republican allies were held behind closed doors, specifically at the home of Republican Action Committee president John Burkhart, as one historian explains, "every Sunday for nine months in 1968."[65] In those closed-door sessions, the so-called kitchen cabinet—including Lugar, Burkhart, Thomas Hasbrook (an Eli Lilly Company executive), Beurt SerVaas (Marion County Council president), and Charles Whistler (Metropolitan Planning Commission president), among others—discussed how to make the city-county merger politically viable, building a formidable base of support along the way.[66] Their publicly stated hope for Unigov, as a journalist later described it, "was to put a bigger, more powerful Indianapolis onto the national map, simplify city services, and grow the city's tax base."[67]

By the end of 1968, the "kitchen cabinet" had more or less finished its work. Unigov, it proposed, would combine the "city and county legislative and executive bodies," would group "related municipal functions . . . into a minimal number of departments," and would use "special taxing and service districts" to expand "municipal services [such as care for streets and sewers] over different areas within the county." Just after the New Year in 1969, the 162-page bill made its way into the state senate, where—given a Republican majority, Republican Action Committee money and influence, and endorsements from the *Star* and *News*—it passed with relative ease, twenty-eight to sixteen. In early March, it cleared the house, sixty-six to twenty-nine, and on March 13, 1969, it was signed into law by Republican governor Edgar Whitcomb, to become effective on January 1, 1970.[68] Adding to its controversy, many labeled the plan undemocratic, especially given the secrecy of the process, not to mention that similar city-county mergers—such as those of Nashville–Davison County in 1958 and Jacksonville–Duvall County in 1967—were voted on in a public referendum. The people of Indianapolis were given no such option.[69]

For all its claims, historian William Blomquist has written, "in reality, the reorganization was considerably less than 'unified,'" and several of its features exacerbated racial inequality in both the city and its schools. To begin with, many African Americans, civil rights leaders, and liberals in Indianapolis recognized that Unigov diluted their political power in the city. Democrats often called the Republican-concocted plan "Unigrab," since it expanded the voting population by 250,000 "mostly white county residents," who tended to vote conservatively. African Americans made up almost 40 percent of the city in the 1970s, for example, but Unigov reduced that figure, when it came to the ballot box, to only 18 percent.[70] Therefore, "just as Cleveland and Gary were electing black mayors," one historian found, "Indianapolis blacks were watching their political strength diminish."[71]

Aside from realigning Indianapolis's politics, Unigov quite conspicuously omitted the city and county school districts from its merger, forcing them (or allowing them, depending on one's perspective) to remain separate entities. Including the schools, several commentators have suggested, would have almost certainly killed its chances, for white voters in suburban Marion County insisted on keeping their districts predominantly white and well funded. Indeed, many white families moved out of the city for that very reason. According to Landrum Shield, who was the first black president of the Indianapolis school board, "To have included schools in Unigov would have raised the specter of racial integration."[72] Even Lugar himself later conceded that "Unigov was not a perfect consolidation." "A good number of [white] people," he continued, "really wanted to keep at least their particular school segregated."[73] While the consolidation may have allowed Indianapolis to prosper financially in an age of suburbanization, it did nothing to address racial equality through the schools. Had it tried, Lugar admitted, it would have never become law.

In July 1971, with Unigov in full swing, the Justice Department's first case against the school system began in United States district judge Samuel Hugh Dillin's courtroom. Dillin was appointed to the court by President John F. Kennedy in 1961. He was a former Democratic Indiana state representative and senator with a reputation for liberal stances and a stern personal style. While the seven-day trial produced few new pieces of evidence (the issues had been debated for years), John Leshy of the Justice Department presented an impressive case, submitting eighty-two pages of evidence and calling nearly a dozen witnesses to the stand. Among the most memorable, according to the local press, was former assistant superintendent Paul Miller (1953 to 1958), who was responsible for drawing the district's boundary lines. In the nearly twenty years since House Bill 242, the school system had redrawn its boundaries a shocking 360 times, none of which, according to Miller's memory, helped to integrate the city's pupils.[74]

On August 18, 1971, Dillin handed down his decision, finding the Indianapolis public schools guilty of unstated, but purposeful, "*de jure* segregation." After penning a long history of "segregation and racial discrimination in . . . the territorial period, through the establishment of segregated schools after the Civil War, to the adoption of the 1949 law abolishing segregation in public education," Dillin described the multiple ways in which the board and administration had maintained an unequal system. From their strategic building plans, to zoning, to the transfer of students from so-called crowded schools, to the recent Shortridge Plan, Dillin found school leaders interested in racial separation. An unjust system, he claimed, was routinely their goal.[75]

Furthermore, Dillin took care to comment extensively on the broader social forces that created problems for the schools, not to absolve its leaders but, as one historian has suggested, "to be able to fashion a remedy that would be more lasting than one that would result from an order for immediate desegregation." As such, Dillin wrote, "it is only fair to say that various factors not of its own making have contributed to that result." For example, racist real estate and housing practices (restrictive covenants, most notably) made integrated "neighborhood schools," especially at the elementary level, difficult.[76]

Borrowing from the arguments laid out by the NAACP in the *Indianapolis Recorder* a half decade earlier, Dillin found that "the failure to assign white children to Attucks had important consequences" for the entire school system, including the elementary schools. Attucks, he found, "had available space during this period, and could, and did, accommodate elementary students from overcrowded Negro schools."[77] While Shortridge was guarding admission with an examination, one that turned away scores of students, Attucks was filled with empty classrooms. Thus, integration could never have been the true, or even meaningful tangential, goal of the Shortridge Plan.

Dillin's critiques of Lugar's actions did not end there. Unigov, Dillin argued, which kept the city and county school systems separate, had promoted educational inequality through residential segregation. "Thus," he summarized, "it [Unigov] leaves the defendant [the school system] . . . exactly where it found it: confined to an area in the central part of the consolidated City of Indianapolis, where it is surrounded by eight township school systems operating independently within the purportedly unified city." More specially, with respect to race, Dillin cited, "for the 1969–1970 school year, the outside school[s] . . . had 73,205 students enrolled, of whom 2.62% were Negro, and together employed 3,037 teachers, of whom 15, or .49%, were Negro."[78] By the numbers alone, little separated Indianapolis's metropolitan schools from strictly enforced apartheid. Dillin may have stopped short of blaming Lugar personally, but he implied that the mayor and his supporters knew full well the consequences of their actions. They knew whom Unigov would help and whom it would hurt. They left school systems out of Unigov because they knew that fervent opposition, based in racism and classism, would have torpedoed their efforts.

To remedy the complicated situation at hand, Dillin eventually "ordered black students in Indianapolis from grades one through nine" to transfer, via busing, to each of Unigov's suburban districts "in such numbers as would cause the total enrollment . . . to approximate 15 percent black students."[79] Not only did his order place the burden of busing solely on black students from the city, but it was also immediately met with fierce opposition by white suburban parents. "I don't pay high taxes to send my child to a low-class school," one parent told a reporter. "I won't allow it." Another parent, in a strange interpretation of history, compared Dillin's "forced busing" order to the *Dred Scott* decision of 1857. Yet another parent claimed that the ruling was reminiscent of "Germany in the 1930s," and that, if the government could "send our children to any school they desire, who is to say that next month or next year it might not be to a [work or concentration] camp of their selection."[80] The hyperbole may have surprised some, but the point was clear to all: emotions ran high among white parents seeking to protect their children's privilege through quasi-segregated housing and quasi-segregated public education. And racially integrated schools would never be a popular idea in the suburbs.

It would take another ten years of legal battles, as well as two efforts to recall Dillin, for the city-county busing program to begin. But Judge Dillin, in both his 1971 opinion and subsequent busing order, gave credence to what generations of citizens in Indianapolis already knew: the school system was organized and maintained with the city's existing inequalities in mind. By this system, that is, Crispus Attucks meant "green and gold," and "African American," and "the Avenue." Shortridge, until the recent past, meant "blue and white," and "affluent," and "North Side." And Manual meant "red and white," and "working class," and "South Side." Each school was given its role to play. Suburbanization and Unigov were changing these schools' reputations and traditions, but the same rules applied. Asking someone, "Where do you go to high school?"—not just in Indianapolis but in America—still revealed a lot.

Conclusion

● ●

> The first year was probably one of the
> worst experiences of my life, if I can be
> honest.
> —LaToya Kirkland, a black high school
> student who was among the first bused
> from Indianapolis to the suburbs in 1981

When fourteen-year-old LaToya Kirkland boarded her school bus in Indianapolis in the fall of 1981, she had no idea what to expect. On the one hand, she was excited, for she was beginning her freshman year in high school at a brand-new school. On the other hand, she was nervous, for she was being bused out of her neighborhood—well out of downtown, for that matter—as part of Judge Samuel Hugh Dillin's court-ordered busing plan, which aimed to achieve greater racial integration by sending black children from the city school district to Unigov's surrounding, mostly white, suburban school districts. While her grade school had been in her neighborhood, just blocks away, she now had a forty-minute ride ahead of her, one that included highways and pockets of dense traffic. "I don't think I had been that far . . . [away from] Indianapolis in my life," recalled Kirkland, one of thousands of affected black students.[1]

When she and her African American classmates pulled into the suburban school's parking lot, however, her sense of excitement was quickly overwhelmed with nervousness. Once they were parked, she recently told a reporter, "dozens of . . . white classmates" approached the bus, "their hands slapping against the yellow metal side panels" as it began to rock back and forth. Seconds later, a window near Kirkland was pelted with an egg, which exploded on impact. Two months later, in October, another black student was injured when a bus window was shattered by white students throwing rocks. "We didn't know what to do with the racism," she explained. After all, they were being sent to integrate a school that was 98 percent white and surrounded by several other predominantly white school districts. She was only a child, but in retrospect, one aspect of her involvement was certain: "The first year," she said, "was probably one of the worst experiences of my life, if I can be honest."[2] Kirkland missed her neighborhood. She hated spending so much time on a bus that year, traveling to and from a school where she did not feel welcome.

While Judge Dillin's busing plan received mixed reviews from the local press, as well as from suburban *and* city parents, it expired at the end of the 2016 school year and was not renewed. As a recent commentator explained, it was set in motion "to give all Marion County kids the same access to quality schools" and "to reduce racial tension," but after thirty-five years, "it's not clear what it achieved." Some black students from the city, of course, had a great experience in their suburban districts, a reality scholars have documented in cases from coast to coast. Other students, like Kirkland, were subjected to appalling acts of racism on a regular basis. And either way, enrollment in the city school system dwindled over the period of court-ordered busing. At its height, in the 1960s, it educated over one hundred thousand children each year. By the mid-1970s, the exit of white families had begun to take its toll, and since the busing plan's first days in 1981, enrollment in the Indianapolis public schools dropped precipitously, from sixty-nine thousand in 1980, to forty-nine thousand in 1990, to fewer than thirty thousand in 2016 (see table C.1).[3]

It has been an all-too-common trend in urban public education. And over the course of those decades, Indianapolis's educational problems were routinely exacerbated by both race- and class-based biases in metropolitan development. Throughout the postwar era, for example, the city, in concert with Indiana University and later Purdue University, began buying land on the northwest side of downtown—in historically black neighborhoods near Indiana Avenue—in an effort to meet the demand for higher education. Eventually, after the piecemeal purchase of much of the area surrounding Crispus Attucks High in the name of "slum clearance" and "urban renewal," city officials welcomed Indiana University–Purdue University Indianapolis (IUPUI) in 1969, merging an undergraduate program with existing medical, law, art, and dental schools.[4]

Table C.1

Enrollment in the Indianapolis Public Schools, 1933–2016 (in thousands)

1933	1965	1970	1975	1980	1985	1990	1993	2016
60	103	108	88	69	53	49	47	26

SOURCE: Bodenhamer and Barrows, eds., *Encyclopedia of Indianapolis* (Bloomington: Indiana University Press, 1994), 1031–1032.

IUPUI was celebrated by Mayor Lugar and other "pro-business" citizens and continued to expand for years, but as anthropologist Paul Mullins explains, "today hundreds of acres of homes that stood in the . . . 1960s are all gone, their heritage is often completely unrecognized, and . . . the university's complicity is ignored or inelegantly remembered."[5]

Recall from chapter 2 that the neighborhoods that developed along "the Avenue" in the early twentieth century did so because black families were denied access to the rest of the city. Once Indianapolis's power brokers found value in them, however, they had little issue displacing whoever or whatever stood in their way. Important black institutions, notably the Walker Theatre and Attucks High, still stand today, yet "the landscape is a remarkably uncontested sea of parking lots and institutional architecture," Mullins notes.[6] Gentrification has taken its toll in Indianapolis, just as it has in New York, Chicago, San Francisco, and nearly every city in between.[7]

The development of the highway system in the metropolitan area, aided significantly by federal money beginning in the 1950s, followed a similar trajectory. Before the end of the 1970s, Indianapolis was crisscrossed by several major highways: I-65, which moves from the northwest to the southeast; I-70, which moves from the southwest to the northeast; and I-465, which intersects with I-65 and I-70 and, as noted in chapter 5, encircles the entire city. As with IUPUI, highway construction disproportionately affected black and working-class neighborhoods: scholars estimate that tens of thousands of people were displaced.[8] Neighborhoods where, for decades, families and loved ones came together to worship, shop, share meals, and engage in recreation were demolished swiftly. They were supplanted by roads that, above all, allowed mostly middle-class and white people to live in the suburbs and find work and entertainment in the city.

Moreover, *second-wave* suburbanization, which was also fully reliant on the tax-supported highways, eventually began to sap even suburban Unigov's once-robust resources. In the two decades after the completion of I-465—spurred by the "great schools" reputation of towns such as Carmel and Fishers—the population of Hamilton County, just north of Marion County (and thus outside Unigov), roughly doubled. In the next two decades, it more than doubled *again*, nearly reaching three hundred thousand in 2010. From 2000 to 2010 alone, downtown Indianapolis lost 13,898 private-sector jobs and suburban Marion County lost another 45,697. Over the same period, the counties around Unigov, including Hamilton, gained 58,082. Once again, affluence and privilege—as with Shortridge in the early 1910s and as with North Central High in the 1960s—had moved north. As local historian Nicole Poletika describes, "My family moved . . . to Carmel in 1992, and the cornfields which then gridlocked our neighborhood are now populated with McMansions. The quaint . . . [s]upermarket down the street quietly closed, and now Carmelites can shop at a store dedicated exclusively to gourmet olive oils in the city's ambitious, if somewhat inauthentic, Arts & Design District."[9]

One wonders where Indianapolis will assign value next, and who will benefit from it. One wonders how high schools will be part of the story, serving as an exceedingly important pawn in a much more complicated game.

It should come as no surprise, then, that the racial, socioeconomic, and educational differences between the Indianapolis schools and the wealthier suburban schools like Carmel remain stark today, despite Dillin's equity-minded busing plan and the efforts of many since. In 2018, for example, the population in the city system was over 75 percent black, Latinx, and multiethnic. More than six out of ten students qualified for a free or reduced-price lunch (meaning they come from a low-income family), and those high school students who sat for the ACT scored an average of 17, which was roughly 3 points below the national average. Conversely, just twenty miles north of the city in the well-to-do Carmel Clay school district, the student population in 2018 was 74 percent white, only 4 percent black, and only 3 percent Latinx. Less than 10 percent of Carmel Clay's students qualified for a free or reduced-price lunch. The average ACT score was 27, which is well within the acceptable range for Indiana University and Butler University (see table C.2).

Scholars have documented this urban-suburban disparity well, including in celebrated books such as Jean Anyon's *Ghetto Schooling* and James Ryan's *Five Miles Away, a World Apart* or, more recently, Ansley Erickson's *Making the Unequal Metropolis* and Walter Stern's *Race and Education in New Orleans*.[10] In the present, moreover, the underlying causes of the spatial divide in public education—namely, housing patterns and the processes of maintaining one's privilege—are being more regularly discussed by news outlets. In 2017, for example, education journalist Nikole Hannah-Jones (a former MacArthur Fellow) gave an interview with public radio's Terry Gross titled, pointedly, "How the Systemic Segregation of Schools Is Maintained by 'Individual Choices.'"[11] Shortly after, Harvard professor Matthew Desmond wrote an extensive and

Table C.2
A Comparison of the Carmel Clay and Indianapolis School Districts, 2018

	% African American	% white	% Hispanic	% Asian	% multiethnic	% free and reduced lunch	Avg. ACT score
Indianapolis Public Schools	44	21	29	1	4	65	17
Carmel Clay Public Schools	4	74	3	13	6	9	27

SOURCE: "SAT & ACT Overview," Indiana Department of Education Compass, accessed July 2019, https://compass.doe.in.gov/dashboard/ceexams.aspx?type=state.

well-received article for the *New York Times Magazine* titled "How Homeownership Became the Engine of American Inequality."[12] Desmond's related book, *Evicted*, was a *New York Times* best seller and won the 2017 Pulitzer Prize for general nonfiction.[13]

In the summer of 2019, even, Democratic presidential contenders Joe Biden and Kamala Harris squared off in a televised debate over—of all issues—the historical importance of busing programs in the decades after *Brown*. Senator Harris, who was herself bused as a child in Berkeley, California, pressed former senator Biden to explain his rationale for opposing busing in the 1970s and 1980s. "There was a little girl in California who was a part of the second class to integrate her public schools," Harris stated, "and that little girl was me." Biden accused Harris of mischaracterizing his position, but few were convinced. No matter his feelings in 2019, he had to accept that he gave an interview in 1975 in which he concluded, to the delight of many white liberals, "To me, [busing] is the most racist concept; what it says is, 'in order for your child with curly black hair, brown eyes and dark skin to be able to learn anything, he needs to sit next to my blond-haired, blue-eyed son.' That's racist!" He continued, "Who the hell do we think we are, that the only way a black man or woman can learn is if they rub shoulders with my white child?"[14] In the days and weeks after the debate, Biden was resolute; so was Harris; and many interested Americans were forced to grapple with how all of this mattered in the twenty-first century.

Whether in politics, in the newspaper, or on the radio, these trends are encouraging. More people talking about schools, housing, and equity is a good thing.

But this is an old story, not a new one. In fact, as this book demonstrates, using systems of public schools—particularly public high schools—to maintain the existing social order is as old as the institution itself. It began in the 1890s, not 1980s; busing plans were only another chapter in the saga, not the beginning. Asking someone, "Where'd you go to high school?" has been demographically revealing since the turn of the century.

In Indianapolis, the city's first public high school (eventually named Shortridge) opened its doors slightly north of the downtown Circle, in a more affluent part of town, in 1864. While it was sometimes attacked for being too elitist, in reality it educated more middle-class children than wealthy ones, and its graduates were as likely to enter the white-collar workforce as they were to go to college. When demand for the high school forced Indianapolis's school leaders to build a second school in 1895, however, they chose a path that set in motion a century of division, inequality, and social reproduction. Instead of building another school like Shortridge, they built a high school that offered some academic courses, but far more courses in manual and industrial education. Furthermore, they chose to place the new school—unapologetically named the Manual Training High School—on the city's more working-class, industrial, and multiethnic South Side. They mapped the secondary school system onto the city's social class divides. They fortified those divisions instead of challenging them.

As a result, children from middle-class families, who tended to live on the North Side, had easy access to Shortridge. There, they wore the school's blue and white colors, and took academic classes that prepared them to enroll in college, if that was what they and their family wanted. Meanwhile, several miles south, children from working-class families had easy access to Manual. There, they wore the school's red and white colors, and took classes in the industrial arts that prepared them to work in respectable, blue-collar jobs. Within a couple of years, the class-based results of this bifurcated system appeared in full force. In 1910, for example, more than 60 percent of Shortridge's students went to college, while roughly 10 percent of Manual's students did so. Moreover, when the two schools met on the football field in those early years, the already-violent game often devolved into bloody, Thanksgiving Day fistfights. In many cases, the fighting continued even after the game, at the downtown Circle, forcing the school board to ban competitions between Shortridge and Manual in 1907. Having sorted the city's high school pupils by class, geographically, and through the curriculum, it should not have been too surprised by the animosity.

By the early 1900s, overcrowding at Shortridge and Manual prompted the opening of a third high school in Indianapolis. This time, rather than building an "academic" school or an "industrial" school, local leaders—in line with national education experts—built a "comprehensive" school, meaning students were offered both of those "tracks" (and a host of other new vocational tracks) on their way toward graduation and a diploma. When the new school, named Arsenal Technical High, welcomed students in 1912, it continued what Shortridge and Manual had started by sorting its students across its multibuilding, seventy-six-acre campus. While Tech, as a truly "comprehensive" high school, slightly obscured the social sorting that had taken place between the North Side and South Side schools, its intentions were the same. Social reproduction was Tech's unstated goal.

Driven by the city's population growth, advances in factory automation, and a succession of child labor laws, the growth in the high school enrollment in Indianapolis was so large in the early 1900s that the student population then included a sizable number of African American students, who had previously only attended in small numbers. As the percentage of black students rose in the 1910s, a number of local white supremacy groups demanded that school leaders build a separate, all-black school. In the 1920s, this demand intensified quickly, as the national resurgence of the Ku Klux Klan reached Indiana and Indianapolis, in particular. In 1925, Klan-backed candidates for the school board swept the fall election (taking the mayor's office, too), and through their efforts, in 1927, the all-black Crispus Attucks High welcomed its first class. Though the impetus for the new school was obviously racism, it was nonetheless in line with the city's decades-old processes of sorting students, whether between the North Side Shortridge, the South Side Manual, or the expansive and "comprehensive" Tech. In order to maintain the social order in an outwardly racist city, it only made sense that Indianapolis would have a racially segregated secondary school system.

In the 1930s, as the Depression sent even more adolescents into the high school, administrators in Indianapolis looked to reform the inner workings of Shortridge, Manual, Tech, and Attucks. And though their goal in this instance was not to divide students from campus to campus or building to building, it was still rooted in maintaining order through public education. During the Depression, school leaders set about "bureaucratizing" adolescence and expanding the high schools' social and cultural significance. By introducing dozens of new clubs and activities and intensifying each school's procedures and regulations, they were able to cultivate cultural homogeneity in the secondary schools. By design, it was a culture rooted in the nation's middle-class, white, Christian, patriarchal, and heteronormative values. Therefore, students who were interested in obtaining the high schools' benefits—a diploma, a job, or a path to college—were forced to embrace this culture. To succeed, they had to follow the high schools' increasingly complex rules.

In the 1940s, Indianapolis's race-related problems once again moved to the fore, as local civil rights leaders began pressing for an end to segregation in the city's public schools. After being blocked on the local level for a number of years, they achieved success in the Indiana state legislature in 1949. In the form of House Bill 242, which was supported by a new Democratic governor, segregated public schools were deemed illegal in every district in the state. As a sign of the city's intransigence on the issue, however, remarkably little changed in Indianapolis's classrooms in the coming years. In 1955, for example, owing to residential segregation, restrictive covenants, and gerrymandered boundary lines, Tech was less than 15 percent black and Manual was less than 2 percent black. Most strikingly, Crispus Attucks was still a completely black school, and would continue to be until 1968.

Moreover, the success of the Attucks boys' basketball team in the 1950s demonstrated the depths of the city's racism. After multiple trips to the state tournament's semifinal game, as well as state championships in 1955 and 1956 (the city's first), Attucks's young men had earned the right to be called "Indianapolis's team," in both white and black neighborhoods. They were heralded as basketball heroes, but as with House Bill 242, the victories proved to be largely symbolic. Indeed, little changed beyond the court, as they were routinely denied the opportunity to be co-workers, or neighbors, or partners with equal rights. They were still representatives of an all-black school, in an all-black neighborhood, within a heavily divided system.

Also in the 1950s, school leaders once more broadened the high school curriculum by embracing the principles of the "life adjustment" movement, which was developed at the national level by the Division of Vocational Education. Based on the notion that preparing graduates for either college or skilled occupations was too limited, courses for life adjustment aimed to teach pupils how to form personal relationships, how to function in a democracy, and how to prepare for low-skill, service-industry jobs, including those in barbering, beauty culture, and commercial food preparation. The life adjustment curriculum made its way into every high school in the city in one form or another (driver's education and mandatory physical education, for example), but, as in the past, school leaders pushed these options most vehemently south of the Circle. By building a new Manual High in 1954 and opening the specialized Harry E. Wood High in the old Manual building, administrators in Indianapolis once again proved that they believed that students on the South Side were better served by a "practical," less academic education.

Meanwhile, the North Side Shortridge became more prestigious in the 1950s and was even named one of the best high schools in the nation by *Time, Newsweek*, and several other publications in 1957. By the early 1960s, however, rapid suburbanization in Indianapolis was making the city's first high school more and more diverse. By 1966, in fact, Shortridge was 75 percent black. In response, the school board, led by Shortridge alumnus and future mayor Richard Lugar, passed the Shortridge Plan, which attempted to stop the influx of low-income and black students by implementing an admissions examination. The effort proved unsuccessful and was ended in 1970, but it proved that school leaders were willing to try almost anything to maintain their divided high school system.

At roughly the same time, the Justice Department sued the Indianapolis public schools for failing to adequately integrate its system, thus violating the Fourteenth Amendment. When United States district judge Samuel Hugh Dillin heard the case, he and the city learned that Indianapolis's administrators had moved the schools' boundary lines 360 times between 1949 and 1970, each in an effort to maintain the city's well-worn racial divisions. Needless to say, Judge Dillin found the district guilty of de jure segregation in 1971, but his decision was, in some respects, moot. The year before, Mayor Lugar had negotiated the passage of Unigov, which united the city and county governments for tax and "efficiency" purposes. To make Unigov politically viable, however, Lugar and his supporters had to exclude the city and suburban school systems, meaning that the metropolitan area—both residentially and educationally—became even more divided. At a time when local politicians were stressing "unity," Indianapolis, between its city and its suburbs, was cementing an ostensibly apartheid system of schools.

In that way, Unigov, especially when it came to education, was an unjust system by a new name. It was the culmination of a process that began in 1895 with the opening of Manual High on the South Side and continued with the "comprehensive" Tech, the all-black Attucks, and the "life adjustment" Wood. Unigov reflected an old—not new—way of thinking about the public high school.

When it comes to the history of educational equality and inequality in the United States, therefore, seeing the connections between the old and the new requires studying multiple, uniquely fashioned high schools—a *system* of schools—over a long period of time. Only then, as observers of this mass institution, can we see that the impulses that created the Shortridge High Schools of yesteryear also created the Carmel Clay High Schools of today. Only when we return to the public high school's roots can we see that it has routinely been used as a tax-supported way for privileged families to maintain their privilege—perhaps not in every case, but in most cases. Perhaps some schools served as levers of social uplift, but they have been the exception, not the rule.

Further, only when we go out of our way to capture the voices of the students themselves can we see that the high school—because it became a mass institution—is just as much a social and cultural institution as an educational one. Without question, young people study while in high school and, in some cases, they learn quite a lot. But if you ask people about their time in an American high school, they are not likely to list off the courses they took, or the midterm exam they aced, or the report on *To Kill a Mockingbird* they wrote. Instead, they will likely tell you about the school dances they nervously attended, the disgusting cafeteria in which they were forced to eat, and the lifelong friendships they formed. What is more, if they attended high school in a metropolitan area, they will probably tell you about their schools' rivals, and what each institution's school colors meant when worn in the community. Some school colors might have meant "North Side" and "wealthy," while others might have meant "South Side" and "working class."

Basically, they are saying that "Where'd you go to high school?" has always been a powerful question. It has always been inexorably bound to educational equality and inequality in the United States.

To end on a note of optimism, it is clear—in spite of decades upon decades of inequity, division, and social reproduction—that the nation's public schools are still called upon to cure society's ills. To this day, politicians and voters, taxpayers and concerned citizens, and parents and their children alike continue to see them as nearly omnipotent change agents. It is too much to expect of our schools alone, to be certain, but the expectation persists. And perhaps for good reason. As historian of education David Tyack suggests in his celebrated book *The One Best System*, "Urban schools did not create the injustices of American urban life, although they had a systematic part in perpetuating them. It is an old and idle hope to believe that better education alone can remedy them. Yet in the old goal of the common school, reimagined in radically reformed institutions, lies a legacy essential to a quest for social justice."[15] That "old goal" was stated loud and clear in Indianapolis as early as 1879, back when the city had just one high school. At the time, board president William Bell declared, "The crowning glory of the public-school system is the *free* High School." For in that institution alone, he trusted, "the child of the humblest citizen can acquire an education that will enable him to compete even-handed in the battle of life with the child of the millionaire."[16] Indianapolis, like its urban peers, never brought Bell's hopes to life, and it was a missed opportunity. But the beauty in that sentiment, although 140 years old, endures. It reveals why Americans remain committed to schools as conceivable sites of social justice.

The potential is too great and too awesome not to.

Acknowledgments

I have several people to thank for supporting me on my path to this book. Because the project grew out of my dissertation, my debt of gratitude stretches back many years. Simply put, I would not be in this position without them.

My primary academic adviser at the University of Wisconsin–Madison, William Reese, is among the kindest and most human people I know. Through his example, guidance, and support, he taught me how to be a historian. He taught me, with patience and care, to be a better writer. He taught me that our stories about the past should be written with purpose, and fairness, and respect for the dead—and, as often as necessary, a healthy dose of irony, and humor, and joy. He taught me that our work is about viewing the diversity of the human experience with empathy, that, as a people, our similarities have always far outweighed our differences. In between these lessons, but perhaps most importantly, Bill has always been up for a chat, often over a beer at the Dane or a PB&J in his office. He asked me how I was doing. He listened to my stories, and he told me stories of his own. He supported me as a person, first and foremost. "Stay in touch," Bill likes to say. I have and I will. But I will never be able to thank him enough.

I was also fortunate to work with my other academic advisers from the beginning to the end of my graduate career. From my course work through my dissertation, I was guided at every step by Michael Fultz, Adam Nelson, and Jennifer Ratner-Rosenhagen. To watch these thoughtful people work as teachers and scholars is humbling. To receive their help on my own teaching and scholarship has been inspiring. While at Madison, I was also supported generously by the History Department Fellowship, the Avril S. Barr Graduate Summer Fellowship, the Mellon-Wisconsin Dissertation Writing Fellowship, a graduate school research travel grant, and the Herbert Kliebard Award for

Scholarly Achievement in Education. As I made my way through the program, each of these proved important.

In Indianapolis, I was met time and again by people who loved to share their city's history and who were remarkably helpful in connecting me to resources. The librarians and staff at the Indiana Historical Society and Indianapolis Public Library were warm, welcoming, and kind—even as I was making my fiftieth request of the day. The administrators of the central offices of the Indianapolis public schools, who were no doubt busy running a complex school system, kindly arranged for me to spend multiple days in the basement archives of the school board. Thanks, too, to the alumni volunteers and administrators at Crispus Attucks High, Arsenal Technical High, and Manual High, who allowed me to spend days in their on-site museums and archives, all three of which are fascinating in their own right. The documentarian, veteran journalist, and all-around awesome person Ted Green invited me to a prescreening of his film *Attucks: The School That Opened a City* on the day we met, one of my first in Indianapolis. In our email and in-person conversations, he connected me to numerous sources that I would have otherwise overlooked. Family friends Dan and Kim Holzhausen of Fishers graciously hosted me on one of my week-long trips. Their hospitality and humor—not to mention the shared food and drinks—made returning from the archives in the evenings a delight.

I fell in love with history at the University of Missouri, in large part because I had the great fortune of working with Carol Anderson (now at Emory), who was my undergraduate thesis adviser. I was inspired to attend graduate school, however, to study history and education policy by my time teaching fourth and fifth grade in South City St. Louis. To my former students—Ezekiel, Mauro, Brandy, Jessica, Amir, Marian, and Anton, among so many others—thank you for showing me what school is really about. I think about our time together often.

Since joining the faculty at the University of Wisconsin Oshkosh, I have had the benefit of the College of Education and Human Services Research Release Program, as well as a faculty development grant, both of which gave me some important time to work on this project. I have also been the beneficiary of several supportive and talented colleagues—Marguerite Penick-Parks and Josh Garrison, in particular—who have helped me settle in as a new faculty member and who, through almost daily impromptu conversations in our offices and shared hallway, have sharpened my thinking about education and equity in America.

My students at the University of Wisconsin–Madison and the University of Wisconsin Oshkosh have also shaped this book in important ways. It is my great honor to work in a state university system, primarily teaching people who want to be teachers. In my experience, they make excellent students, and they demand from historians of education a clarity, relevance, and enthusiasm that makes the field better. Through their questions and insights, they helped improve my own telling of this story, as well as how it might matter in the present. Likewise, a number of my colleagues in history and education policy have discussed my research with me, and some have even read chapters, large sections, or all of this book. Brad Baranowski, Brett Bertucio, Erin Cantos, Sam Gale, Robbie Gross, Liz Hauck, Amato Nocera, Matt Reiter, Cam Scribner, Jenny Seelig, Walter Stern, Nick Strohl, and Derek Taira, among many others: I am deeply grateful for your time and care with my work and your friendship throughout.

I am indebted to Ben Justice for providing indispensable feedback on an early draft of this book, as well as for recommending it for the New Directions in the History of Education series at Rutgers University Press. Lisa Banning, my editor at Rutgers, helped move this project through its many phases, always responding to my questions quickly, accurately, and professionally. Greg Hyman, too, my production editor, made many helpful and incisive comments in the book's final stages. I cannot imagine working with a more thoughtful and talented group of people. I will be forever thankful for the time they devoted to this project.

To my dad and mom, Mike and Jan Steele, thank you—well, for everything. The truth is, as a kid, I never really cared about the academic parts of school. My indifference is one of my earliest memories. The fact that I ended up working in academia is just as much a testament to you as it is to me. I have studied education long enough to know that I would not have gotten here without you. Not even close. Dad: thank you for proving to me that showing up on time and truly, sincerely trying your best can sometimes open doors in life. Mom: thank you for guiding me with boundless patience and grace, and showing me the beauty in seeing the best in other people.

Finally, this book is for Emily, my wife and best friend. I could not have planned it this way, but, given my research interests, it is fitting that she and I met in high school. I sneaked out of fifth period freshman year at Francis Howell North to "ask her out," as we used to say. I still recall my nervousness. Thankfully, she said yes, and from that day, we have been inseparable.

People say that love is putting someone else's needs before your own. If that is right, and I think it is, then Emily loves as much as anyone I know. When I decided to go to grad school but had to first finish teaching grade school in St. Louis, Emily got a new job so fast (of course) that she had to spend the summer in Madison by herself, sleeping on an air mattress. She never complained; she told me to do what I love; she told me to go for it. Since that first summer, she has given birth to a beautiful daughter and two beautiful sons, and climbed the ladder at work. And every day—every single day—she supported me completely, with all her heart. Her strength, and smarts, and beauty, and wit made the journey from that summer to today an absolute joy. So, thank you, Em. This is for you.

Notes

Introduction

1 "Where You *Should've* Gone to High School," *Riverfront Times* (St. Louis), February 16, 2012. The author prefaced the quiz by writing, "A disclaimer: This chart is, of course, based on gross stereotypes, but isn't that part of what the high school question is about?"

2 This is paraphrased from William Reese, *America's Public Schools: From the Common School to "No Child Left Behind"* (Baltimore: Johns Hopkins University Press, 2011).

3 Jeffrey Mirel, "The Traditional High School: Historical Debates over Its Nature and Function," *Education Next* 6, no. 1 (Winter 2006): 15. For more on these trends with respect to Detroit, see David Angus and Jeffrey Mirel, "Equality, Curriculum, and the Decline of the Academic Ideal: Detroit, 1930–1968," *History of Education Quarterly* 33, no. 2 (Summer 1993): 177–207. While scholars emphasize different reasons for the increase in the student population, Reese describes factors such as significant immigration (especially in the Progressive Era), factory automation, an escalating standard of living for segments of the working class, a number of child labor laws, and the declining involvement of young people in industry. See Reese, *America's Public Schools*, 118–120. Further, the authors of *Recent Social Trends*, a federally commissioned study of the United States, remarked, "Of those high school age, about fifty percent are now in school—evidence of the most successful single effort which government in the United States has ever put forth." President's Research Committee on Social Trends, *Recent Social Trends in the United States*, vol. 1 (New York: McGraw-Hill, 1933), xlvii.

4 Deborah Fallows, "Why We Never Get Over High School," *Atlantic*, February 23, 2014.

5 That the American high school is the product of both national trends and local governing structures is fairly well established in the historiography; see, for example, Edward Krug, *The Shaping of the American High School*, vol. 1, *1880–1920*, and vol. 2, *1920–1941* (Madison: University of Wisconsin Press, 1969, 1972). For an

example of this from 1940 on, see Robert Hampel, *The Last Little Citadel: American High Schools since 1940* (Boston: Houghton Mifflin, 1986).

6   Patrick Ottenhoff, "Where Does the South Begin?," *Atlantic*, January 28, 2011. Also see Joel Garreau, *The Nine Nations of North America* (New York: Houghton Mifflin, 1981).

7   While the degree to which any of this thinking matters is debatable, the intent is significant. Ironically, the motto has its roots in turn-of-the-century Indianapolis. As James Divita writes, "The leadership preferred to advertise Indianapolis as the 'Crossroads of America,' 'this 100 percent American town,' and 'the Capitol of the land of opportunity.' In 1910 the Commercial Club . . . declared, 'There is almost a total absence of the foreign floating element.'" James Divita, "Overview: Demography and Ethnicity," in *The Encyclopedia of Indianapolis*, ed. David Bodenhamer and Robert G. Barrows (Bloomington: Indiana University Press, 1994), 55.

8   The historiography of the twentieth-century American high school has most often focused on changes to the curriculum that developed in step with the swelling student population. In many ways, Krug's two volumes of *The Shaping of the American High School*, covering 1880 to 1920 and 1920 to 1941, respectively, continue to be exemplars in this regard, although they were published more than forty years ago. This trend in the scholarship, though at times too top-down and analytically one-dimensional, is vital, since curricular matters profoundly shaped the character of the high school. But it is also understandable, since the historical actors who debated and decided the fate of the curriculum—college professors, members of educational associations, school board members, and superintendents and administrators—often left meticulous records, which have been, and continue to be, well suited for interpretation.

9   For more on youth culture, which is rarely connected to the high school in an explicit sense in the literature, see Beth Bailey, *From Front Porch to Back Seat: Courtship in Twentieth-Century America* (Baltimore: Johns Hopkins University Press, 1988); Paula Fass, *The Damned and the Beautiful: American Youth in the 1920s* (New York: Oxford University Press, 1979); Thomas Hine, *The Rise and Fall of the American Teenager: A New History of the American Adolescent Experience* (New York: Perennial, 2000); and William Graebner, *Coming of Age in Buffalo: Youth and Authority in the Postwar Era* (Philadelphia: Temple University Press, 1990).

10 Rare examples of historians using yearbook data include, among very few others, chapter 3 of Paula Fass's *Outside In: Minorities and the Transformation of American Education* (New York: Oxford University Press, 1989); and Paul Harbach, "Student Life in Milwaukee High Schools, 1920–1985," in *Seeds of Crisis: Public Schooling in Milwaukee since 1920*, ed. John L. Rury and Frank A. Cassel (Madison: University of Wisconsin Press, 1993). Even more recently, see Jon Hale, *The Freedom Schools: Student Activists in the Mississippi Civil Rights Movement* (New York: Columbia University Press, 2016), as well as Pamela Grundy, *Color and Character: West Charlotte High and the American Struggle over Educational Equality* (Chapel Hill: University of North Carolina Press, 2017).

11 William Reese, "Overview: Education," in Bodenhamer and Barrows, *Encyclopedia of Indianapolis*, 74–77. In describing the high school's development, the school system's 1934 internal report, Indianapolis Public Schools, *Survey Findings: Senior High School Division Secondary School* (Indianapolis: Indianapolis Board of School Commissioners, 1934), included a section called "Brief History of the

Indianapolis Public Schools." On the earliest forms of manual education (and its distinction from vocational education) in the high school, see Herbert Kliebard, *Schooled to Work: Vocationalism and the American Curriculum, 1876–1946* (New York: Teachers College Press, 1999), 24–25.

12 Reese, "Overview: Education," 79; for more, see Laura Sheerin Gaus, *Shortridge High School, 1864–1981, in Retrospect* (Indianapolis: Indiana Historical Society, 1985), 130–135.

13 The National Education Association commissioned a report titled the *Cardinal Principles of Secondary Education* in 1918. Principally written by a former high school teacher, Clarence Kingsley, the report argued that the current model of secondary education failed to meet the needs of both individual students and society. Though laden with vague language, the report clearly advocated for an expansion of the vocational and nonacademic curricula, which, it suggested, would cultivate the nation's "industrial growth," "efficiency," and "democracy." Underlying the report's conclusion was the assumption that the era's "new" students were less intelligent than previous generations had been, and, consequently, demanding that they follow a college-preparatory path was both futile and wasteful. Upon the release of Kingsley's report, historian Jeffrey Mirel notes, it was "not hard to see where the battle lines would have been drawn" regarding the future of the curriculum ("The Traditional High School," 15). As the 1920s wore on, however, despite ongoing disagreements at the local and national levels, it was apparent that school leaders had reached a compromise of sorts. Indicative of the compromise, most large urban systems, particularly in the North, featured multiple educational "tracks," or paths to graduation, some of which were purely academic (reflecting the preferences espoused in the report of the Committee of Ten, which was commissioned by the National Education Association in 1892), and some of which were purely vocational (reflecting the preferences outlined in the *Cardinal Principles*). In many cities, all the various tracks were housed in expansive, typically new, high school buildings—called "comprehensive" schools—though several cities also opened separate vocational, "manual," or "industrial" schools.

14 For more on this tension among civil rights leaders—created by segregation and integration in public education—see Jerald Podair, *The Strike That Changed New York: Blacks, Whites, and the Ocean Hill–Brownsville Crisis* (New Haven, CT: Yale University Press, 2002).

15 Throughout, *racism* will be used to connote feelings of racial superiority among white people. For more, see Edward Bonilla-Silva, *Racism without Racists: Color-Blind Racism and the Persistence of Racial Inequality in America* (Lanham, MD: Rowman and Littlefield, 2018). The use of *white supremacy* is informed by the work of Carol Anderson, in particular *White Rage: The Unspoken Truth of Our Racial Divide* (New York: Bloomsbury, 2017). Anderson notes, "White rage is not about visible violence, but rather it works its way through the courts, the legislatures, and a range of government bureaucracies. It wreaks havoc subtly, almost imperceptibly. Too imperceptibly, certainly, for a nation consistently drawn to the spectacular—to what it can *see*. It's not the Klan. White rage doesn't have to wear sheets, burn crosses, or take to the streets. Working the halls of power, it can achieve its ends far more effectively, far more destructively" (3).

16 Quoted in Reese, *America's Public Schools*, 286–287. Reese also notes that, in 1983, Vonnegut told a group of students, "Every joke I've ever told, every attitude I've

ever struck, came from school 43 [his elementary school] and Shortridge. I've never needed any new material from any place" (287).

Chapter 1   Shortridge, Then Manual, Then Arsenal

1   Milo Stuart, "The Manual-Training School," in *Types of Schools for Boys*, by Alfred E. Stearns et al., Childhood and Youth Series (Indianapolis: Bobbs-Merrill, 1917), 135.

2   Milo Stuart, *The Organization of a Comprehensive High School: A Presentation of Plans and Devices of the Arsenal Technical Schools, Indianapolis, whereby the Interest of the Individual Is Kept Paramount* (New York: Macmillan, 1926), 1.

3   Reese, *America's Public Schools*, 192.

4   David Tyack, *The One Best System: A History of American Urban Education* (Cambridge, MA: Harvard University Press, 1974), esp. 126–176. By tackling the question of the high school's new student population head on, the *Cardinal Principles* marked a key turning point in the maturation of secondary education. Its skillful rhetoric, furthermore, successfully united multiple reform agendas around a common cause. To the conservative "developmentalists" and nearly all proponents of a "socially efficient" curriculum, the report reiterated the need for a broadly conceived program of study, one that included multiple academic and nonacademic "tracks." Further, by justifying curricular differentiation with the emerging "science" of intelligence testing—notably methods pioneered by E. L. Thorndike—the report also grabbed the attention of Tyack's middle-class "administrative progressives." Not only was this group predisposed to the report's quantitative, business-minded style of sorting students, but it also regularly held the power and political will to modify the organizational structure of the schools, which was key in bringing many of Kingsley's recommendations to fruition. Eventually, because of this alliance—for bureaucracy, differentiation, and testing—most districts added "comprehensive" high school buildings, facilities for vocational education, and more professionals to staff their new mechanisms of guidance and assessment.

5   Reese, *America's Public Schools*, 191.

6   Reese, 182.

7   For generations, a very small group of adolescents attended the public high school, and even then, the experience was anything but uniform. For some, "high school" meant opulent, cathedral-like structures led by large and accomplished faculty. For others, it meant a dozen or so students studying together on the top floor of a grammar school. And for others still, it simply meant a handful of students learning algebra, as Reese describes it, "next to abecedarians in drafty one-room schools." See William Reese, *The Origins of the American High School* (New Haven, CT: Yale University Press, 1995), 80. Also, as Michael Katz notes, there is real "danger in overstressing uniformity among early high schools." Michael Katz, review of *The Origins of the American High School*, by William J. Reese, *History of Education Quarterly* 36, no. 4 (Winter 1996): 521.

8   Dugdale's writing included in "A Clearing in the Forest," in *Arsenal Tech Memories* (Indianapolis: Arsenal Technical High School, 1994), 26.

9   "Clearing in the Forest," 27.

10 "Clearing in the Forest," 26.

11 A "free high school, the Central High of Indianapolis," operated sporadically in 1853 and 1854 in the County Seminary building on University Square. It was

common for high schools to open and close in the antebellum period, so it is more useful to begin the story with the first permanent high school. Quote and information from Emmett A. Rice, *A Brief Story of Shortridge and Her Forbears* (Indianapolis: Shortridge High School, 1935).

12 Reese, *America's Public Schools*, 220. Reese also writes extensively about the first public high school in America, Boston's English Classical School, which was founded in 1821. Historians have found that towns and cities with strong ties to the marketplace were generally receptive to the ideas of Whig and Republican reformers and, consequently, served as sites of early high school development. Unsurprisingly, given Boston's legacy, other commercial centers within Massachusetts were among the first to act, including Lowell, Springfield, Worchester, and Salem, such that by 1856, nearly three-fourths of the Bay State's population lived in towns with public high schools. In neighboring New York State, scholars have found that the most dynamic period of growth was in the 1850s and 1860s, when the number of high schools grew from twenty-two to fifty-nine, eventually surpassing "academies in number of institutions by 1875 and in number of students by 1880." See Carl Kaestle, *Pillars of the Republic: Common Schools and American Society, 1780–1860* (New York: Hill and Wang, 1983), 120–121. In due course, Philadelphia (1838), Baltimore (1839), Hartford (1847), and scores of other cities fell in line with their New England peers. A similar pattern unfolded outside the Northeast. In Cleveland, the first public high school opened under the guidance of the city's Whig mayor in 1846, only decades after the Ohio and Erie Canals connected the city to distant markets through the Great Lakes and Ohio River. Likewise, Cincinnati, which blossomed throughout the nineteenth century as a commercial hub between free and slave states, established its first high school in 1847. Even on the West Coast, San Francisco, following the Gold Rush and the continual westward expansion of the railroads, graduated its first class of pupils in 1859. What this trend reveals, historians have observed, is that cities and burgeoning towns outside the South regularly exhibited the features that made public secondary schooling more feasible and palatable to voters: they had sturdy foundations of political support in the form of Whig and Republican activism; they had healthy tax bases, aside from economic panics in 1837, 1857, and 1873; they had high-density populations, which made age-graded and hierarchical school systems possible; and they had a robust middle-class, whose members most easily identified with—and stood to gain the most from—the institution's bourgeois culture and objectives. Also see Carl Kaestle, *The Evolution of an Urban School System: New York City, 1750–1850* (Cambridge, MA: Harvard University Press, 1973), 174–175.

13 Gaus, *Shortridge High School*, 18.

14 Reese, *Origins of the American High School*, 60–62.

15 Gaus, *Shortridge High School*, 30.

16 Indianapolis Board of School Commissioners, *Report of the President* (Indianapolis: Indianapolis Board of School Commissioners, 1879), 10.

17 William Reese, *History, Education, and the Schools* (New York: Palgrave Macmillan, 2007), 84.

18 Reese, 86.

19 Reese, 87. Others included "Man's happiness or misery are, in great measure, put into his own hands." Reese notes that these textbooks were often challenged by opponents of the high school, as well as various Catholic organizations.

20 While Indianapolis High was not named Shortridge High until the early 1900s, this chapter uses its permanent name earlier for continuity.

21 Reese, *Origins of the American High School*, 103–106, 136–141. Also see David Labaree, *The Making of an American High School: The Credentials Market and the Central High School of Philadelphia, 1838–1939* (New Haven, CT: Yale University Press, 1988), 14–16. For rates of college attendance, see Edward Krug, *The Secondary School Curriculum* (New York: Harper and Brothers, 1960), 35.

22 Indianapolis Public Schools, *Survey Findings*, 17–18.

23 The four "desires" of the high school are taken from Labaree, *Making*, 12–27. Also see Kaestle, *Pillars of the Republic*, 73–103.

24 Gaus, *Shortridge High School*, 25–27.

25 Gaus, 25–27.

26 James Madison, "Overview: Economy," in Bodenhamer and Barrows, *The Encyclopedia of Indianapolis*, 62–64. For another midwestern expression of commercialism, in Chicago, see William Cronon, *Nature's Metropolis: Chicago and the Great West* (New York: W. W. Norton, 1991). For more on the context of Milwaukee, which rivaled Chicago in growth until the 1870s, see Bayrd Still, *Milwaukee: The History of a City* (Madison: State Historical Society of Wisconsin, 1948).

27 Madison, "Overview," 62–64.

28 Elizabeth Brand Monroe, "Overview: Built Environment," in Bodenhamer and Barrows, *Encyclopedia of Indianapolis*, 28–30.

29 Monroe, 28–30.

30 Quoted in Frederick Kershner Jr., "From Country Town to Industrial City: The Urban Pattern in Indianapolis," *Indiana Magazine of History* 45, no. 4 (December 1949): 330. Historian Robert Wiebe writes, "Moreover, the very process of urban living generated its own special values. The individualism and casual cooperation of the towns still had their place in the city. But new virtues—regularity, system, continuity—clashed increasingly with the old. The city dweller could never protect his home from fire or rid his street of garbage by the spontaneous voluntarism that had raised cabins along the frontier." Wiebe, *The Search for Order, 1877–1920* (New York: Hill and Wang, 1967), 14.

31 Lamont J. Hulse, "Overview: Neighborhoods and Communities," in Bodenhamer and Barrows, *Encyclopedia of Indianapolis*, 133.

32 David G. Vanderstel, "General Entries: Irish," in Bodenhamer and Barrows, *Encyclopedia of Indianapolis*, 827–828.

33 James Divita, "Overview: Demography and Ethnicity," in Bodenhamer and Barrows, *Encyclopedia of Indianapolis*, 55.

34 Hulse, "Overview," 133.

35 William Reese, "Overview: Education," in Bodenhamer and Barrows, *Encyclopedia of Indianapolis*, 74–77. On the earliest forms of manual education (and its distinction from vocational education) in the high school, see Kliebard, *Schooled to Work*, 24–25.

36 Rice, *Brief Story of Shortridge*.

37 Carolyn Griffin, *Emmerich Manual High School: A History, 1895–1969* (Indianapolis: Manual High School, 1969), 8. In the late nineteenth century, Germany was the nation's fiercest competitor in industry and the world's leader in manual education.

38 Griffin, 11. Manual was originally called the Industrial Training High School, but, as Griffin also notes, changed its name because the latter "brought many inquiries regarding its works as a reformatory."

39 Griffin, 10–11.

40 Indianapolis Board of School Commissioners, *Catalogue of the Industrial Training School* (Indianapolis: Indianapolis Board of School Commissioners, 1899), 6.

41 Kliebard notes that the NEA was "at the time the nation's most important forum for debating education policy and a place where local school people could become acquainted with what was going on in leading urban centers such as Boston and Chicago." Further, in addressing the NEA, Woodward would soften his message regarding manual training, in Kliebard's words, characterizing "traditional education as a two-legged stool, needing the leg of manual training to make it stable." Kliebard, *Schooled to Work*, 8–9.

42 Kliebard, 8–9. Also see Krug, *Secondary School Curriculum*, 365–370.

43 *Mind and Hand* (Indianapolis: Manual Training High School, 1897), 7–9.

44 *Mind and Hand* (Indianapolis: Manual Training High School, 1896), 3.

45 Indianapolis Public Schools, *Shortridge High School Textbook List, Revised June 1914* (Indianapolis: Indianapolis Public Schools, 1914), 4.

46 Gaus, *Shortridge High School*, 42.

47 Gaus, 38–44.

48 *Daily Echo* (Shortridge High School, Indianapolis), September 26, 1898, 1.

49 Indianapolis Public Schools, *Annual Report, 1905–1906* (Indianapolis: Indianapolis Public Schools, 1906), 56.

50 Indianapolis Public Schools, 56–57.

51 "Teams Anxious for the Whistle," "Coaches Give Charges Last Bit of Advice," "Teams Ready to Fight like Tigers," *Indianapolis Sun*, November 24, 26, 30, 1906.

52 An exception, though it focuses on all high school sports and their use to keep "control" of children in the Progressive Era, is Robert Pruter, *The Rise of American High School Sports and the Search for Control, 1880–1930* (Syracuse, NY: Syracuse University Press, 2013).

53 Brian Ingrassia, *The Rise of Gridiron University: Higher Education's Uneasy Alliance with Big-Time Football* (Lawrence: University of Kansas Press, 2015), 3–4.

54 Theodore Roosevelt, *The Strenuous Life: Essays and Addresses* (New York: Century, 1900), 3–5. He continued, to his audience in Chicago, "I ask only that what every self-respecting American demands from himself and from his sons shall be demanded of the American nation as a whole. Who among you would teach your boys that ease, that peace, is to be the first consideration in their eyes—to be the ultimate goal after which they strive?"

55 "Hears Football Men; Coaches in Conference with President Roosevelt," *Washington Post*, October 10, 1905.

56 "Hears Football Men." On the subject, in 1905, Roosevelt said, "I believe in outdoor games, and I do not mind in the least that they are rough games, or that those who take part in them are occasionally injured."

57 *Indianapolis Sun*, November 24, 1906.

58 *Indianapolis Times*, Manual Training Anniversary Edition, February 17, 1945, 2.

59 Tom Koch, "A History of Football at Shortridge," *Daily Echo*, supplement, September 1943. This supplement, which was produced by the *Echo* staff but sold separately during the football season, was primarily written by former graduate, then Butler University student, Koch.

60 *Daily Echo*, November 23, 1907, 1.

61 *Daily Echo*, November 22, 1907, 1.

62 *Daily Echo*, November 23, 1905, 1.

63 Koch, "History of Football at Shortridge," 11.

64 *The Mirror* (Indianapolis: Manual High School, 1907), 18–19.

65 Fourteen Shortridge students were suspended in 1910 for playing a game against Manual without permission. See Gaus, *Shortridge High School*, 92.

66 Indianapolis Public Schools, *Annual Report, 1908–1909* (Indianapolis: Indianapolis Public Schools, 1909), 50.

67 Indianapolis Public Schools, *Annual Report, 1915–1916* (Indianapolis: Indianapolis Public Schools, 1916), 57; Gaus, *Shortridge High School*, 94 (this figure was reported in the *Echo*).

68 Gaus, *Shortridge High School*, 94.

69 Gaus, 91, 94–97.

70 Indianapolis Public Schools, *Annual Report, 1908–1909*, 54.

71 Indianapolis Public Schools, 119.

72 Indianapolis Public Schools, 141–142.

73 Michelle D. Hale, "School Finance," in Bodenhamer and Barrows, *Encyclopedia of Indianapolis*, 1224–1226.

74 Indianapolis Public Schools, *Annual Report, 1908–1909*, 143. This financial arrangement was reminiscent of the Cleveland Plan, which, approved in 1899, was meant to limit the local board's control of funding.

75 Indianapolis Public Schools, *Annual Report, 1915–1916*, 66.

76 "The New Arsenal Technical Schools at Indianapolis, Ind.," *Architectural Forum*, February 1919, 55.

77 Indianapolis Public Schools, *Annual Report, 1915–1916*, 65–66.

78 Stuart's daughter's words included in "Clearing in the Forest," 7.

79 Reese, *America's Public Schools*, 191. For more, see David Angus and Jeffrey Mirel, *The Failed Promise of the American High School, 1890–1995* (New York: Teachers College Press, 1999), 13–16.

80 To historian Herbert Kliebard, the report "reflected with reasonable accuracy the winds of change that had swept through the educational world in the previous quarter-century." This point is made in Reese, *America's Public Schools*, 192. Also see Krug, *Shaping*, 2:25.

81 *Cardinal Principles*, quoted in Krug, *Shaping*, 2:53.

82 *Cardinal Principles*, quoted in David Tyack and Larry Cuban, *Tinkering toward Utopia: A Century of School Reform* (Cambridge, MA: Harvard University Press, 1995), 51.

83 Stuart, *Organization*, 3.

84 Stuart, 3–4.

85 Mirel, "Traditional High School," 17.

86 Indiana State Board of Education, *Report of the Indianapolis Survey for Vocational Education* (Indianapolis: Fort Wayne Printing, 1917), 87.

87 Indiana State Board of Education, 150.

88 Indiana State Board of Education, 150–151.

89 Indiana State Board of Education, 152.

90 *Arsenal Cannon*, September 24, 1925, 1.

91 Indianapolis Public Schools, *Annual Report, 1915–1916*, 89–90.

Chapter 2   Forced Segregation and the Creation of Crispus Attucks High School, 1919-1929

1 *The Attucks (1928)* (Indianapolis: Crispus Attucks High School, 1928).
2 *The Attucks (1928)*, 5. For more on Nolcox's appointment, see "Local Man Heads New High School," *Indianapolis Recorder*, May 14, 1927.
3 *The Attucks (1928)*, 6.
4 *The Attucks (1928)*, 6; Leonard J. Moore, *Citizen Klansmen: The Ku Klux Klan in Indiana, 1921–1928* (Chapel Hill: University of North Carolina Press, 1991), 144–150.
5 *The Attucks (1928)*, 8.
6 Emma Lou Thornbrough, *Indiana Blacks in the Twentieth Century* (Bloomington: Indiana University Press, 2001), 14–15. For more, see Beverly Lowry, *Her Dream of Dreams: The Rise and Triumph of Madam C. J. Walker* (New York: Vintage, 2004). Born in Louisiana to former slaves, Walker was an orphan at seven, a wife at fourteen, and a widow at twenty. To support herself and her daughter, she had worked as a laundress in St. Louis, Missouri, selling hair care and beauty products in her spare time. She moved to Indianapolis in 1910 and built her business with her associate and lawyer Freeman B. Ransom.
7 See A'Lelia Bundles, *Madame Walker Theatre Center: An Indianapolis Treasure* (Charleston, SC: Arcadia, 2013).
8 *The Attucks (1928)*, 9–10.
9 Thornbrough, *Indiana Blacks*, 25–26. For more on DeFrantz, see Faburn DeFrantz, "'To Kathy and to David': The Memoir of Faburn E. DeFrantz," *Indiana Magazine of History* 108, no. 2 (June 2012): 104–145. After years of rejection by the city's central YMCA branch, blacks organized their own in 1900, which gained full membership in the state association in 1902. When Sears, Roebuck, and Company president and philanthropist Julius Rosenwald offered $25,000 to any city that could raise $75,000 of its own for the construction of a "Negro Y.M.C.A.," Indianapolis and its black leaders leapt at the chance.
10 Thornbrough, *Indiana Blacks*, 26. Thornbrough includes an image of the dedication, in which Washington is standing shoulder to shoulder with Madam C. J. Walker, Freeman B. Ransom, newspaperman George Knox, and five others. Though DeFrantz only mentions DuBois once in his memoir, as having attended one of his meetings related to the Y, the DuBois Papers reveal that the two men corresponded throughout their careers.
11 *The Attucks (1928)*, 12, 13, 15.
12 Richard Pierce makes this point explicit in *Polite Protest: The Political Economy of Race in Indianapolis, 1920–1970* (Bloomington: Indianan University Press, 2005), 2–3.
13 Davison M. Douglas, *Jim Crow Moves North: The Battle over Northern School Desegregation, 1865–1954* (New York: Cambridge University Press, 2005), 228. For a more expansive view on race in the North, including facets of life beyond the schoolhouse, see Thomas Sugrue, *Sweet Land of Liberty: The Forgotten Struggle for Civil Rights in the North* (New York: Random House Trade Paperbacks, 2009).
14 As a marker of African American exclusion, Eric Jackson notes that an 1855 law "banned Black students from being counted as school children and proclaimed that no school taxes be collected from any African American residents." Eric R. Jackson, "The Endless Journey: The Black Struggle for Quality Public Schools

in Indianapolis, Indiana, 1900–1949" (PhD diss., University of Cincinnati, 2000), 18.

15 Emma Lou Thornbrough, "African Americans," in Bodenhamer and Barrows, *Encyclopedia of Indianapolis*, 5–7.

16 Emma Lou Thornbrough, "Segregation in Indiana during the Klan Era of the 1920s," *Mississippi Valley Historical Review* 47, no. 4 (March 1961): 596. She notes that an 1885 civil rights law prohibiting discrimination in public spaces was a "dead letter."

17 Pierce, in *Polite Protest*, 11–12, makes clear that there were three black districts at the turn of the century, though the area along Indiana Avenue was the "largest and best-known." This area was sometimes referred to as "Pat Ward's Bottoms," and "the Avenue" is sometimes written as "the Avenoo."

18 Thornbrough, *Indiana Blacks*, 12–16.

19 Paul Mullins and Glenn White, *The Price of Progress: IUPUI, the Color Line, and Urban Displacement* (Indianapolis: IUPUI Office of External Affairs, 2010), 23. Patrice Abdullah, who is quoted by Mullins and White, was born in 1943, but the sentiment matches well what previous generations of residents thought of the Avenue and its environs.

20 Jackson, "Endless Journey," 45–46.

21 Thornbrough, "Segregation in Indiana," 597. George L. Knox, the owner of the *Freeman*, once wrote that the way for blacks to end prejudice was to prove "their capacity for patience, industry, economy, and virtuous living." Knox, *Slave and Freeman: The Autobiography of George L. Knox*, ed. Willard B. Gatewood Jr. (Lexington: University Press of Louisville, 1979), 17.

22 Jackson, "Endless Journey," 45–46. Jackson notes that Washington visited Anderson, Indiana, in 1900, urging the state's residents to continue in their support of the Republican Party.

23 Thornbrough, *Indiana Blacks*, 24–25.

24 Thornbrough, 26–27. This is the title of the first chapter of the final book of her career.

25 For more on the complexity of Washington's actions and political strategy, see, for example, Louis Harlan, "Booker T. Washington and the Politics of Accommodation," in *Black Leaders of the Twentieth Century*, ed. John Hope Franklin and August Meier (Urbana: University of Illinois Press, 1982), 1–18.

26 Much has been written about the early use of restrictive covenants and racist real estate practices in the 1910s and 1920s. For more on the long-term implications of this strategy in St. Louis, see Richard Rothstein, "The Making of Ferguson," *American Prospect*, Fall 2014, 1–19.

27 Pierce, *Polite Protest*, 59.

28 For more on the Chicago race riots, see William Tuttle, *Race Riot: Chicago in the Red Summer of 1919* (New York: Atheneum, 1970).

29 Pierce, *Polite Protest*, 59. Also see Thornbrough, "Segregation in Indiana," 597–599.

30 By 1926, segregationist groups, allied with the Klan, managed to pass a housing ordinance. Although it was eventually overturned in court, it stated that, "in the interest of public peace, good order and general welfare, it is advisable to foster the separation of [the] white and negro residential community." For a short time, it was illegal for whites to "establish a home-residence . . . in a negro community or . . . the municipality inhabited . . . by negroes." Quoted in Thornbrough, *Indiana Blacks*, 52–53.

31 Jackson, "Endless Journey," 68–70.

32 Jackson, 70.

33 Jackson, 70–72. Black parents in Indianapolis considered de jure segregation their clearest target, but historians have since taken care to explain that the mechanisms that drove (and would continue to drive) de facto segregation were still indeed based in laws and carried out by state actors. Thus, to call them de facto in the present is misleading. For more on this work, see, among others, Matthew Lassiter and Joseph Crespino, eds., *The Myth of Southern Exceptionalism* (New York: Oxford University Press, 2009); and Ansley Erickson, *Making the Unequal Metropolis: School Desegregation and Its Limits* (Chicago: University of Chicago Press, 2016).

34 Shortridge is quoted in Frederick K. Gale, "The First Twenty-Five Years of Crispus Attucks High School, Indianapolis, Indiana, 1927–1952" (master's thesis, Ball State Teachers College, 1955), 12–13.

35 Gale, 13.

36 Stanley Warren, *Crispus Attucks High School: "Hail to the Green, Hail to the Gold"* (Virginia Beach, VA: Donning, 1998), appendix 2.

37 For more, see W. T. Lhamon Jr., *Raising Cain: Blackface Performance from Jim Crow to Hip Hop* (Cambridge, MA: Harvard University Press, 2000).

38 "The '99 Entertainment," in *The High School Annual* (Indianapolis: Shortridge High School, 1899), 56.

39 Gaus, *Shortridge High School*, 76.

40 Jackson, "Endless Journey," 41.

41 Douglas, *Jim Crow Moves North*, 123–166.

42 Indianapolis School Board, school board minutes, September 1922, Indianapolis public schools. The presentation at the September meeting was a reiteration of the committee's remarks at a board meeting in June 1922. It "deemed it wise to renew its request."

43 Indianapolis School Board, school board minutes, March 1925.

44 Thornbrough, *Indiana Blacks*, 54–55.

45 Indianapolis School Board, school board minutes, January 1925.

46 Indianapolis School Board, school board minutes, December 1922.

47 Indianapolis School Board, school board minutes, December 1922.

48 Leonard J. Moore, "Ku Klux Klan," in Bodenhamer and Barrows, *Encyclopedia of Indianapolis*, 879.

49 For a discussion of these values as they related to the development of the public school system, see Kaestle, *Pillars of the Republic*.

50 See Wyn Craig Wade, *The Fiery Cross: The Ku Klux Klan in America* (London: Simon and Schuster, 1987). Also see Jackson, "Endless Journey," 80–85.

51 Moore, *Citizen Klansmen*, 150.

52 N.E.A. Indianapolis, "A Suggestion of the Purposes and Accomplishments of the Indianapolis Public Schools," 1925, Indianapolis Public Library.

53 Moore, *Citizen Klansmen*, 148–149.

54 "Board Fails to Relieve High School Congestion," *Fiery Cross*, December 19, 1924. For more on the role private schools play in shaping the educational landscape, see Michelle Purdy, *Transforming the Elite: Black Students and the Desegregation of Private Schools* (Chapel Hill: University of North Carolina Press, 2018).

55 Moore, *Citizen Klansmen*, chap. 6.

56 Indianapolis School Board, school board minutes, November 1922.

57 Indianapolis School Board, school board minutes, November 1922.

58 Thornbrough, *Indiana Blacks*, 57.

59 For more on the early years of the NAACP, see Charles Flint Kellogg, *NAACP: A History of the National Association for the Advancement of Colored People* (Baltimore: Johns Hopkins University Press, 1973).

60 W. E. B. DuBois to Faburn DeFrantz, June 16, 1921, W. E. B. Du Bois Papers, 1803–1999, Special Collections and University Archives, University of Massachusetts Amherst Libraries.

61 Jackson, "Endless Journey," 78.

62 Thornbrough, "Segregation in Indiana," 604–605. Also see Jackson, "Endless Journey," 70–78.

63 Indianapolis School Board, school board minutes, November 1922.

64 Indianapolis School Board, school board minutes, November 1922.

65 Jackson, "Endless Journey," 95–96.

66 "Local Man Heads New High School," *Indianapolis Recorder*, May 14, 1927.

67 Gale, "First Twenty-Five Years," 16.

68 Gale, 78.

69 *The Attucks (1938)* (Indianapolis: Crispus Attucks High School, 1938), 50–51.

70 *The Attucks (1929)* (Indianapolis: Crispus Attucks High School, 1929).

71 *The Attucks (1928)*, 15.

Chapter 3   The High School Moves to the Center of the American Adolescent Experience, 1929–1941

1 Indianapolis Public Schools, *Survey Findings*, 2.

2 "Clearing in the Forest," 45.

3 "Clearing in the Forest," 49.

4 Deborah Markisohn, "Great Depression," in Bodenhamer and Barrows, *Encyclopedia of Indianapolis*, 637.

5 Markisohn, 636–639.

6 Mirel, "Traditional High School," 18.

7 See David Tyack, Elisabeth Hansot, and Robert Lowe, *Public Schools in Hard Times: The Great Depression and Recent Years* (Cambridge, MA: Harvard University Press, 1984), 189. They write, "Was the depression a watershed? The simplest answer—which needs some qualification—is no. In comparison with the private economy, in which employment and the GNP fluctuated radically, public schooling remained remarkably stable in funding. The depression did not deflect much the long-term trends of institutional expansion from 1920 to 1950." With regard to custodialism, this chapter describes the Depression as indeed a "watershed" moment in public secondary education.

8 Thomas Hine, *The Rise and Fall of the American Teenager*, 204.

9 Indianapolis Public Schools, *The Senior High School . . .* (Indianapolis: Board of School Commissioners, 1939), 40.

10 Indianapolis Public Schools, 40.

11 Drawn from the yearbooks of Shortridge, Manual, Tech, and Attucks from 1915, 1925, 1935, and 1945. They are all available in the Education Section of the Digital Indy Archive, which is part of the Indianapolis Public Library, http://www.digitalindy.org/cdm/ (accessed December 2016).

12 Robert Lynd and Helen Lynd, *Middletown: A Study in American Culture* (New
    York: Harcourt, 1929), 54. They continue,

    > Here the social sifting devices of their elders—money, clothes, personal
    > attractiveness, male physical prowess, exclusive clubs, election to positions of
    > leadership—are all for the first time set going with a population as yet largely
    > undifferentiated save as regards their business class and working class parents.
    > This informal training is not a preparation for a vague future that must be
    > taken on trust, as is the case with so much of the academic work; to many of
    > the boys and girls in high school this is "the life," the thing they personally like
    > best about going to school. The school is taking over more and more of the
    > child's waking life. Both high school and grades have departed from the
    > attitude of fifty years ago, when the Board directed: "Pupils shall not be
    > permitted to remain on the school grounds after dismissal. The teachers shall
    > often remind the pupils that the first duty when dismissed is to proceed quietly
    > and directly home to render all needed assistance to their parents." Today the
    > school is becoming not a place to which children go from their homes for a few
    > hours daily but a place from which they go home to eat and sleep. (54)

13 See Graebner, *Coming of Age in Buffalo*. As Graebner writes, "To a considerable
    degree, youths were the objects of middle-class, adult efforts to shape and contain
    youth culture and subcultures" (26).

14 See Penelope Eckert, *Jocks and Burnouts: Social Categories and Identity in the High
    School* (New York: Teachers College Press, 1989). Eckert famously described how
    high school students whom she called "the jocks" adopted a pro-school, middle-
    class culture, while "the burnouts" adopted an anti-school, working-class culture.
    The former group, therefore, had access to all of the social and cultural capital
    maintained by the high school, which was significant.

15 For more on the potency of the American high school as a powerful transmitter of
    cultural values, see Frederick Wiseman's film *High School* (Cambridge, MA:
    Zipporah Films, 1968). Film scholar Barry Keith Grant writes of the film,
    "Wiseman has said that his first impression upon seeing the school was that it
    looked like a factory, a perception that informs the structure of the entire film.
    From the opening sequence, with the camera approaching Northeast's fences and
    tall smokestack, to the ending, in which the school principal reads a letter from a
    former student about to be parachuted into Vietnam, the film suggests that the
    educational system is like an impersonal assembly line manufacturing consent,
    more concerned with socialization than knowledge." Barry Keith Grant, *Five
    Films by Frederick Wiseman: Titicut Follies, High School, Welfare, High School II,
    Public Housing* (Berkeley: University of California Press, 2006), 51. Similarly, see
    Michel Foucault, *Discipline and Punish: The Birth of the Prison* (New York:
    Vintage Books, 1995).

16 Angus and Mirel, *Failed Promise*, 57. Also see Kliebard, *Schooled to Work*; and
    Robert Church, "The Progressive Era High School," in *Education in the United
    States: An Interpretive History* (New York: Free Press, 1976).

17 Department of the Interior, Bureau of Education, *Cardinal Principles of Secondary
    Education: A Report of the Commission on the Reorganization of Secondary
    Education* (Washington, DC: Government Printing Office, 1918), 9.

18 Indianapolis Public Schools, *Survey Findings*, 14.

19 Angus and Mirel, *Failed Promise*, 57.

20 Indianapolis Public Schools, *Survey Findings*, 14.

21 Indianapolis Public Schools, 14. For more on the history of home economics, see Sarah Stage and Virginia Vincenti, eds., *Rethinking Home Economics: Women and the History of a Profession* (Ithaca, NY: Cornell University Press, 1997); and Megan Elias, *Stir It Up: Home Economics in American Culture* (Philadelphia: University of Pennsylvania Press, 2010).

22 Indianapolis Public Schools, 19–22.

23 Indianapolis Public Schools, 8.

24 Indianapolis Public Schools, *Senior High School*, 40.

25 Indianapolis Public Schools, 40. Italics added.

26 Indianapolis Public Schools, 40.

27 Indianapolis Public Schools, 48.

28 Michelle D. Hale, "School Finance," in Bodenhamer and Barrows, *Encyclopedia of Indianapolis*, 1224–1226.

29 See Tyack, Hansot, and Lowe, *Public Schools in Hard Times*.

30 Indianapolis Public Schools, "Amount Expenditure; Instruction—Cont." (June 1931 through December 1931), 11.

31 Indianapolis Public Schools, *Survey Findings*, 328–329.

32 *The Tech Way* (Indianapolis: Arsenal High School, 1938), 5.

33 *Tech Way*, 13–14.

34 *Tech Way*, 14.

35 *Tech Way*, 15.

36 *Tech Way*, 17. For more on "moral education," broadly conceived, in the United States, see B. Edward McClellan, *Moral Education in America: Schools and the Shaping of Character from Colonial Times to the Present* (New York: Teachers College Press, 1999).

37 See Eckert, *Jocks and Burnouts*.

38 *Facts for Freshmen* (Indianapolis: Manual Training High School, 1942), 1.

39 Charles Chaplin, dir., *Modern Times* (Los Angeles: United Artists, 1936).

40 Indianapolis Public Schools, *Survey Findings*, 206. The exact number of lockers in 1933 was 6,208. *Facts for Freshmen*, 2.

41 *Facts for Freshmen*, 3.

42 *The Viewpoint* (Indianapolis: Crispus Attucks High School, 1930), 4.

43 *Viewpoint*, 9.

44 *Booster* (Manual Training High School, Indianapolis), June 1926, 23.

45 *The Attucks* (Indianapolis: Crispus Attucks High School, 1928), 49.

46 *Daily Echo* (Shortridge High School, Indianapolis), October 28, 1928, 1.

47 *Viewpoint*, 9.

48 *Facts for Freshmen*, 10.

49 Much of this took place in the 1920s; Stuart left Tech to become a district administrator in 1930. See Indianapolis School Board, school board minutes, November 1922–1929.

50 For more on the history of the public school lunch, a product of the Progressive Era, see Susan Levine, *School Lunch Politics: The Surprising History of America's Favorite Welfare Program* (Princeton, NJ: Princeton University Press, 2008).

51 "Not to Be Read before Lunch," *Arsenal Cannon* (Arsenal Technical High School, Indianapolis), May 25, 1933, 6.

52 For more on women's high school basketball, see Pamela Grundy, *Learning to Win: Sports, Education, and Social Change in Twentieth-Century North Carolina* (Chapel Hill: University of North Carolina Press, 2001).

53 *Tech Way*, 109.

54 *Tech Way*, 109.

55 For more on the evolution of this thinking, see Lizabeth Cohen, *A Consumers' Republic: The Politics of Mass Consumption in Postwar America* (New York: Vintage Books, 2004). Cohen argues that, during the 1930s, several New Deal programs, such as the Consumer Advisory Board—which played a role in the short-lived National Recovery Administration's code setting—created a firm link between consuming and citizenship by championing consumer protections (what she calls "citizen consumers"). On the other hand, a growing number of economists and government officials, often operating with Keynesianism in mind, called for Americans to better the nation by spending rather than asserting themselves politically (as "purchaser consumers"). During the war, Cohen notes, the link between citizenship and consumption was further fortified. Federal programs like the Office of Price Administration, women who adapted their domestic and civic activities around the war effort (through liberty gardens and rationing), and African Americans who, because of Jim Crow, were denied access to multiple sites of consumption, including theaters, department stores, and restaurants, all engaged in shaping the American consumer landscape. It would not be until after the war, however, that the dilemma of the "citizen consumer" versus the "purchaser consumer" would give way to the formation of the consumer's republic, which looked to "the mass consumption marketplace, supported by government resources," to deliver "not only economic prosperity but also loftier social and political ambitions for a more equal, free, and democratic nation" (6–15).

56 *Tech Way*, 108.

57 *The Attucks* (Indianapolis: Crispus Attucks High School, 1938), 41.

58 *Facts for Freshmen*, 13.

59 Hine, *Rise and Fall*, 188.

60 Gaus, *Shortridge High School*, 161.

61 See Bailey, *From Front Porch*.

62 For more on the Y on college campuses, on which it operated similarly, see David Setran, *The College "Y": Student Religion in the Era of Secularization* (New York: Palgrave Macmillan, 2007).

63 "A Thanksgiving Prayer for Renewed Faith," *Arsenal Cannon*, November 24, 1948, 1.

64 *Daily Echo*, October 24, 1932, 4.

65 *Attucks* (1938), 42.

66 *The Attucks* (Indianapolis: Crispus Attucks High School, 1935), 25.

67 *Attucks* (1938), 30.

68 Mary Louise Harry, "The Contribution of the Negro to American Civilization" (student research report, Crispus Attucks High School, Indianapolis, 1941), 14.

69 *Tech Way*, 110–111.

70 *Tech Way*, 106. Italics added.

71 *Tech Way*, 107.

72 So-called social clubs also exploded during the Depression. While the city's top administrators rooted out and banned high school fraternities and sororities in the early 1900s (for their secrecy and their resemblance to their college peers), social clubs in the 1930s were welcomed. In the 1943 Shortridge yearbook, over one hundred such clubs were listed.

73 *Techtown* (Indianapolis: Arsenal High School, 1938), 55.

74 See Eckert, *Jocks and Burnouts.*

75 For a more specifically "antischool" reaction to this culture after World War II, see Graebner, *Coming of Age in Buffalo.*

76 "Arsenal Cannon Subscription Statistics," *Arsenal Cannon*, April 6, 1939, 1.

77 See, for example, *Daily Echo*, September 27, 1932, 1.

78 "Arsenal Cannon Subscription Statistics," *Arsenal Cannon*, April 6, 1939, 1. *Booster*, June 1939, 50.

79 "Tech's Public Enemies," *Arsenal Cannon*, April 6, 1932, 7.

80 *Booster*, June 1933, 3.

81 *Daily Echo*, February 6, 1932, 2.

82 *Daily Echo*, November 17, 1932, 3.

83 *Daily Echo*, November 17, 1932, 4.

84 "An Authority Discusses Problems in Make-Up," *Arsenal Cannon*, March 2, 1932, 4. For more on the 1920s, see Hine, *Rise and Fall*, especially chap. 10, "Dancing Daughters."

85 "Reasons Why (You Should Vote for the May Queen)," *Booster*, June 1931, 2.

86 "Freshmen's Diary," *Daily Echo*, November 18, 1932, 3.

87 "Freshmen's Diary," *Daily Echo*, November 18, 1932, 3.

88 "Our Tiny Freshmen," *Arsenal Cannon*, October 2, 1922, 1.

89 *Daily Echo*, February 2, 1944, 3.

90 *The Attucks* (Indianapolis: Crispus Attucks High School, 1943), 28.

91 "Our Tiny Freshmen," *Arsenal Cannon*, October 2, 1922, 1.

92 For more on the coming rebelliousness and its effects on the broader culture, see Hine, *Rise and Fall*, 237–244.

Chapter 4 An End to De Jure School Segregation, Crispus Attucks Basketball Success, and the Limits of Racial Equality, 1941–1955

1 Indianapolis Public Schools, "Application for Membership in the Indianapolis High School Victory Corps," 1942, Arsenal Technical High School Archives.

2 *TechTown* (Indianapolis: Arsenal Tech High School, 1945), 15.

3 *The Attucks* (Indianapolis: Crispus Attucks High School, 1944), 2.

4 *The Booster* (Indianapolis: Manual Training High School, 1943), 1. Later in the yearbook: "Room 216 won a plaque for buying the most war stamps last semester. On Pearl Harbor Day, December 7, Manual sold $1,086 in 'slaps at the axis.' Last semester totals reached $6,553.25, and we're out to top that. Does that sound like home front backing for you all?" Also, "One of the most successful feats was the volunteering of Manual girls to fill more than two hundred posts in neighborhood shows. They collected money for the Red Cross. You see, Mr. Barnhart is Victory Corps director for all city high schools. Physical education is on the 'must' list for membership, and oh, my 'muskles!'" (25).

5 *Annual* (Indianapolis: Shortridge High School, 1945), 102.

6 Lamont J. Hulse, "Overview: Neighborhoods and Communities," in Bodenhamer and Barrows, *Encyclopedia of Indianapolis*, 137. Also see Ira Katznelson, *When Affirmative Action Was White: An Untold History of Racial Inequality in Twentieth-Century America* (New York: W. W. Norton, 2005).

7 Gunnar Myrdal, *An American Dilemma: The Negro Problem and Modern Democracy* (New York: Harper Brothers, 1944), xx. Also see John Morton Blum, *V Was for Victory: Politics and American Culture during World War II* (New York:

Harcourt, 1976); David M. Kennedy, *Freedom from Fear: The American People in Depression and War* (New York: Oxford University Press, 1998); and Neil A. Wynn, *The Afro-American and the Second World War* (New York: Holmes and Meier, 1993).

8   Lois Quinn, "An Institutional History of the GED" (unpublished manuscript, University of Wisconsin–Milwaukee, 2001).

9   Indianapolis Public Schools, *Educational Services for Veterans* (Indianapolis: Indianapolis Public Schools, 1946), foreword. By 1946, the program had provided guidance for three thousand veterans, and one thousand students were enrolled in day and evening classes.

10 Pierce, *Polite Protest*, 35.

11 Pierce, 35.

12 The emphasis in this chapter on the boys' basketball team at Attucks is not meant to distract from the many other meaningful activities in the school. Basketball is not inherently more important than academics at Attucks or anywhere else, but within Indianapolis's dominant culture, it was far more important. Indeed, it was the popularity of basketball in the city and state that allowed young men at Attucks to be heroes on the court but—because of white supremacy—never neighbors or co-workers on equal footing off the court.

13 The story of the path to ending segregation in the Indianapolis public schools has been told remarkably well by Emma Lou Thornbrough, *The Indianapolis Story: School Segregation and Desegregation in a Northern City* (Indianapolis: Indiana Historical Society, 1993).

14 "School Fire Advances an Issue," *Indianapolis Recorder*, January 19, 1946, 2.

15 Jackson, "Endless Journey," 178–179.

16 Pierce, *Polite Protest*, 33.

17 "School Board Plans Program of Building," *Indianapolis Recorder*, January 5, 1946, 1; Pierce, *Polite Protest*, 33.

18 Jackson, "Endless Journey," 178–180.

19 "School Board Blamed in Students' Clamor," *Indianapolis Recorder*, October 19, 1946, 1. Also, as Thornbrough notes, the busing of students to Attucks, in and of itself, had to be won. In fact, she sees it as the one clear victory for civil rights in the 1930s: "The segregation policies adopted by school boards in the 1920's remained unchanged until World War II. One small favor granted to blacks was a law enacted by the state legislature in 1935 which provided that 'cities of the first class' (i.e. Indianapolis), which required students to attend segregated schools, must furnish transportation for students who traveled more than half a mile farther than the distance to the nearest public school" (*Indianapolis Story*, 44).

20 Jackson, "Endless Journey," 178.

21 "Board Gives Slight to Protest of Citizens," *Indianapolis Recorder*, February 16, 1946, 1–2. The *Recorder* reported, "The spirit of Abraham Lincoln was given the brush-off on the Great Emancipator's birthday Tuesday night at a meeting of the Indianapolis Board of School Commissioners." Ransom spoke that night, too. The paper added, "Attorney Ransom painted in graphic terms the dangers to life and health of the little children who are being carried in busses across busy streets and a dangerous railroad intersection. 'Who can say how long the little fellows will have to stand in snow, sleet and rain?' Ransom demanded. 'The icy winds of March are just around the corner. And we cannot assume that these children are healthier than the average. No, these children are ill-housed, ill-fed and

ill-clothed, because of the employment discrimination which is directed against their parents.'" Also see Pierce, *Polite Protest*, 34.

22 As Pierce notes, there were four black members of the CSC. *Polite Protest*, 38.

23 Thornbrough, *Indianapolis Story*, 60.

24 Thornbrough, 62–63. As part of the effort, Thornbrough notes, "there was no real discussion of issues affecting educational policies at board meetings and no effort to sound out public opinion. The . . . [CSC] rarely nominated a member to serve for a second term, thereby removing a method by which voters might have shown approval or disapproval for conduct or policies" (63).

25 Thornbrough, 61.

26 Thornbrough, 63. As Thornbrough notes, the *Times* also wrote, "While its anonymity shields the group from badgering by politicians, pressure groups, and office seekers and their friends, it also allows a choice of candidates favorable to a low tax rate" (63).

27 Thornbrough, 63.

28 Thornbrough, 63. Emblematic of her depth of knowledge of the city and its politics, she writes,

> Members of the legal profession were most numerous among the men. Others were drawn from middle management ranks of banks and large corporations and owners of small businesses. Occasionally a foreman or managerial employee of a factory was named, but very few union men. The women members were frequently described as "club women." Spokesmen for the Citizens Committee said the slates of candidates represented all the geographical sections of the city, but as critics pointed out, a disproportionate number came from the wealthier section on the Northside, a smaller number from the well-to-do neighborhoods on the far Eastside, and only a few from the Southside and Westside. No black was ever named or even considered, nor did blacks have a voice in the choice of candidates although two or three conservative black Republicans were members of the whole committee. (27)

29 Thornbrough, 63.

30 Pierce, *Polite Protest*, 40–41.

31 See "Introduction," Mapping Inequality, accessed June 2019, https://dsl.richmond .edu/panorama/redlining/#loc=13/43.083/-89.401&city=madison-wi&text=intro. The website is maintained by the University of Richmond's Digital Scholarship Lab, which has digitized many of the HOLC maps. Also see Thomas J. Sugrue, *Origins of the Urban Crisis: Race and Inequality in Postwar Detroit* (Princeton, NJ: Princeton University Press, 1996).

32 See Indianapolis map and comments, Mapping Inequality, accessed June 2019, https://dsl.richmond.edu/panorama/redlining/#loc=11/39.787/-86.208&city =indianapolis-in&adview=full. Also see Richard Rothstein, *The Color of Law: A Forgotten History of How Our Government Segregated America* (New York: W. W. Norton, 2017).

33 Pierce, *Polite Protest*, 38–39.

34 Pierce, 39. Also, Thornbrough notes of Niblack's biography,

> Born in the small town of Wheatland, Indiana, Niblack graduated from Indiana University and Benjamin Harrison Law School after a stint in the United States Navy during World War I. A reporter for the Indianapolis *Times* during the 1920's, he also began the practice of law. Active in Republican politics, he was elected four times as judge of Superior Court in Marion

County, and in 1956 began the first of three six year terms as Judge of the Circuit Court. In 1929, he served as executive secretary of the Citizens School Committee in the campaign that ousted the Klan board; in 1938 he was designated executive vice president of the committee, a position he held continuously until 1964, when he resigned, but did not relinquish his power. (*Indianapolis Story*, 60)

35 Pierce, *Polite Protest*, 40. Niblack also reportedly stated, "It's a mighty hard job to get people to run for the school board. It's a tremendous job for which they're paid absolutely nothing." He continued, "It wouldn't make any difference to me if they were all Democrats or all Republicans. But in the interest of the general public, we have to split it up." Thornbrough, *Indianapolis Story*, 103.

36 Pierce, *Polite Protest*, 40.

37 Pierce, 40.

38 Pierce, 40. The *Recorder* wrote that there was "heavy responsibility . . . to put a more democratic slate in the field and thus give the voters a choice on election day." Thornbrough, *Indianapolis Story*, 104.

39 Pierce, 40.

40 Pierce, 36. For more on voting among African Americans, see Darryl Pinckney, *Blackballed: The Black Vote and US Democracy* (New York: New York Review Books, 2014).

41 Thornbrough, *Indianapolis Story*, 97; Pierce, *Polite Protest*, 36.

42 Evansville, Indiana, was the only other city with segregated schools and a large African American population.

43 Thornbrough, *Indianapolis Story*, 98.

44 Thornbrough, 98.

45 Pierce, *Polite Protest*, 37. Stinebaugh also implied that liberals and civil rights leaders, if successful in the schools, would eventually come for all the city's institutions. It was an anti-integration tactic that would be lasting because, as several scholars have found, it challenged one's right to choose—neighbors, children's classmates, social club confederates, etc.

46 For more on segregation and jobs for black teachers, see Jack Dougherty, *More Than One Struggle: The Evolution of Black School Reform in Milwaukee* (Chapel Hill: University of North Carolina Press, 2004), especially chap. 1.

47 Pierce, *Polite Protest*, 36.

48 Thornbrough, *Indianapolis Story*, 99–100.

49 See, for example, James Patterson, *Brown v. Board of Education: A Civil Rights Milestone and Its Troubled Legacy* (New York: Oxford University Press, 2001).

50 Pierce, *Polite Protest*, 41; Thornbrough, *Indianapolis Story*, 82.

51 Thornbrough, Indianapolis Story, 104–105.

52 Pierce, *Polite Protest*, 41. As historians have noted, this was (and would be) the Legal Defense Fund's strategy nationally, notably in cases at the University of Missouri (*Missouri ex rel. Gaines v. Canada*, 1938), the University of Oklahoma (*McLaurin v. Oklahoma State Regents*, 1950), and the University of Texas (*Sweatt v. Painter*, 1950). See Patterson, *Brown v. Board of Education*.

53 Kenneth Clark and Mamie Clark's "doll study" was instrumental in the *Brown* (1954) decision. See Patterson *Brown v. Board of Education*.

54 Pierce, *Polite Protest*, 42.

55 Thornbrough, *Indianapolis Story*, 107.

56 Pierce, *Polite Protest*, 43. As Thornbrough notes, "Wolff, a consultant on

community interrelationships of the American Jewish Congress, [was invited] to make a preliminary survey. After meeting with school officials and interviewing a variety of people, including black and white ministers, the former head of the Church Federation, visiting some schools, and obtaining data from the school offices and the Chamber of Commerce, Wolff wrote a brief report in which he pointed out some of the inequities and hardships resulting from segregation." *Indianapolis Story*, 111.

57 Pierce, *Polite Protest*, 44.

58 Historians have found that the switch to the Democratic Party began earlier in Indianapolis than in the country as a whole (as early as the 1920s). See William Griffin, "The Political Realignment of Black Voters in Indianapolis, 1924," *Indiana Magazine of History* 78 (June 1993): 133–180. Also, the black population increased at twice the rate of the total population from 1940 to 1950. From 1950 to 1960, it grew at five times the rate.

59 Pierce, *Polite Protest*, 44.

60 Pierce, 45. Roselyn Richardson gave this interview to Pierce himself.

61 Pierce, 46–47. House Bill 242 was very clear in its stance on segregation, noting, "That it is hereby declared to be public policy in the State of Indiana to provide, furnish, and make available equal, non-segregated, non-discriminatory educational opportunities and facilities for all regardless of race, creed, national origin, color or sex; to provide and furnish public schools and common schools equally open to all and prohibited or denied to none because of race, creed, color, or national origin." Exact language from Jackson, "Endless Journey," 188.

62 Pierce, *Polite Protest*, 48.

63 Pierce, 45–48. The limits were clear by 1953. As Thornbrough notes, "In 1953, about two-thirds of the students in the city attended schools with racially mixed enrollments. Of fifty-three elementary schools reported as being 'integrated,' blacks were in a minority in forty-nine; whites a minority in only four. In two of these there was a single white pupil. In two other 'integrated' schools there was only one Negro in the entire student body. About one hundred seventy-five black pupils were still being bused outside their residential district." *Indianapolis Story*, 129.

64 Quoted in David Martin, "Gymnasium or Coliseum? Basketball, Education, and Community Impulse in Indiana in the Early Twentieth Century," in *Hoosier Schools: Past and Present*, ed. William Reese (Bloomington: Indiana University Press, 1989), 129.

65 For more, see Rob Rains, *James Naismith: The Man Who Invented Basketball* (Philadelphia: Temple University Press, 2009).

66 Quote taken from an excellent documentary film about Attucks by Ted Green titled *Attucks: The School That Opened a City* (Indianapolis: WFYI Public Television, 2016).

67 Aram Goudsouzian, "'Ba-ad, Ba-a-ad Tigers': Crispus Attucks Basketball and Black Indianapolis in the 1950s," *Indiana Magazine of History* 96, no. 1 (March 2000): 16.

68 Goudsouzian, 15–16, 9–10. Also see Randy Roberts, *"But They Can't Beat Us": Oscar Robertson and the Crispus Attucks Tigers* (Indianapolis: Indiana Historical Society, 1999).

69 For more on Lane, see Rosie Cheatham Mickey, "Russell Adrian Lane: Biography of an Urban Negro School Administrator" (PhD diss., University of Akron, 1983).

70 Goudsouzian, "'Ba-ad, Ba-a-ad Tigers,'" 17. For more on Indianapolis's jazz scene,

see David Leander Williams, *Indianapolis Jazz: The Masters, Legend, and Legacy of Indiana Avenue* (Charleston: History Press, 2014). As one community member recalled,

> The dust bowl was started sometime around 1945, 1946, 1947 . . . somewhere in that area. The reason it was a 'dust bowl' was because it was played on gravel and just dirt. And as the kids would run up and down the courts and whatnot the dust would rise up from the dirt. So, as a result of that it became known as the dust bowl. In the early 50s, half of the area was asphalted and a blacktop was put on the other half. Some of the best basketball players lived in and around Lockefield. As it became better known, guys from all over the city would come and to play in Lockefield, you know. You would come over there with your boys and you know—'we got next' or something like that. . . . Later on when the dust bowl got its notoriety, there would be some White kids that would come in from different high schools to play in the dust bowl tournaments. (Mullins and White, *Price of Progress*, 56)

For more on the comparisons between jazz and basketball in the city, see Phillip Hoose, *Hoosiers: The Fabulous Basketball Life of Indiana* (Indianapolis: Guild Press of Indiana, 1995); and Nelson George, *Elevating the Game: Black Men and Basketball* (New York: HarperCollins, 1992).

71 Goudsouzian, "'Ba-ad, Ba-a-ad Tigers,'" 19.
72 Oscar Robertson, *The Big O: My Life, My Times, My Game* (New York: Rodale, 2003), 16–17.
73 Pierce, *Polite Protest*, 18.
74 Robertson, *Big O*, 17–19; Pierce, *Polite Protest*, 18–19.
75 Pierce, *Polite Protest*, 20.
76 *An Appreciation* (Indianapolis: Board of School Commissioners, 1951).
77 Pierce, *Polite Protest*, 22.
78 "Attucks Tigers and Hoosier Democracy," *Indianapolis Recorder*, March 17, 1951, 1, 4. It continued, "You don't like it when you think Attucks is getting a bad deal from the officials in a basketball game; shouldn't the same standards of fair play and equality be applied to the other fields in this great game of life?"
79 Robertson, *Big O*, 18.
80 Goudsouzian, "'Ba-ad, Ba-a-ad Tigers,'" 29.
81 Goudsouzian, 30.
82 Goudsouzian, 30.
83 Robertson, *Big O*, 25.
84 Green, *Attucks*.
85 Green.
86 Green.
87 Robertson, *Big O*, 52.
88 Robertson, 53.
89 Robertson, 53.
90 Robertson, ix.

Chapter 5   "Life Adjustment" Education, Suburbanization, Unigov, and an Unjust System by a New Name, 1955–1971

1 Indianapolis Public Schools, *Living and Learning in the Indianapolis Public Schools* (Indianapolis: Indianapolis Public Schools, 1954), 5–7.

2   Indianapolis Public Schools, 2.
3   Indianapolis Public Schools, 8–10.
4   Angus and Mirel, *Failed Promise*, 80.
5   Angus and Mirel, 73.
6   Diane Ravitch, *The Troubled Crusade: American Education, 1945–1980* (New York: Basic Books, 1985), 65. Prosser said, "Never in all the history of education has there been such a meeting as this one. . . . Never was there such a meeting where people were so sincere in their beliefs that this was the golden opportunity to do something that would give to all American youth their educational heritage so long denied."
7   Ravitch, 64–65.
8   Angus and Mirel, *Failed Promise*, 80.
9   Ravitch, *Troubled Crusade*, 67–69.
10 Indianapolis Public Schools, *Living and Learning*, 2.
11 Between 1954 and 1961, Wood High's black student population grew from thirty-three students (about 12 percent) to 266 students (about 20 percent). See local historian John Loughlin's "A Critical History of Harry E. Wood High School" (unpublished paper, 1980). The author provided a copy.
12 Indianapolis Public Schools, *Living and Learning*, 2.
13 Indianapolis Public Schools, *For a New Century, a New School* (Indianapolis: Indianapolis Public Schools, 1954).
14 Indianapolis Public Schools.
15 Indianapolis Public Schools.
16 Indianapolis Public Schools.
17 William Reese, "Overview: Education," in Bodenhamer and Barrows, *Encyclopedia of Indianapolis*, 83.
18 *The Harry E. Wood School* (Indianapolis: Indianapolis Public Schools, 1953).
19 *Harry E. Wood School.*
20 *Harry E. Wood School.*
21 William Reese, "Urban Schools in Postwar Indiana," in *Hoosier Schools: Past and Present*, ed. William Reese (Bloomington: Indiana University Press, 1989), 157.
22 Ted Stahly, "High Schools," in Bodenhamer and Barrows, *Encyclopedia of Indianapolis*, 676.
23 *The Wood Log* (Indianapolis: Harry E. Wood High School, 1957), 19.
24 Angus and Mirel, *Failed Promise*, 112–114. Angus and Mirel see Conant's influence on the debate over diversification and nonacademic subjects as monumental. They write, "His report . . . essentially ended the raging debate about the high school curriculum in the 1950s and determined how the institution would respond to the challenges of the 1960s and early 1970s" (113).
25 James Bryant Conant, *Conference on the Indiana High School: An Address* (Bloomington: School of Education, Indiana University and Indiana School Boards Association, 1958).
26 Reese, "Urban Schools in Postwar Indiana," 154. To Angus and Mirel, it was a "vision in which both curriculum and guidance would operate to lower the career aspirations of the majority of students." *Failed Promise*, 82. For more, see Hampel, *Last Little Citadel*, 61–65.
27 Indianapolis Public Schools, *Educational Opportunities in the Indianapolis Public Schools* (Indianapolis: Indianapolis Public Schools, Fall 1953), 1.

28 Indianapolis Public Schools, 2, 6.
29 "Shortridge Is Rated in Top 38 Schools," *Indianapolis Star*, October 8, 1957, 16.
30 "Shortridge Is Rated," 16.
31 Gaus, *Shortridge High School*, 224–225.
32 Gaus, 221.
33 Gaus, 227.
34 Gaus, 228.
35 Gaus, 219–220.
36 Gaus, 222.
37 Lamont J. Hulse, "Overview: Neighborhoods and Communities," in Bodenhamer and Barrows, *Encyclopedia of Indianapolis*, 222.
38 Gaus, *Shortridge High School*, 223, 224. This seems unlikely, given the school's eventual name.
39 Gaus, 224.
40 Helen Jean McClelland Nugent, "Schools, Religious," in Bodenhamer and Barrows, *Encyclopedia of Indianapolis*, 1235–1239. Also see "School History," Cathedral High School, accessed June 2019, https://www.gocathedral.com/about /school-history.
41 Hulse, "Overview," 138.
42 See, among many works, Cohen, *Consumers' Republic*; and Thomas Sugrue, "Structures of Urban Poverty: The Reorganization of Space and Work in Three Periods of American History," in *The "Underclass" Debate: Views from History*, ed. Michael Katz (Princeton, NJ: Princeton University Press, 1993).
43 Pierce, *Polite Protest*, 75. Pierce explains, "The BTNA sought and received a $60,000 grant from Neighborhood Housing Opportunities (NHO), a non-profit corporation organized to promote integrated housing throughout Marion Country," but their attempts to keep the area integrated eventually failed.
44 Gaus, *Shortridge High School*, 238–239.
45 Gaus, 238.
46 Pierce, *Polite Protest*, 112.
47 Gaus, *Shortridge High School*, 244.
48 Gaus, 244. This last line was an obvious gesture to Barry Goldwater's 1960 book *The Conscience of a Conservative*; Goldwater had just lost the 1964 election to Lyndon Johnson. The announcement stated, "The Indianapolis Board of School Commissioners wishes to affirm that it is important to the strength of the Indianapolis Public School system that the tradition of academic excellence and achievement at Shortridge High School be maintained. To further this aim, the Indianapolis Board of School Commissioners . . . desires that Shortridge High School shall be an academic high school with faculty and curriculum chosen to challenge those students who will benefit from a college preparatory course of study" (244).
49 Many historians suggest that "magnet schools" began in Tacoma, Washington, in 1969 as "a nationwide experiment to integrate public schools using market-like incentives instead of court orders." While the Shortridge Plan in many ways operated inversely—hoping to stem black enrollment through a prohibitive test rather than attract white enrollment though special programs—its intentions were similar. See Christine Rossell, "Magnet Schools: No Longer Famous but Still Intact," *Education Next* 5, no. 2 (Spring 2005): 44.
50 Gaus, *Shortridge High School*, 247.

51 Andrew Ramsey, "Shortridge Uber Alles," *Indianapolis Recorder*, February 26, 1966, 9. Ramsey maintained a regular column on this and a variety of political issues throughout the period of study.

52 "NAACP, School Board Clash at Meet," *Indianapolis Recorder*, January 15, 1966, 1, 2.

53 *Timeline: Mapleton-Fall Creek Neighborhood, 1843–1995* (Indianapolis: Polis Center at IUPUI, 1995), 5. The Human Relations Council was still meeting as late as 1968 to discuss the Shortridge Plan. See "HRC to Initiate Membership Drive," *Daily Echo*, September 12, 1968, 1.

54 Richard Lugar, interview by Philip Scarpino, professor of history and director of oral history for the Randall L. Tobias Center for Leadership Excellence at Indiana University–Purdue University Indianapolis, September 30, 2016. Available online at https://tobiascenter.iu.edu/research/oral-history/audio-transcripts/lugar -richard.html (accessed July 2019). Lugar continued,

> As a person, as a father, why, I became involved because after this desegregation occurred, my two sons who were in high school age were assigned to Crispus Attucks High School. They attended there and played football. My wife became a volleyball coach and so forth. So we were right in the middle of the desegregation with our own family, literally. When I was elected to the Senate; why, we all moved over to Washington, and they went to school there at McLean High School [words inaudible]. As I say, it was simply one of these things where we tried awfully hard to change the course of things on the School Board and succeeded, and it played out in the federal courts.

55 Gaus, *Shortridge High School*, 245.

56 Gaus, 248.

57 Janet Cheatham Bell, *The Time and Place That Gave Me Life* (Bloomington: Indiana University Press, 2007), 145.

58 Gaus, *Shortridge High School*, 254.

59 Scott D. Seay, "The Shortridge Incident," *Encounter* 68, no. 1 (2007): 63. Seay notes, "Word of the altercation spread quickly in the neighborhood, and nervous parents made sure that just over two hundred of their children were 'absent' the next day, February 26."

60 Ted Green, dir., *Attucks: The School That Opened a City* (Indianapolis: WFYI Public Television, 2016).

61 Thornbrough, *Indianapolis Story*, 167.

62 Thornbrough, 234.

63 Pierce, *Polite Protest*, 50; Thornbrough, *Indianapolis Story*, 234.

64 Thornbrough, *Indianapolis Story*, 236–237.

65 Pierce, *Polite Protest*, 114.

66 Pierce, 114.

67 Shaina Cavazos, "Racial Bias and the Crumbling of a City," *Atlantic*, August 17, 2016.

68 William Blomquist, "Unigov, Creation Of," in Bodenhamer and Barrows, *Encyclopedia of Indianapolis*, 1351–1352.

69 For more, see Nicole Poletika, "The Undemocratic Making of Indianapolis," *Belt*, March 2019. Also, on Nashville, see Erickson, *Making the Unequal Metropolis*.

70 Blomquist, "Unigov, Creation Of," 1352.

71 Pierce, *Polite Protest*, 120–121.

72 Cavazos, "Racial Bias."

73 Cavazos.

74 Thornbrough, *Indianapolis Story*, 286–287. She adds, "The first witness, Virgil Stinebaugh, the superintendent when the 1949 law was passed, now in his seventies, could not recall that the school board had ever opposed desegregation and was vague and forgetful on other questions."

75 Thornbrough, 284.

76 Thornbrough, 284.

77 United States v. Bd. of Sch. Com'rs, Indianapolis, 332 F. Supp. 655, 668 (S.D. Ind. 1971). Dillin added, "During the post-1954 period, the Board perpetuated segregation through the use of option attendance zones. Specifically, in areas of mixed residential patterns students were given options between predominantly Negro and predominantly white elementary schools, and where the entire elementary districts covered both Negro and white neighborhoods, graduates were given options between predominantly Negro and predominantly white high schools. Students in Negro elementary schools were given options to Crispus Attucks when other, predominantly white high schools were closer and more accessible. White students in optional zones almost always attended white schools."

78 *Bd. of Sch. Com'rs, Indianapolis*, 332 F. Supp. at 676.

79 Pierce, *Polite Protest*, 54.

80 Thornbrough, *Indianapolis Story*, 290–291.

Conclusion

1 Shaina Cavazos, "The End of Busing in Indianapolis," *Atlantic*, July 5, 2016.

2 Cavazos.

3 Hence the title of Jeffrey Mirel's celebrated book, *The Rise and Fall of an Urban System: Detroit, 1907–1981* (Ann Arbor: University of Michigan Press, 1993).

4 See Paul Mullins and Lewis Jones, "Race, Displacement, and Twentieth Century University Landscapes: The Archeology of Urban Renewal and Urban Landscapes," in *The Materiality of Freedom: Archaeologies of Postemancipation Life*, ed. Jodi A. Barnes (Columbia: University of South Carolina Press, 2011), 250–262.

5 Mullins and Jones, 251.

6 Paul Mullins, "Racializing the Commonplace Landscape: The Archeology of Urban Renewal along the Color Line," *World Archaeology* 38, no. 1 (2006): 61.

7 See Eve Ewing, *Ghosts in the Schoolyard: Racism and School Closings on Chicago's South Side* (Chicago: University of Chicago Press, 2018); P. E. Moskowitz, *How to Kill a City: Gentrification, Inequality, and the Fight for the Neighborhood* (New York: Nation Books, 2018); and Cary McClelland, *Silicon City: San Francisco in the Long Shadow of the Valley* (New York: W. W. Norton, 2018).

8 Mullins, "Racializing the Commonplace Landscape," 61–69.

9 Nicole Poletika, "The Undemocratic Making of Indianapolis," *Belt*, March 29, 2019. Poletika continues, "Suburbanites commuted to Indianapolis for work and recreation, and retreated to communities recognized nationally for their safety and education."

10 See Jean Anyon, *Ghetto Schooling: A Political Economy of Urban Educational Reform* (New York: Teachers College Press, 1997); James Ryan, *Five Miles Away, a World Apart: One City, Two Schools, and the Story of Educational Opportunity in*

Modern America (New York: Oxford University Press, 2011); Ansley Erickson, *Making the Unequal Metropolis: School Desegregation and Its Limits* (Chicago: University of Chicago Press, 2016); and Walter Stern, *Race and Education in New Orleans: Creating the Segregated City* (Baton Rouge: Louisiana State University Press, 2018).

11 "How the Systemic Segregation of Schools Is Maintained by 'Individual Choices,'" *Fresh Air*, hosted by Terry Gross, produced by WHYY-FM, Philadelphia, broadcast January 16, 2017.

12 Matthew Desmond, "How Homeownership Became the Engine of American Inequality," *New York Times Magazine*, May 9, 2017.

13 Matthew Desmond, *Evicted: Poverty and Profit in the American City* (New York: Crown, 2016).

14 Matt Stevens, "What We Know about Joe Biden's Record on School Busing," *New York Times*, June 28, 2019.

15 Tyack, *One Best System*, 12.

16 Indianapolis Board of School Commissioners, *Report of the President*, 10.

Bibliography

Manuscript Collections and Archives

Argus [student newspaper for Emmerich Manual High School], 1896–1910, Indiana Historical Society

Arsenal Technical High School Archives, Arsenal Technical High School

Crispus Attucks High School Museum Archives, Crispus Attucks High School

Daily Echo [daily student newspaper of Shortridge High School], 1898–1981, Indiana Historical Society

Emmerich Manual Training High School Time Capsule Collection, 1896–1920, Indiana Historical Society

Harry E. Wood Collection, Indiana Historical Society

Henry J. Richardson [lawyer and civil rights leader] Papers, 1910–1992, Indiana Historical Society

Indianapolis Board of School Commissioners, *Annual Report of the Public Schools of the City of Indianapolis*, 1890–1954

Indianapolis Board of School Commissioners, *Manual of the Public Schools of the City of Indianapolis with Rules and Regulations of the Board of School Commissioners*, 1895–1954

Ivian [yearbook for Emmerich Manual High School], 1901–1920, Indiana Historical Society

Manual Training High School Archives, Emmerich Manual Training High School

Riparian [student newspaper for Broad Ripple High School], 1944–1964, Indiana Historical Society

Shortridge High School *Annuals*, 1894–1980, Indiana Historical Society

Shortridge High School Collection, 1870–1981, 1995, Indiana Historical Society

W. E. B. Du Bois Papers, 1803–1999, Special Collections and University Archives, University of Massachusetts Amherst Libraries

Periodicals

Architectural Forum
Atlantic Monthly
Freeman
Indianapolis News
Indianapolis Star
Indianapolis Times
New York Times
New York Times Magazine
Recorder
Washington Post

Published Materials

Angus, David, and Jeffrey Mirel. "Equality, Curriculum, and the Decline of the Academic Ideal: Detroit, 1930–1968." *History of Education Quarterly* 33, no. 2 (Summer 1993): 177–207.

———. *The Failed Promise of the American High School, 1890–1995.* New York: Teachers College Press, 1999.

Anyon, Jean. *Ghetto Schooling: A Political Economy of Urban Educational Reform.* New York: Teachers College Press, 1997.

Bailey, Beth. *From Front Porch to Back Seat: Courtship in Twentieth-Century America.* Baltimore: Johns Hopkins University Press, 1988.

Bell, Janet Cheatham. *The Time and Place That Gave Me Life.* Bloomington: Indiana University Press, 2007.

Blum, John Morton. *V Was for Victory: Politics and American Culture during World War II.* New York: Harcourt, 1976.

Bodenhamer, David, and Robert G. Barrows, eds. *The Encyclopedia of Indianapolis.* Bloomington: Indiana University Press, 1994.

Bundles, A'Lelia. *Madame Walker Theatre Center: An Indianapolis Treasure.* Charleston, SC: Arcadia, 2013.

"A Clearing in the Forest." In *Arsenal Tech Memories,* 2–79. Indianapolis: Arsenal Technical High School, 1994.

Cohen, Lizabeth. *A Consumers' Republic: The Politics of Mass Consumption in Postwar America.* New York: Vintage Books, 2004.

Conant, James Bryant. *Conference on the Indiana High School: An Address.* Bloomington: School of Education, Indiana University and Indiana School Boards Association, 1958.

Cronon, William. *Nature's Metropolis: Chicago and the Great West.* New York: W. W. Norton, 1991.

Cuban, Larry. *How Teachers Taught: Constancy and Change in American Classrooms, 1890–1990.* New York: Teachers College Press, 1984.

DeFrantz, Faburn. "'To Kathy and to David': The Memoir of Faburn E. DeFrantz." *Indiana Magazine of History* 108, no. 2 (June 2012): 104–145.

Department of the Interior, Bureau of Education. *Cardinal Principles of Secondary Education: A Report of the Commission on the Reorganization of Secondary Education.* Washington, DC: Government Printing Office, 1918.

Desmond, Matthew. *Evicted: Poverty and Profit in the American City.* New York: Crown, 2016.

Dougherty, Jack. *More Than One Struggle: The Evolution of Black School Reform in Milwaukee*. Chapel Hill: University of North Carolina Press, 2004.

Douglas, Davison M. *Jim Crow Moves North: The Battle over Northern School Desegregation, 1865–1954*. New York: Cambridge University Press, 2005.

Eckert, Penelope. *Jocks and Burnouts: Social Categories and Identity in the High School*. New York: Teachers College Press, 1989.

Elias, Meghan. *Stir It Up: Home Economics in American Culture*. Philadelphia: University of Pennsylvania Press, 2010.

Erickson, Ansley. *Making the Unequal Metropolis: School Desegregation and Its Limits*. Chicago: University of Chicago Press, 2016.

Ewing, Eve. *Ghosts in the Schoolyard: Racism and School Closings on Chicago's South Side*. Chicago: University of Chicago Press, 2018.

Fallows, Deborah. "Why We Never Get Over High School." *Atlantic*, February 23, 2014.

Fass, Paula. *The Damned and the Beautiful: American Youth in the 1920s*. New York: Oxford University Press, 1979.

———. *Outside In: Minorities and the Transformation of American Education*. New York: Oxford University Press, 1989.

Foucault, Michel. *Discipline and Punish: The Birth of the Prison*. New York: Vintage Books, 1995.

Franklin, John Hope, and August Meier, ed. *Black Leaders of the Twentieth Century*. Urbana: University of Illinois Press, 1982.

Fresh Air. "How the Systemic Segregation of Schools Is Maintained by 'Individual Choices.'" Hosted by Terry Gross. Produced by WHYY-FM, Philadelphia. Broadcast January 16, 2017.

Gale, Frederick K. "The First Twenty-Five Years of Crispus Attucks High School, Indianapolis, Indiana, 1927–1952." Master's thesis, Ball State Teachers College, 1955.

Garreau, Joel. *The Nine Nations of North America*. New York: Houghton Mifflin, 1981.

Gaus, Laura Sheerin. *Shortridge High School, 1864–1981, in Retrospect*. Indianapolis: Indiana Historical Society, 1985.

George, Nelson. *Elevating the Game: Black Men and Basketball*. New York: Harper-Collins, 1992.

Goudsouzian, Aram. "'Ba-ad, Ba-a-ad Tigers': Crispus Attucks Basketball and Black Indianapolis in the 1950s." *Indiana Magazine of History* 96, no. 1 (March 2000): 4–43.

Graebner, William. *Coming of Age in Buffalo: Youth and Authority in the Postwar Era*. Philadelphia: Temple University Press, 1990.

———. "Outlawing Teenage Populism: The Campaign against Secret Societies in the American High School, 1900–1960." *Journal of American History* 74, no. 2 (September 1987): 411–435.

Grant, Barry Keith. *Five Films by Frederick Wiseman: Titicut Follies, High School, Welfare, High School II, Public Housing*. Berkeley: University of California Press, 2006.

Green, Ted, dir. *Attucks: The School That Opened a City*. Indianapolis: WFYI Public Television, 2016. DVD.

Griffin, Carolyn. *Emmerich Manual High School: A History, 1895–1969*. Indianapolis: Manual High School, 1969.

Griffin, William. "The Political Realignment of Black Voters in Indianapolis, 1924." *Indiana Magazine of History* 78 (June 1993): 133–180.

Grundy, Pamela. *Color and Character: West Charlotte High and the American Struggle over Educational Equality*. Chapel Hill: University of North Carolina Press, 2017.

———. *Learning to Win: Sports, Education, and Social Change in Twentieth-Century North Carolina*. Chapel Hill: University of North Carolina Press, 2001.

Hale, Jon. *The Freedom Schools: Student Activists in the Mississippi Civil Rights Movement*. New York: Columbia University Press, 2016.

Hampel, Robert. *The Last Little Citadel: American High Schools since 1940*. Boston: Houghton Mifflin, 1986.

Harbach, Paul. "Student Life in Milwaukee High Schools, 1920–1985." In *Seeds of Crisis: Public Schooling in Milwaukee since 1920*, edited by John L. Rury and Frank A. Cassel, 193–228. Madison: University of Wisconsin Press, 1993.

Hine, Thomas. *The Rise and Fall of the American Teenager: A New History of the American Adolescent Experience*. New York: Perennial, 2000.

Hoose, Phillip. *Hoosiers: The Fabulous Basketball Life of Indiana*. Indianapolis: Guild Press of Indiana, 1995.

Indianapolis Board of School Commissioners. *Catalogue of the Industrial Training School*. Indianapolis: Indianapolis Board of School Commissioners, 1899.

———. *Report of the President*. Indianapolis: Indianapolis Board of School Commissioners, 1879.

———. *Report of the Principal of the High School*. Indianapolis: Indianapolis Board of School Commissioners, 1880.

Indianapolis Public Schools. *Educational Services for Veterans*. Indianapolis: Indianapolis Public Schools, 1946.

———. *For a New Century, a New School*. Indianapolis: Indianapolis Public Schools, 1954.

———. *Shortridge High School Textbook List, Revised June 1914*. Indianapolis: Indianapolis Public Schools, 1914.

———. *Survey Findings: Senior High School Division Secondary Schools*. Indianapolis: Indianapolis Board of School Commissioners, 1934.

Indiana State Board of Education. *Report of the Indianapolis Survey for Vocational Education*. Indianapolis: Fort Wayne Printing, 1917.

Ingrassia, Brian. *The Rise of Gridiron University: Higher Education's Uneasy Alliance with Big-Time Football*. Lawrence: University of Kansas Press, 2015.

Jackson, Eric R. "The Endless Journey: The Black Struggle for Quality Public Schools in Indianapolis, Indiana, 1900–1949." PhD diss., University of Cincinnati, 2000.

Kaestle, Carl. *The Evolution of an Urban School System: New York City, 1750–1850*. Cambridge, MA: Harvard University Press, 1973.

———. *Pillars of the Republic: Common Schools and American Society, 1780–1860*. New York: Hill and Wang, 1983.

Katz, Michael. Review of *The Origins of the American High School*, by William J. Reese. *History of Education Quarterly* 36, no. 4 (Winter 1996): 518–522.

Katznelson, Ira. *When Affirmative Action Was White: An Untold History of Racial Inequality in Twentieth-Century America*. New York: W. W. Norton, 2005.

Kellogg, Charles Flint. *NAACP: A History of the National Association for the Advancement of Colored People*. Baltimore: Johns Hopkins University Press, 1973.

Kennedy, David M. *Freedom from Fear: The American People in Depression and War*. New York: Oxford University Press, 1998.

Kershner, Frederick, Jr. "From Country Town to Industrial City: The Urban Pattern in Indianapolis." *Indiana Magazine of History* 45, no. 4 (December 1949): 327–338.

Kliebard, Herbert. *Schooled to Work: Vocationalism and the American Curriculum, 1876–1946*. New York: Teachers College Press, 1999.

———. *The Struggle for the American Curriculum, 1835–1958.* 2nd ed. New York: Routledge, 1995.

Knox, George L. *Slave and Freeman: The Autobiography of George L. Knox.* Edited by Willard Gatewood Jr. Lexington: University Press of Louisville, 1979.

Koch, Tom. "A History of Football at Shortridge." *Daily Echo* (Shortridge High School, Indianapolis), supplement, September 1943.

Krug, Edward. *The Shaping of the American High School.* Vol. 1, *1880–1920.* Madison: University of Wisconsin Press, 1969.

———. *The Shaping of the American High School.* Vol. 2, *1920–1941.* Madison: University of Wisconsin Press, 1972.

Labaree, David. *The Making of an American High School: The Credentials Market and the Central High School of Philadelphia, 1838–1939.* New Haven, CT: Yale University Press, 1988.

Lareau, Annette. *Unequal Childhoods: Class, Race, and Family Life.* Berkeley: University of California Press, 2003.

Lassiter, Matthew, and Joseph Crespino, eds. *The Myth of Southern Exceptionalism.* New York: Oxford University Press, 2009.

Levine, Susan. *School Lunch Politics: The Surprising History of America's Favorite Welfare Program.* Princeton, NJ: Princeton University Press, 2008.

Lhamon, W. T., Jr. *Raising Cain: Blackface Performance from Jim Crow to Hip Hop.* Cambridge, MA: Harvard University Press, 2000.

Lowry, Beverly. *Her Dream of Dreams: The Rise and Triumph of Madam C. J. Walker.* New York: Vintage, 2004.

Lynd, Robert, and Helen Lynd. *Middletown: A Study in American Culture.* New York: Harcourt, 1929.

McClellan, B. Edward. *Moral Education in America: Schools and the Shaping of Character from Colonial Times to the Present.* New York: Teachers College Press, 1999.

McClelland, Cary. *Silicon City: San Francisco in the Long Shadow of the Valley.* New York: W. W. Norton, 2018.

Mickey, Rosie Cheatham. "Russell Adrian Lane: Biography of an Urban Negro School Administrator." PhD diss., University of Akron, 1983.

Mintz, Steven. *Huck's Raft: A History of American Childhood.* Cambridge, MA: Harvard University Press, 2004.

Mirel, Jeffrey. *The Rise and Fall of an Urban System: Detroit, 1907–1981.* Ann Arbor: University of Michigan Press, 1993.

———. "The Traditional High School: Historical Debates over Its Nature and Function." *Education Next* 6, no. 1 (Winter 2006): 14–21.

Moore, Leonard J. *Citizen Klansmen: The Ku Klux Klan in Indiana, 1921–1928.* Chapel Hill: University of North Carolina Press, 1991.

Moskowitz, P. E. *How to Kill a City: Gentrification, Inequality, and the Fight for the Neighborhood.* New York: Nation Books, 2018.

Mullins, Paul. "Racializing the Commonplace Landscape: The Archeology of Urban Renewal along the Color Line." *World Archaeology* 38, no. 1 (2006): 60–71.

Mullins, Paul, and Lewis Jones. "Race, Displacement, and Twentieth Century University Landscapes: The Archeology of Urban Renewal and Urban Landscapes." In *The Materiality of Freedom: Archaeologies of Postemancipation Life,* edited by Jodi A. Barnes, 250–262. Columbia: University of South Carolina Press, 2011.

Mullins, Paul, and Glenn White. *The Price of Progress: IUPUI, the Color Line, and Urban Displacement.* Indianapolis: IUPUI Office of External Affairs, 2010.

Myrdal, Gunnar. *An American Dilemma: The Negro Problem and Modern Democracy.* New York: Harper Brothers, 1944.

Ottenhoff, Patrick. "Where Does the South Begin?" *Atlantic*, January 28, 2011.

Patterson, James. *Brown v. Board of Education: A Civil Rights Milestone and Its Troubled Legacy.* New York: Oxford University Press, 2001.

Pierce, Richard. *Polite Protest: The Political Economy of Race in Indianapolis, 1920–1970.* Bloomington: Indiana University Press, 2005.

Podair, Jerald. *The Strike That Changed New York: Blacks, Whites, and the Ocean Hill–Brownsville Crisis.* New Haven, CT: Yale University Press, 2002.

President's Research Committee on Social Trends. *Recent Social Trends in the United States.* Vol. 1. New York: McGraw-Hill, 1933.

Pruter, Robert. *The Rise of American High School Sports and the Search for Control, 1880–1930.* Syracuse, NY: Syracuse University Press, 2013.

Purdy, Michelle. *Transforming the Elite: Black Students and the Desegregation of Private Schools.* Chapel Hill: University of North Carolina Press, 2018.

Quinn, Lois. "An Institutional History of the GED." Unpublished manuscript, University of Wisconsin–Milwaukee, 2001.

Rains, Rob. *James Naismith: The Man Who Invented Basketball.* Philadelphia: Temple University Press, 2009.

Ravitch, Diane. *The Great School Wars: A History of the New York Public Schools.* New York: Basic Books, 1974.

———. *The Troubled Crusade: American Education, 1945–1980.* New York: Basic Books, 1985.

Reese, William J. *America's Public Schools: From the Common School to "No Child Left Behind."* Baltimore: Johns Hopkins University Press, 2011.

———. *History, Education, and the Schools.* New York: Palgrave Macmillan, 2007.

———, ed. *Hoosier Schools: Past and Present.* Bloomington: Indiana University Press, 1998.

———. *The Origins of the American High School.* New Haven, CT: Yale University Press, 1995.

Reynolds, Maureen Anne. "Politics and Indiana's Public Schools during the Civil War Era, 1850–1875." PhD diss., Indiana University, 1997.

Rice, Emmett. *A Brief Story of Shortridge and Her Forbears.* Indianapolis: Shortridge High School, 1935.

Ricos, Nick. *A History of Basketball at Shortridge.* Indianapolis: Indiana Historical Society, 1944.

Riverfront Times (St. Louis). "Where You *Should've* Gone to High School." February 16, 2012.

Roberts, Randy. *"But They Can't Beat Us": Oscar Robertson and the Crispus Attucks Tigers.* Indianapolis: Indiana Historical Society, 1999.

Robertson, Oscar. *The Big O: My Life, My Times, My Game.* New York: Rodale, 2003.

Roosevelt, Theodore. *The Strenuous Life: Essays and Addresses.* New York: Century, 1900.

Rossell, Christine. "Magnet Schools: No Longer Famous but Still Intact." *Education Next* 5, no. 2 (Spring 2005): 44–49.

Rothstein, Richard. *The Color of Law: A Forgotten History of How Our Government Segregated America.* New York: W. W. Norton, 2017.

Rury, John. *Education and Women's Work: Female Schooling and the Division of Labor in Urban America, 1870–1930.* Albany: State University of New York Press, 1991.

Ryan, James. *Five Miles Away, a World Apart: One City, Two Schools, and the Story of Educational Opportunity in Modern America*. New York: Oxford University Press, 2011.

Setran, David. *The College "Y": Student Religion in the Era of Secularization*. New York: Palgrave Macmillan, 2007.

Stage, Sarah, and Virginia Vincenti, eds. *Rethinking Home Economics: Women and the History of a Profession*. Ithaca, NY: Cornell University Press, 1997.

Stearns, Alfred, L. R. Gignilliat, Milo H. Stuart, Eric Parson, and J. J. Findlay. *Types of Schools for Boys*. Childhood and Youth Series. Indianapolis: Bobbs-Merrill, 1917.

Stern, Walter. *Race and Education in New Orleans: Creating the Segregated City*. Baton Rouge: Louisiana State University Press, 2018.

"The Story of Technical High School: Supplement to the Arsenal *Cannon*." Indianapolis: Arsenal Technical High School, 1916.

Stuart, Milo. *The Organization of a Comprehensive High School: A Presentation of Plans and Devices of the Arsenal Technical Schools, Indianapolis, Whereby the Interest of the Individual Is Kept Paramount*. New York: Macmillan, 1926.

Sugrue, Thomas J. *Origins of the Urban Crisis: Race and Inequality in Postwar Detroit*. Princeton, NJ: Princeton University Press, 1996.

———. *Sweet Land of Liberty: The Forgotten Struggle for Civil Rights in the North*. New York: Random House Trade Paperbacks, 2009.

Thornbrough, Emma Lou. *Indiana Blacks in the Twentieth Century*. Bloomington: Indiana University Press, 2001.

———. *The Indianapolis Story: School Segregation and Desegregation in a Northern City*. Indianapolis: Indiana Historical Society, 1993.

———. "Segregation in Indiana during the Klan Era of the 1920s." *Mississippi Valley Historical Review* 47, no. 4 (March 1961): 590–604.

Tuttle, William. *Race Riot: Chicago in the Red Summer of 1919*. New York: Atheneum, 1970.

Tyack, David. *The One Best System: A History of American Urban Education*. Cambridge, MA: Harvard University Press, 1974.

Tyack, David, and Larry Cuban. *Tinkering toward Utopia: A Century of School Reform*. Cambridge, MA: Harvard University Press, 1995.

Tyack, David, Elisabeth Hansot, and Robert Lowe. *Public Schools in Hard Times: The Great Depression and Recent Years*. Cambridge, MA: Harvard University Press, 1984.

Wade, Wyn Craig. *The Fiery Cross: The Ku Klux Klan in America*. London: Simon and Schuster, 1987.

Warren, Stanley. *Crispus Attucks High School: "Hail to the Green, Hail to the Gold."* Virginia Beach, VA: Donning, 1998.

Wiebe, Robert. *The Search for Order, 1877–1920*. New York: Hill and Wang, 1968.

Index

About the Author

KYLE P. STEELE teaches undergraduate and graduate courses in the history of education, education for social justice, and education policy at the University of Wisconsin Oshkosh. A native of St. Louis, Missouri, Steele has a joint PhD (history and educational policy studies) from the University of Wisconsin–Madison. Before his career in academia, he taught the world's most delightful fourth and fifth graders in South City St. Louis.